CHANNELS
&
CYCLES:
A Tribute to
J.M. Hurst

by
Brian J. Millard

Traders Press, Inc.®

BOOKS BY THE AUTHOR

Millard On Stocks and Shares (4th Edition)

Millard on Traded Options (2nd Edition)

Millard on Profitable Charting Techniques (2nd Edition)

Millard on Channel Analysis (2nd Edition)

Millard on Winning on the Stock Market (2nd Edition)

Visit our Website at http://www.traderspress.com

• *View our latest releases*
• *Browse our updated catalog*
• *Access our Gift Shop for investors*
• *Read our book reviews*

Contact us for our hardcopy 100 page catalog.

TRADERS PRESS, INC.
PO Box 6206

Greenville, SC 29606

Tradersprs@aol.com

800-927-8222

Fax 864-298-0222

ISBN: 0-934380-50-3

Published January 1999

Editing and Cover Design by
Margaret Ros Hudson, Editor and Graphic Designer
Teresa Darty Alligood, Assistant Editor and Graphic Designer

TRADERS PRESS, INC.®
PO BOX 6206
Greenville, SC 29606

*Books and Gifts
for Investors and Traders*

800-927-8222 Fax 864-298-0221 864-298-0222 Tradersprs@aol.com
http://www.traderspress.com

Publishers Comments

For many years I have heard how valuable the work of J M Hurst has proven to those interested in the use of cycles in the pursuit of market profits. Many **Traders Press** customers have advised me how valuable any material would prove to them that would shed any additional light on the work of Hurst. It is with great pride that we present the work of Brian Millard, *Channels and Cycles,* which clarifies the original work of Hurst as well as updating it and bringing it forward to the present time. Millard, like other market technicians such as Jim Tillman and Peter Eliades, found the work of Hurst of such seminal importance in influencing his approach to market analysis that it became the cornerstone of his methodology.

It is hoped that this work will prove valuable to the members of the investment community who are interested in the application of cycles and the work of Hurst.

It should also be noted that **Traders Press** has recently reprinted the full-fledged training course on cycles authored by J M Hurst. This extensive course, which consists of 10 lessons encompassing nearly 1,600 pages (including hundreds of 11 x 17 foldout charts) and 11 audio tapes, is the most comprehensive and practical material available anywhere for those interested in understanding how to use cycles to their benefit in investing and trading. It shows how to actually apply Hurst's methods to actual trading situations, including actual buying and selling rules and applications. A fuller description of this course is included in the back of this book. This course is available exclusively through **Traders Press.**

Edward D Dobson, President
Traders Press, Inc.

Greenville, SC
January 7, 1999

FOREWORD BY PETER ELIADES

Before my stock market life, I had a life as a law school graduate and a professional musician-singer. The latter profession led to a vast mental storehouse of song lyrics. From the preface to his book Brian Millard echoes the sentiment I have expressed often in the past. Jimmy Web wrote a lyric that said, *Sometimes a single moment changes all the ones that follow.* How true. For me it was the discovery of J. M. Hurst's book, *The Profit Magic of Stock Transaction Timing.* When I read in Brian Millard's preface that he felt the same way, that Hurst's book was responsible for changing his life, I was drawn immediately to the promise of what Millard might be able to add to the Hurst legacy. It turns out he has offered much.

From his explanation of the importance of the concept that trends of different periodicity's are additive through his detailed explanation of the Hurst envelopes, he prepares the reader for the main course of his book, namely the basis and applications of numerical analysis as applied to the markets.

For the thousands of Hurst students worldwide and for anyone interested in the serious study of technical analysis, Brian Milliard's book *of "Channels and Cycles"* is a wonderful addition to your technical libraries.

Preface

Until 1979 my career followed the established path of university scientists and teachers the world over—writing papers, teaching students, presenting my work at conferences and visiting other workers in my field of scientific research. Then I was invited to spend a year as visiting scientist with the Food and Drug Administration in Washington, D.C., bringing my family with me.

Since I had an interest in the stock market, mainly from the scientific aspect of using digital filters to market data, I naturally paid a visit to the local library to see what was available on the subject of investment. I was astonished to find almost a whole wall of books devoted to this topic, at a time when there would have been probably none, or at best a couple of books on this subject back home in our local library in England.

Imagine my delight and pleasure when after about three months I came across J.M. Hurst's book *The Profit Magic of Stock Transaction Timing* (published by Prentice Hall). Unknown to me, Hurst had been putting into practice for years methods of analysis of market data that I had only recently begun to look at. Hurst was a mathematical analyst with an engineering background and he employed techniques familiar to me as a scientist where I frequently analyzed the noisy output of various instruments. He also, in his book, satisfied the slight reservations I had as a scientist about the predictability of the stock market by providing a great deal of evidence in support of the author's theories about cycles and

channels in stock price movement.

If I had any criticism of the book at all, it was simply that the average investor, picking it up and quickly scanning through its pages, would perhaps feel that it was too mathematically orientated, and replace it on the shelf, because it contained terms such as *Fourier Analysis*, *modulated side-bands*, etc. The investor would then be missing an important contribution to the subject of technical analysis. However, a reader who took the trouble to study the book in depth would grasp that Hurst's' work was based on five main concepts. These were:

1. Maximum profits are obtained from shorter trades
2. Some 23% of price motion is based on cyclic movements in nature
3. These cycles are additive
4. The cycles can be seen clearly if envelopes are constructed around the price movement
5. The ideal buying point is when several such cyclic components are reaching their low points

Now, some 20 years later, Hurst's pioneering work is as valid as ever, and his concepts form a solid foundation for profitable investment. To my regret, I never had the opportunity of meeting Hurst, but I can truly say that he was responsible for changing my life, because once I returned to England I used his basic principles as a starting point for my own line of research into price movements. This soon became my full time occupation.

Of course, I have the advantage over Hurst of state-of the-art computers and vast amounts of price data from markets all around the world on stocks, commodities, currencies and futures. However, these markets all have one thing in common—the methods described in this book apply to all of them, as will be seen by the examples used to illustrate the various chapters.

In this book I have employed the general principle of putting forward a concept and then applying it to artificial data before using it on real market data. The reason for this is quite simple—predictive techniques must be shown to work with totally predictable data, i.e. artificial data, so that the accuracy of the predictions can be checked. It is only then that these same techniques can be applied to less predictable market data.

A great deal of space has also been taken by a full discussion of moving averages and their properties. Moving averages are not only simple to calculate, they are also extremely powerful tools, but unfortunately the majority of investors have no idea of how to harness this power. It is to be hoped that the treatment given here will enable readers to avoid the mistakes made by using them incorrectly.

Finally, although the majority of investors have access to computers and programs to carry out various calculations and plot charts, computers are not absolutely essential for channel analysis, and the investor with only a pencil, paper and calculator can still achieve a great improvement in performance.

Brian J. Millard
Bramhall
Cheshire
England

CHAPTER 1

Money Management and Other Disciplines

Since the stock market is subject to a certain amount of random, *i.e.* unpredictable, movement, it is impossible to be correct in all of your investment decisions. Because of this fact, it is imperative that certain basic rules are followed in order to prevent the incorrect decisions that you will inevitably make having a disproportionate effect on your capital base. In other words, the aim should be to reduce the overall risk to your portfolio.

INVESTMENT RISK

There are many forms of investment risk, but as far as we are concerned we can reduce these to three. There is the overall market risk, there is the risk attached to a particular sector of the market, for example oil stocks, and there is the risk attached to an individual stock. Although the concept of risk can be addressed mathematically, we can avoid this approach by taking the view that the risk is reflected by the performance of these three components. Taking the very simplest way of looking at things, when the market has become overbought and is due for a reversal, then the market risk is high. When a sector has become overbought and is due for reversal following a rise, then the sector risk is high. Finally, the same argument applies to the individual stock, making the individual stock risk high.

Later in this book we will see how to determine the most probable direction of the trend in stock price, sector and market. This will give us some idea of the risks attached to each of the three components. There is an interplay between them that can be crystallized by the '80:20 rule.' Research on the UK stock market has shown that in a normal falling market, 80% of the component stocks of that market will also fall, and the same rule applies to sectors of the market. In a severely falling market this percentage can rise to 100% or very near 100%. Thus it is imperative that the investor is aware of the probable market and sector direction when invested in a stock. **It is taking an unacceptable risk to invest in a stock if the market direction is down or about to turn down and its market sector is also in the same situation.** Conversely of course, the overall risk is lowest when the market, market sector, and stock have just begun to rise.

Quite clearly, the way to reduce each of these risks to zero is to exit the market if the market risk is high, exit the sector if the sector risk is high, and exit the individual stock if the individual stock risk is high. However, the partially random behavior of the stock market means that each of these risks can increase dramatically and so quickly that it is impossible to take immediate action. Because of this potential for disaster we must have another way of reducing the overall risk. This is achieved by diversification.

If all the available capital is placed in one stock, then all three component risks will apply. If the capital is placed in a number of stocks, and these stocks are all in the same market sector, then the risk attached to an individual stock is diluted by a factor which is proportional to the number of stocks. Although the risk is reduced, the total holding is still subject to the market risk and the market sector risk. It is obvious that spreading one's holdings across a number of market sectors can reduce the overall risk even further. An item of bad news that would affect a complete sector would then have a reduced effect on the total holdings.

The ideal would be to invest in individual sectors and individual stocks with very little correlation to each other. By this we mean that many factors that can affect one sector or stock will then either have no effect or indeed the opposite effect on other sectors or stocks.

Opinions vary as to how many stocks an investor should diversify into, but the number should obviously be large enough to reduce significantly the overall risk to the portfolio from the various component risks. The greater the number of stocks, the smaller is the effect on the whole portfolio of an individual losing stock. On the other hand, a large number of stocks will cause the portfolio to behave more and more like the market itself, and the effect of making some good investment decisions will become diluted. Since we are going to show in this book how investors can easily outperform the market itself, then we need to concentrate our efforts on just a handful of stocks. This will also have the advantage of making it much less tiresome to continue to monitor and manage the portfolio. The experience of this author and many others is that a portfolio consisting of eight stocks is the ideal. Such a portfolio is fairly robust towards the occasional loser, but will allow the outstanding winner to make a large contribution to the overall value.

FULL INVESTMENT

The portfolio of eight stocks that make up the ideal diversification represents the maximum position when all the available capital has been invested. In practice, this position is rarely attained, since the investor will be trading fairly constantly over a period of time. The risk to the portfolio will be minimized when the capital is evenly divided between the eight stocks, *i.e.* each represents one eighth of the total value.

KEEP IN BALANCE

As time moves on, individual stocks will make individual gains, with the occasional losses, so that the value of each one will cease to be exactly one eighth of the total. The investor should try to keep the portfolio in rough balance if possible. Retaining a cash reserve can only do this.

Thus, if one holding, once liquidated because a selling signal has been given, represents a large proportion of the total capital, then it would be inappropriate to re-invest the whole of the proceeds into the next stock. It would be better to use an amount representing roughly one eighth of the total portfolio and cash value, and keep the rest in this cash reserve. This reserve can then be used to top up the selling proceeds from an under-performing stock whose representation has fallen below the one-eighth level so that the next investment will restore the balance.

Of course, if the first stock to be sold were an under-performing one, then the proceeds would not be enough when re-invested to buy a hold-ing that would amount to one eighth of the whole. In such a case, it is best to wait until one or two other stocks have been sold so that the increased amount of cash will make it easier to balance the whole port-folio.

It is important to realize that one should not spend too much time and effort trying to maintain more than a rough balance of one eighth of the total for any one stock. Avoid at all costs the temptation to sell a stock simply to maintain this balance. **A stock should only be sold when its price movement dictates that it is time to sell.**

STAY DISCIPLINED

Besides this question of money management, there are a number of other rules that the investor should obey in order to stay disciplined. The greatest barrier to success in the stock market is *investor psychology*. This mani-fests itself in two ways. In the first, the investor ignores the selling signal generated by a stock because the feeling is that the downturn in price is simply a temporary aberration in the long upward trend, which will be resumed tomorrow, next week, or the week after that. In the second, the investor is subject to impulse buying. A stock becomes attractive for a variety of reasons, and the investor rushes in to buy, totally ignoring the fact that a buying signal has not been given by any of the methods devel-oped in this book. Sometimes one of the reasons for buying is because advice has been given by a friend, a broker, or simply by a press comment. It is perfectly in order to listen to such advice, but it is vital that the stock being pushed is checked by these well proven methods before it is bought.

The methods in this book have stood the test of time in various markets throughout the world. They move the balance of probabilities in favor of the investor. Over the short term of just a few transactions, the investor might find that results might not be favorable, but over a larger number of transactions the investor comes out ahead. For this reason it is essential that the investor follow the methods without question, does not stay inactive when action is required, and does not give in to the urge to take action when inactivity is called for. If the investor does not do this, the balance of probabilities will move the wrong way, and may not just have the effect of reducing the profit made, but could cause serious losses over the long term.

CHAPTER 2

The Importance of the Trading Interval

A surprising number of investors still hold the view that the best strategy is to buy and hold. They can point to the substantial profits that would have been accumulated by an investment in most stocks if they had been held for say five years. This gain would have occurred over any five-year period for most stocks, irrespective of when it started in the last fifteen years, even including the eve of the 1987-market crash. This, in retrospect, is now viewed as just a blip in the market's long upward trend, as can be seen from the chart of some twenty years of the weekly closing values of the Dow Jones Index in Figure 2.1.

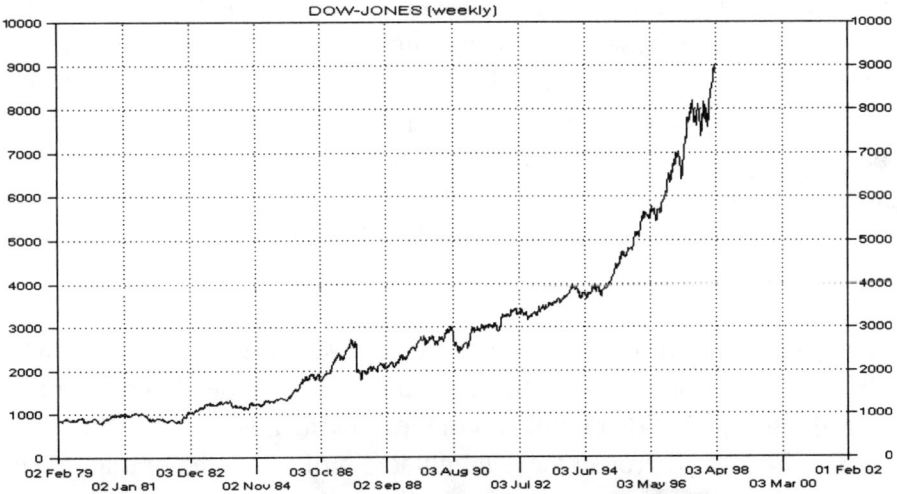

Figure 2.1. *A chart of the Dow Jones Index since February 1979.*

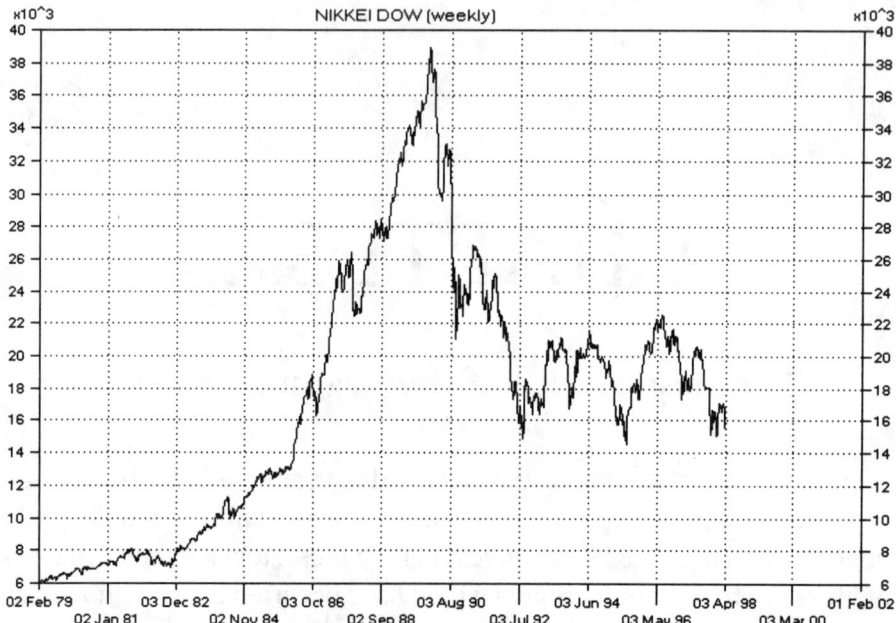

Figure 2.2. *A chart of the Nikkei-Dow Index since February 1979.*

Underpinning this strategy is the assumption that the underlying long term trend in the market will always be upwards, and that minor fluctuations in stock prices are simply temporary aberrations in the long march to substantial profit. There is of course no fundamental law of nature that says the stock market will rise indefinitely, and so a strategy based on this concept is subject to some risk. A Japanese investor will understand this only too well, as can be seen by comparing the chart of some twenty years of the closing values of the **Nikkei Dow Index** in Figure 2.2 with the chart in Figure 2.1. The **Nikkei** is now less than half of what it was in late 1989.

It is important that investors have a clear objective. The investor who stays in for the long term has the unclear though commendable objective of making profits. What is not part of the thinking is how to maximize the profit, and how to protect the accumulated profit. The factor that makes it possible to improve and protect profits from all markets, stocks, currencies and commodities alike, is that the movements in these markets are not straight line rises, but show shorter term rises and falls grafted on to the underlying long term trend. An investor who utilizes the short term rises and is not in the market during the short term falls will achieve much better results than the buy-and-hold investor. Using this approach, it is even possible to make profits from some markets by buying and selling (not going short) while the long term trend is down!

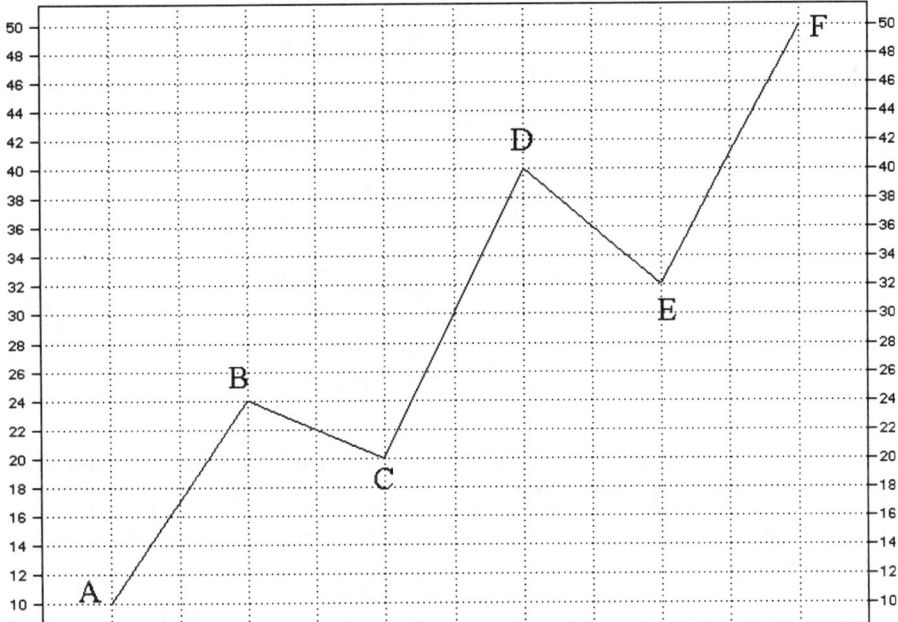

Figure 2.3. *Rises and falls in a stock starting at $10 and rising to $50 over a period of time.*

We will soon see that some unexpected conclusions will follow from a closer examination of short term trends. The starting point for this is to take a simple view, such as that shown in Figure 2.3, for a stock which starts at say $10 and eventually reaches $50 over a period of time.

The time axis is not labeled since it is not relevant to the immediate discussion, but we can take it to represent a period of years rather than weeks or days.

THE BUY-AND-HOLD INVESTOR

The investor who buys at $10 and reaches the end of the period of time without selling will see the price rise to $50, for a profit of 500% for the period.

THE FREQUENT TRADER

If we assume that the price moves in irregular steps such as those shown in the figure, then a (mythical) investor selling at each peak and buying at each trough would pass through the following sequential positions:

> Point A: Buy 100 shares @ $10, pays $1000
> Point B: Sell 100 shares @ $24, receives $2400
> Point C: Buy 120 shares @ $20, pays $2400
> Point D: Sell 120 shares @ $40, receives $4800
> Point E: Buy 150 shares @ $32, pays $4800
> Point F: Sell 150 shares @ $50, receives $7500

This investor turned $1000 into $7500 in the same period of time that the buy-and-hold investor turned the $1000 into $5000. Thus a gain of half as much again has been made by riding the short term up trends and exiting for the short term down trends. Since the starting price and ending price are exactly the same in both cases, the reason for the increased profit is the second investor ended up holding more shares than the first investor, 150 compared with 100.

It is illuminating to look more closely at the reason why more shares are being obtained by the approach of more frequent trading. It is the percentage amount by which the price falls from the intermediate high point to the next low point that is responsible. The example in Figure 2.3 showed two intermediate falls, the first from $24 to $20, a fall of 16.7%, while the second was from $40 to $32, a fall of 20%. The peak prices of $24 and $40 are irrelevant in isolation, as are the trough prices of $20 and $32. **It is the relationship between the peak and the trough that is the deter-**

mining factor. This means the same result would be obtained if we changed the value of the peak values and trough values as long as the fall from the first peak remained at 16.7% and the fall from the second peak remained at 20%. As an example, we could take intermediate peak prices of $30 and $45 and intermediate trough prices of $25 and $36. These also give falls of 16.7% and 20%. The position would then be:

> Buy 100 shares @ $10, pays $1000
> Sell 100 shares @ $30, receives $3000
> Buy 120 shares @ $25, pays $3000
> Sell 120 shares @ $45, receives $5400
> Buy 150 shares @ $36, pays $5400
> Sell 150 shares @ $50, receives $7500

We see quite clearly that the end result is the same in terms of the overall number of shares held at the end of the period and the percentage gain made. It is only if a trader cuts short the exercise that the intermediate peak prices have any meaning, since, for example the trader could exit with $5400 at point D in the second case compared with $4800 at point D in the first case.

We have now arrived at a surprising result. For a trader who trades in and out of one stock, the increased profit compared with the buy and hold investor depends *not* on the intermediate price rises, but on the intermediate price falls!

The vast majority of investors do not of course dip in and out of the same stock, but will sell one share to move into another one. Even so, the same principle applies that better returns will be made by frequent trading rather than staying with the same stock for many years. What is not obvious, since Hurst did not address the issue in any great depth, is what is meant by frequent trading. Is it a transaction every day, or every week or every month?

THE FREQUENCY OF TRADING

Since each price fall leads to an increased amount of stock being obtained, then it appears that the more frequently we trade, the larger our holding will be. This is partly true, but three assumptions have been made, which will have to be examined closely in order to decide how far we can take this method:

1. Dealing costs in buying and selling stock have been ignored.

2. The shorter term rises and falls in the example used are fairly extensive.

3. Perfect timing of buying and selling have been achieved, with the investor hitting the exact peaks and troughs in the price.

In practice, we will reach a limit when no profit will be made. This is because as we move to shorter and shorter trading intervals between peaks and troughs, the average percentage falls (and of course rises) in price get smaller and will no longer be sufficient to offset the dealing costs.

TYPICAL RISES AND FALLS

These are illustrated for the Dow 30 constituents in Table 2.1, where a nominal trading interval of 25 days was used. The data was obtained by using a 25-day centered average of the daily closing values to determine the approximate turning points in the trends, and then the lowest daily closing value within a few days either side of the turn taken as the start of the up trend. Similar logic was used in determining the start of the downtrend. The Table shows the average lengths of these down trends and up trends for a five year period in each of the stocks and the average percentage falls and rises in the stock price over the time span of the trend. For clarity, the percentage falls are shown as negative numbers.

The stock with the shortest down trend was **Allied Signal**, with an average of 15 days for the nominal 25 day trends, while the stock with the longest was **Woolworth** with 29.7 days. Across the whole group of 30 the average for down trends was 20.75 days.

The stock with the shortest up trend was **Westinghouse** at 16.8 days, while the stock with the longest was **United Technologies** at 36.1 days. Across the whole group the average was 26.7 days.

As far as the actual percentage rises and falls are concerned, you can see the largest average fall during the down trends was **Bethlehem Steel** at 18.6%, while the largest rise was also for **Bethlehem Steel** at 22.3%. Across the whole group the average fall was 10.3% and the average rise 14.6%.

It is interesting to see what happens as we shorten the trading interval, down to say a nominal 5 days. The method of determining the down trends and up trends is the same as before, except we are using a 5-day centered average. The data is given in Table 2.2.

The stock with the shortest down trend was **American Express**, with an average of 4.3 days for the nominal 5-day trends, while the stock with the longest was **Westinghouse** with 6.7 days. Across the whole group of 30 the average for down trends was 5.16 days.

The stock with the shortest up trend was **Bethlehem Steel** at 4.8 days, while the stock with the longest was **Union Carbide** at 6.2 days. Across the whole group the average for up trends was 5.53 days.

For the percentages, the largest faller was again Bethlehem Steel, with an average fall of 7.52%; this stock was also the largest riser at 8.01%.

You can quite clearly see that the result of shortening the trading interval from a nominal 25 days down to 5 days is to reduce the amount by which the average stock fell during a down trend from 10.26% to 4.6%. The amount by which the average stock rose during an up trend was also reduced from 14.6% to 5.5%.

Stock	days falling	% fall	days rising	%rise
A T & T	20.1	- 8.88	23.0	12.84
Allied Signal	15.0	- 8.25	24.2	12.82
Aluminum Co	23.5	- 11.71	29.0	16.05
American Express	20.3	-10.10	27.6	15.39
Bethlehem Steel	28.8	-18.59	21.7	22.26
Boeing Company	21.2	- 9.87	23.5	12.99
Caterpillar Inc	21.4	-11.60	32.6	19.20
Chevron Corp	16.3	- 7.69	28.3	10.72
Coca Cola	16.6	- 8.64	32.8	14.64
Disney	20.2	- 9.51	24.3	14.73
Du Pont	23.5	- 9.36	26.6	13.74
Eastman Kodak	21.6	-10.81	26.3	14.18
Exxon	17.4	- 6.50	30.4	9.72
General Electric	18.8	- 7.24	27.4	12.38
General Motors	24.7	-12.21	24.5	16.11
Goodyear Tire	21.1	- 9.98	26.5	15.69
IBM	27.3	-14.02	30.3	21.05
Internl Paper Co	19.2	-10.09	23.5	2.55
J P Morgan	17.7	- 8.59	26.5	11.78
MacDonalds	20.1	- 8.36	26.3	12.67
Merck & Co	23.2	-11.20	28.8	15.86
Minnesota M M	19.9	- 7.53	26.2	10.37
Philip Morris	19.7	-11.27	32.4	15.86
Proctor & Gamble	14.6	- 7.25	25.0	11.88
Sears Roebuck	18.4	-10.94	28.4	16.70
Texaco Inc	18.1	- 6.60	3.5	8.55
Union Carbide	20.7	-12.38	25.7	16.96
United Technols	19.2	- 9.14	36.1	14.68
Westinghouse	24.4	-13.65	16.8	16.52
Woolworth Corp	29.7	-15.69	21.3	19.37
Averages	20.75	-10.26	26.65	14.60

Table 2.1. *Dow 30 Constituents. The analysis of nominal 25-day trends over the 5 year period to mid 1998. Shown is the average length in days of a falling trend, the average percentage fall of falling trends (given a negative value), the average length in days of a rising trend and the average percentage rise.*

Stock	days falling	% fall	days rising	%rise
A T & T	5.7	-4.10	5.2	4.99
Allied Signal	4.9	-4.33	5.7	5.57
Aluminum Co	5.7	-5.19	6.0	6.21
American Express	4.3	-4.37	5.3	5.69
Bethlehem Steel	6.1	-7.52	4.8	8.01
Boeing Company	5.0	-4.32	5.5	5.27
Caterpillar Inc	5.1	-4.99	5.4	6.21
Chevron Corp	4.7	-3.80	5.9	4.55
Coca Cola	4.7	-3.78	6.0	5.08
Disney	5.0	-4.27	5.4	5.24
Du Pont	5.0	-4.12	5.6	5.08
Eastman Kodak	4.9	-4.44	5.4	5.06
Exxon	4.4	-3.11	5.2	3.59
General Electric	4.9	-3.43	5.7	4.49
General Motors	5.8	-5.57	5.2	6.18
Goodyear Tire	4.7	-4.40	5.6	5.75
IBM	5.6	-5.51	6.0	6.63
Internl Paper Co	5.2	-4.74	5.9	5.32
J P Morgan	4.9	-3.91	5.1	4.55
MacDonalds	4.7	-3.90	5.5	4.88
Merck & Co	5.4	-4.77	5.6	5.85
Minnesota M M	4.9	-3.36	5.3	3.82
Philip Morris	5.0	-4.73	6.0	5.60
Proctor & Gamble	5.3	-3.94	5.5	5.05
Sears Roebuck	5.0	-5.15	5.5	6.41
Texaco Inc	5.1	-3.31	5.0	3.75
Union Carbide	5.1	-5.38	6.2	6.65
United Technols	4.9	-3.97	5.8	5.29
Westinghouse	6.7	-6.55	5.7	7.07
Woolworth Corp	6.2	-6.42	5.0	6.65
Averages	5.16	-4.58	5.53	5.48

Table 2.2. Dow 30 Constituents. The analysis of nominal 5-day trends over the 5 year period to mid-1998. Shown is the average length in days of a falling trend, the average percentage fall of falling trends (given a negative value), the average length in days of a rising trend and the average percentage rise.

RELATIONSHIP BETWEEN TREND LENGTH AND PERCENTAGE CHANGE

In order to get a better grasp of the relationship between the length of trends and the amounts by which the price rises or falls during the duration of the trend, we show the results, in Figure 2.4, for up trends running from 3 days up to nearly one year. For trends of 50 days and longer, there is a steady increase in the percentage gains, although it is not a one-for-one relationship in the sense that doubling the length of time doubles the percentage gain. Below 50 days, there is a rapid fall off in the amount of gain.

THE EFFECT OF COMPOUNDING

If we just take the typical average gains and average length of the up trends in the Dow 30 constituents, we can look at the performance at the end of one year of our perfect investor who re-invests the proceeds from one deal into the next.

We will make the assumption that as soon as one trade is closed another is immediately opened. Assuming there are 260 business days in the year, the number of trades carried out in the year will be 260 divided by the length of the up trend. As well as the nominal 5 day and 25 day trends discussed earlier, data has also been obtained for nominal 3, 9, 15, 51, 101 and 201 days. Odd numbers have been used so the moving average, used to give an approximate position for the start of the trends, can be centered. The data, part of which was used to generate Figure 2.4, is now collected in Table 2.3.

It can be seen that the compounding effect results in a steady rise in gain for a year's trading as we shorten the trading interval, moving from 72.8% for the trading interval of 232.4 days up to a massive 1654.6% for a very short trading interval of 3.76 days. As with Tables 2.1 and 2.2, the trading interval is not a convenient whole number of days because it is the average of large numbers of trends within each stock and the average of these values for all 30 stocks. Since we are simply trying to establish an overall picture for the effect of compounding, this does not matter.

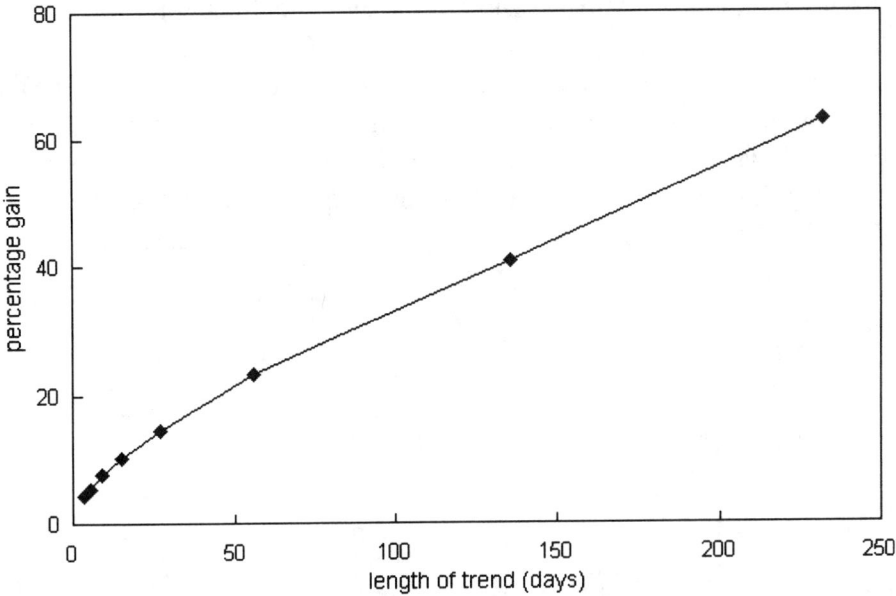

Figure 2.4. *How the percentage gain for up trend increases with the length of the trend.*

This compounding effect is naturally very impressive, and seems to confirm quite clearly that the frequent trader, for example using a trend of 3.76 days which results in nearly 70 trades in a year, will make about 22 times as much profit as the trader who makes just one trade in the year. As a general principle this is correct, but as we will soon see, when more realistic figures are used, there will be a lower limit to the frequency of trading.

ADJUSTING FOR REAL LIFE

There are two modifications to be made to the figures. First, we have ignored the effect of dealing costs, the spread of prices and some value placed on the investor's time. As a round figure, we should consider these to add up to about 5% of the capital employed. Thus the investor has to achieve a gain of 5% per trade in order to cover costs and make the exercise worthwhile in terms of time and effort. Second, we have been discussing the perfect trader who buys at the exact beginning and end of the up trend. Bearing in mind that we cannot know when a trend has started until the price moves up from its previous falls in order to give us a trough price, and cannot know when a trend has ended until the price moves down to generate a peak price, then our definition of a perfect investor should change to that of an investor who enters the trend one day after the lowest price and exits one day after the highest price. This will of course lower the amount of gain made from each up trend.

Nominal trend (days)	Rise time (days)	Average % rise	Compounded rise % per annum
3	3.8	4.23	1654.6
5	5.5	5.48	1128.5
9	9.1	7.64	713.8
15.1	10.27	437.7	437.7
25	26.7	14.6	277.9
51	55.9	23.1	163.1
101	135.3	40.8	93.1
201	232.4	63.07	72.8

Table 2.3. *The effect of compounding over one year the rises from various lengths of up trends if all of the rise is available*

Nominal days	Rise time (days)	Avge % Rise	Compounded % rise annum	Adjusted for 5% costs
3	3.8	4.23	1654.6	-41.4
5	5.5	5.48	1128.5	25.3
9	9.1	7.64	713.8	110.0
15	15.1	10.27	437.7	142.0
25	26.7	14.6	277.9	144.6
51	55.9	23.1	163.1	117.0
101	135.3	40.8	93.1	80.1
201	232.4	63.07	72.8	66.9

Table 2.4. *How applying a minimum gain of 5% to cover dealing costs, etc. reduces the compounded gain dramatically.*

By using these two modifications of a lower gain per trend, and removing 5% from the gain per trend in order to cover for costs, the data shown in Table 2.5 are obtained. These data establish an important point. As we lower the trading interval, the gains made over one year start to increase, then start to decrease again. Thus, there is an optimum trading interval to provide the maximum gain over one year for the frequent trader. In Table 2.5 this is for a nominal period of 51 days.

This optimum period of 51 days applies to our perfect trader who manages to get into a stock the day after it bottoms out and leaves it the day after it tops out. Moreover, the investor does this for each and every trade. To bring a bit of realism into the exercise it is necessary to look at a more typical investor. This typical investor captures only a proportion of the available gain made during the up trends. It is a matter of conjecture as to how much this proportion is, but one difficulty is that it will vary with the length of trend, since a day or two late in entering and leaving a trend of 5 days duration will have a greater effect on the profit made than the same delay applied to a long term trend of say 100 days duration. This can be seen by comparing Tables 2.4 and 2.5 for the gains made from each up trend. The gain from the 5-day trend was reduced from 5.48% to 2.28%, *i.e.* effectively halved by entering and leaving one day after the start and end of the trends. For the 101-day trend the effect was to reduce the gain from 40.82% to 31.14%. Because of this decreasing effect as we move to longer trading intervals, we must use a sliding scale, although this can be fairly crude since we are only trying to establish a principle. Noting that the typical investor will do worse than the investor who was a day late entering and leaving the trend, we can for the sake of progressing the argument, put the levels of gain actually achieved, to those shown in Table 2.6. These would result over the one year period in a heavy loss of 91.5% for the 3-day trader to a maximum gain of 62.4% for the trader taking advantage of 51 day trends, falling back to 51.5% for the trader using the 201 day trends.

Nominal days	Rise time (days)	Average % rise	Avge %rise (1 day late)	Compounded 5% costs/trend
3	3.8	4.23	1.75	-89.8
5	5.5	5.48	2.83	-64.4
9	9.1	7.64	4.85	-4.2
15	15.1	10.27	7.28	47.4
25	26.7	14.6	11.32	81.8
51	55.9	23.14	19.27	86.5
101	135.3	40.82	36.14	68.4
201	232.4	63.07	57.36	60.2

Table 2.5. *If the investor enters and leaves the trends one day late the average rise per trend is reduced. The effect on the compounded gains is more severe for the shorter trends.*

Obviously, the length of up trends which give the maximum return over a one year period (and of course over any periods longer than this) are very dependent upon the exact gains made for these trends. Since we have been taking an average view of the whole 30 constituent stocks, we would expect to find stocks that give a higher maximum return and others that give a lower return and that these occur at different trading intervals for the various stocks. As we saw for the individual Dow 30 constituents, the length of the trends will vary considerably from one stock to another, as will the gains made for these trends. If we take **Bethlehem Steel** as an example, the annual gain for up trends is best for a trading interval of around 75 days and gives an annual compounded gain of around 150%.

In general, the conclusion we have come to is that the relationship between trading interval and the gain achieved by compounding the individual trades will have the shape shown in Figure 2.5. For the investor who seeks a gain of more than 5% per trade in order to offset dealing costs, etc., we expect the maximum return for a stock to occur for trading intervals of between say 50 and 100 days, although there may be some that fall outside of this range. It is not possible to give any idea of the percentage gain that will be achieved at this optimum point; it can vary substantially.

The investor who is prepared to take a smaller gain per trade than the 5% minimum we have been considering so far will see the maximum return occur at a lower trading interval, although due to the rapid fall off of the percentage gain with trend length as this interval will not be much lower than this range of 50 to 100 days.

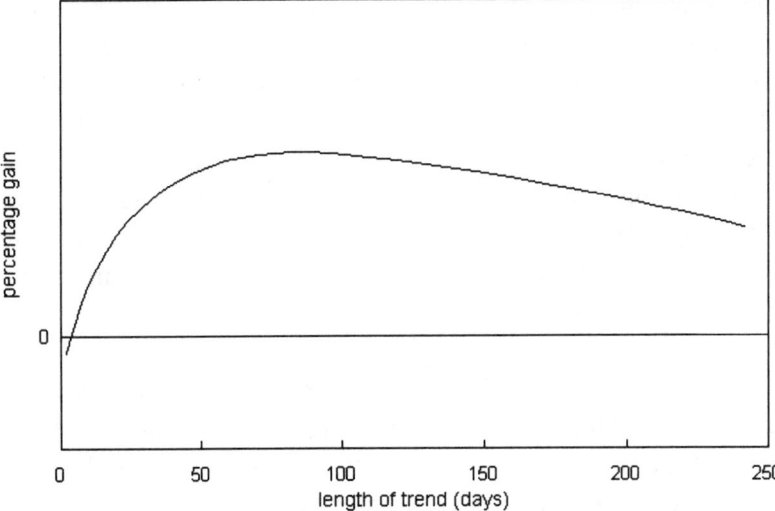

Figure 2.5. *The relationship between trading interval and the gain compounded over one year. The maximum return is given by trading intervals of between 50 and 100 days.*

Nominal days	Rise time (days)	Average% rise	Possible% rise	Compounded -5%costs/trend
3	3.8	4.23	1.5	-91.5
5	5.5	5.48	2.5	-69.6
9	9.1	7.64	4.0	-24.9
15	15.1	10.27	6.0	0
25	26.7	14.6	9.0	46.6
51	55.9	23.14	16.0	62.4
101	135.3	40.82	32.0	58.3
201	232.4	63.07	50.0	51.5

Table 2.6. *A more realistic view of the gains which might be achieved. It is assumed that only a proportion of the rise for each up trend is captured by the investor. The column headed 'Possible % rise captured' are simply guesses to illustrate the overall effect.*

Finally, in the development of this theory of the optimum trading interval, we must not forget that we have been considering an investor who has only been trading on up trends. Inevitably any investor will suffer losing trades, although the methods shown in later chapters of this book will reduce this number. The overall effect of introducing some losing trades into the compounding effect will be to reduce the annual gain made. The effect on the optimum trading interval is not as easy to determine. If, on balance, an investor makes more winning trades than losing trades, then with only a few trades in one year there is a sporting chance that none of them will be losers. As the number of trades made in one year rises, the probability of making a losing trade in the sequence of trades increases. Thus there will be a greater effect in reducing the annual profit as the trading interval decreases. The net effect is to shift the optimum to a longer trading interval.

We will take this concept of the maximum trading interval, approximately between 50 and 100 days, forward in the rest of this book. It will modify our view of the optimum cycles and channels to use when deciding the best entry and exit points for individual stocks.

CHAPTER 3

How Prices Move

There are two schools of thought on price movement and how to predict it. The fundamentalists believe the way to make a successful investment is to concentrate on methods of determining the value of a company. This is done by studying the way that it is managed, the various financial statements emanating from the company, the markets in which its products are being sold, comparisons with other companies operating in the same field, and so on. On the other hand, technical analysts base their predictions on historic price movement, although most of them would agree that there is some value in the fundamental approach. The technical analysts are of the opinion that the positive and negative aspects of a company are reflected in the stock price, and that a lot of unnecessary effort in studying the fundamentals can be avoided if you carry out the correct price analysis.

The major difficulty with technical analysis is there are a hundred and one ways to use it. In its simplest form it consists of plotting charts of the historical price data to see if there are any patterns developing that give an indication of movement in the near future. In its more complex form, it requires a computer to carry out extensive mathematical calculations before the analyst can decide what might happen to the stock price. Many of the indicators used to show the best times to buy or sell were developed in the past for particular types of markets. A major pitfall is that investors still apply such indicators to markets quite different in behavior from those based on the indicator for the original research and development. Many indicators based on fairly simple mathematics were developed by non-mathematicians, who applied them incorrectly. The use of moving averages is a case in point, as will be shown later in this book. Used incorrectly, moving averages can seriously damage your wealth!

The difficulty with the fundamentalist approach is that the investor might have to wait a long time before realizing a profit. Although you discover that a company is undervalued, and that its stock price ought to be much higher, and until other investors come to the same conclusion, the price cannot be expected to move down in the required direction. This composite view of investors towards the company is not being measured by an analysis of the fundamentals. However, technical analysis correctly applied will give a reasonable indication that the weight of outside opinion about the company is either optimistic, pessimistic or neutral. From that knowledge the investor can determine whether to buy, sell or do nothing. Of course, opinions about a stock, sector, or market can change rapidly, leaving the investor to base his decision on outdated materials. By giving the investor an early warning sign technical analysis is subjected to its severest test.

Some technical analysis methods are far too simplistic. In their most trivial form they come down to a set of rules that should be obeyed without any other understanding of the meaning behind them. Typical of such rules are those of the form 'buy when the stock price rises above the x-day average' or 'sell when the y-day average falls below the x-day average,' where x and y depend upon which technician you are speaking to. The difficulty with rules such as these is that they may have been formulated for a market quite different from that in which they are being applied. It is only when the investor starts to ask what lies behind these rules that an understanding begins to develop. This understanding is invaluable in deciding whether or not the current market is the type in which these rules should be applied.

By adopting a logical approach, gradually developing the idea of cycles and channels in stock prices, foreign currencies and commodities as we proceed through this book, the investor will come to understand quite clearly that we will have arrived at a method that is universal in its application.

ARE STOCK PRICES RANDOM?

The answer to this question should be 'no,' since billions of dollars, pounds, yen, marks, francs, crowns, etc. are invested in stocks at any one time. We must make the assumption that the people who invest these vast sums are not simply putting their money into a 100% unpredictable lottery. As well as these actual investors, further amounts of dollars, pounds, yen, marks, francs and crowns are being paid to institutions, stockbrokers, financial commentators and the like in the form of commissions and salaries.

Financial commentators play an interesting part in the market. If in their absence, markets behaved in a totally random fashion, then the presence of such commentators would induce an indeterminate number of investors to buy or sell the particular stocks being commented on. This action would then mean that the market in those particular stocks ceased to be totally random. From this concept it follows we should be able to accept the idea if stock prices move randomly most of the time, there will be occasions when press, radio and TV comment will cause them to move in an ordered fashion.

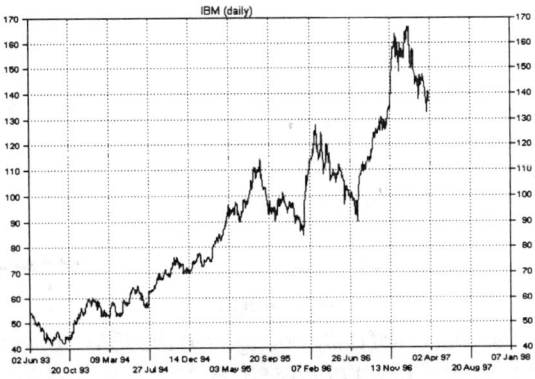

Figure 3.1. *A chart of the daily closing prices of IBM since June 1993.*

It will help to clarify our thinking if we restate this idea as follows:

• Stock prices contain random day-to-day movement

• Stock prices contain upwards and downwards trends

• The start and end of an individual trend is itself a random event

The word 'trend' means an underlying price movement that lasts between a few minutes and many years.

At this point we have taken the comments of the financial commentator to be the trigger for converting aimless random movement in a stock price to something which is non-random. This is a rather simple view, since many other triggers can be envisaged. to illustrate the point, a few examples of triggers that produce a rise in price will suffice. Thus there is the trigger caused by a broker telephoning clients to tell them to invest in stock X; there is the trigger of followers of the chart of stock X seeing that the price has started to climb and taking action to get on board; there is the trigger of the company issuing financial figures which are far better than had been expected, and so on.

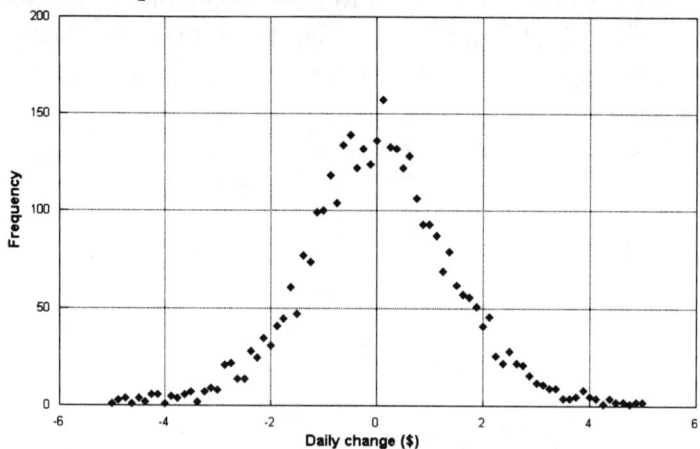

Figure 3.2. *The distribution of daily changes in the IBM closing price. A total of 3600 daily changes have been analysed. A rise of $1/8 is the most common, followed by a fall of $1/2. A zero change is the third most common.*

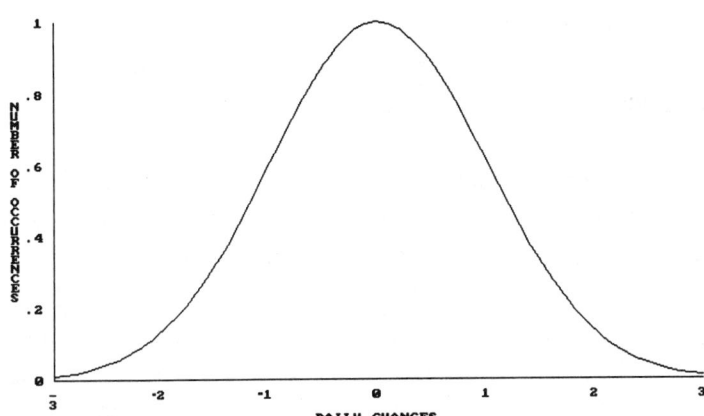

Figure 3.3. *A random distribution of daily changes would conform to this envelope.*

Although the argument just put forward is a logical one, it is not easy to demonstrate whether the price movements in a particular stock are random or not. Before doing this we need to decide on our time scale. This could be minutes, days, weeks or intervals of many weeks. Whichever we take, the intervals must be constant. We will take the day as our unit of time.

A good starting point is to look at the daily changes in the closing prices for a stock over a long period of time. In Figure 3.1 we show a chart of **IBM** daily closing prices since June 1993. The chart is characterized by a lengthy rise punctuated by three short-lived corrections. One way in which the data can be investigated is to analyze the changes in the closing price from one business day to the next. The smallest change in the data is $\$^1/_8$, but there are of course many occasions when the closing price is unchanged for the next day. In Figure 3.2 the data is presented for **IBM** stock for a period of 3600 days, giving sufficient data to draw a conclusion. The central vertical line in Figure 3.1 represents a change of zero, *i.e.* those occasions in which a day's closing value was the same as the previous day. The horizontal scale covers daily changes from a fall of $6 to a rise of $6. A few extreme values which occurred on the occasion of the 1987 crash have been left out in order not to extend the horizontal scale more than is necessary. The vertical scale represents the number of occasions when a particular change has occurred. As an example, a rise of exactly $2 occurred on 41 occasions and a fall of $2 on 31 occasions.

As far as we are concerned, it is not the exact values in Figure 3.2 that are important, but the shape of the envelope outlined by the plotted points. If the daily price changes were completely random, then the shape of the envelope would be like that shown in Figure 3.3. which is the classic probability shape. While it is not exactly the same, there is enough similarity to draw the conclusion that there is a high degree of random behaviour in the daily price changes in **IBM**. As more data points are used, the plot of daily changes will be more similar to the probability curve. Just as a probability curve is defined by two quantities known as the mean and standard deviation, so can the daily changes in a stock be described by two such quantities. Such a plot can be used to estimate the probabilities of various price changes occurring between one day and the next. Changes other than those from one day to the next can be analyzed in this way, for example changes over a 30 day period or even one year period. With a reasonable amount of data, it is possible to estimate the probability of a certain change occurring, so, for example, it should be possible to make a statement such as 'there is a 7.5% probability of a fall of $3.50 in the stock price by 30 days time." However, this is not the objective of the current exercise, it is to see whether stock prices move in a random fashion or not. Quite clearly, the day-to-day movement in the **IBM** stock price is highly random. This is also the case for the day-to-day movement in any other stock analyzed over a long period of time.

At this stage in our thinking we come to the conclusion that investing in the stock market behaves purely according to the laws of chance. Whether we make a profit or not lies in the lap of the Gods.

SEQUENCES OF DAILY CHANGES

Investors do not normally buy a stock with the aim of selling it the next day. They envision holding that stock for a period of time, from a few days to a few years. Since the change from one day to the next is highly random, it would appear logical to assume that the change in price from the beginning to the end of the holding period is also random.

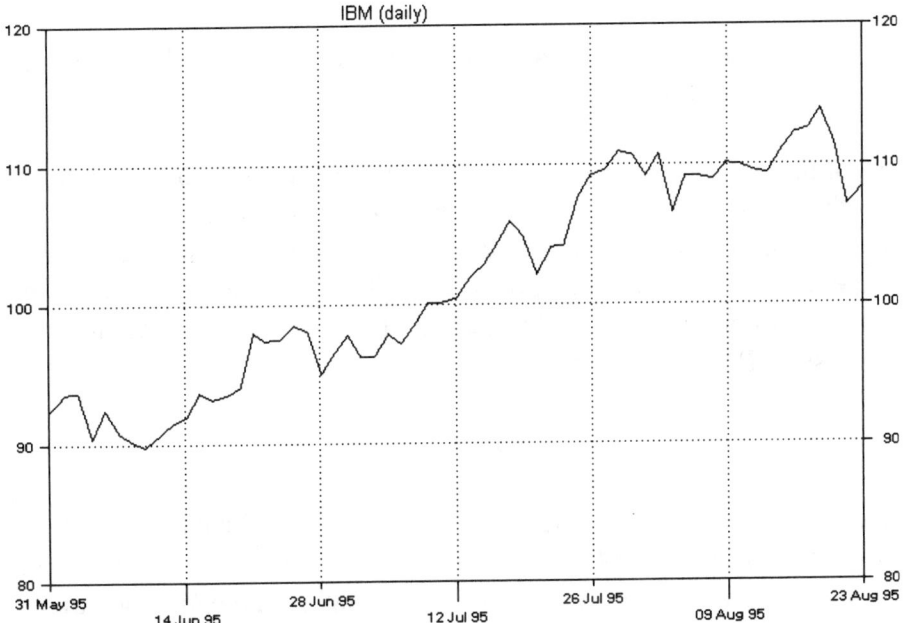

Figure 3.4. *A period of rising price in IBM stock.*

Fortunately the logic is faulty, because we cannot extrapolate from individual daily changes to the change over a period in this way. **The actual sequence of daily changes may not be random.** If we look at a change in price over a lengthy period, where the final price is higher than the starting price, then the price ends up higher because the sum of all the daily rises is greater than the sum of all the daily falls during this period. There are two reasons why this should be so:

1. There are more daily rises than falls.

2. The individual daily rises tend to be greater than the individual daily falls.

In the case of a period where the final price is lower than the starting price, then the reasons would be:

3. There are more daily falls than rises.

4. The individual daily falls tend to be greater than the individual daily rises.

All of these may occur, and of course they may occur by chance, but it is worth exploring the idea of sequences to see if we can establish that sequences of upward or downward moves in a stock might be caused by something other than random behavior. This can be done by comparing a period when prices rose with a period of similar time span when prices fell, using **IBM** as an example.

Price rise

Such a period is shown in the chart in Figure 3.4 in which the **IBM** stock prices from May 31, 1995 to August 23, 1995 are plotted. The actual rise started on June 8 with the closing price at $89³/₈ and ended on August 17, 1995. Out of 47 daily changes during this period there were 32 daily rises and 15 daily falls. The average daily rise was $1.348 and the average fall $1.258.

Price fall

Such a period is shown in Figure 3.5, where the price fell from $112¹/₈ on May 20, 1996 to $90.25 by July 23, 1996. This particular period was chosen because the length of time is similar to that of the rise with which it is to be compared. Out of 42 daily changes during this period, there were 27 daily falls and 15 daily rises. The average daily fall was $1.36 and the average daily rise was $0.99.

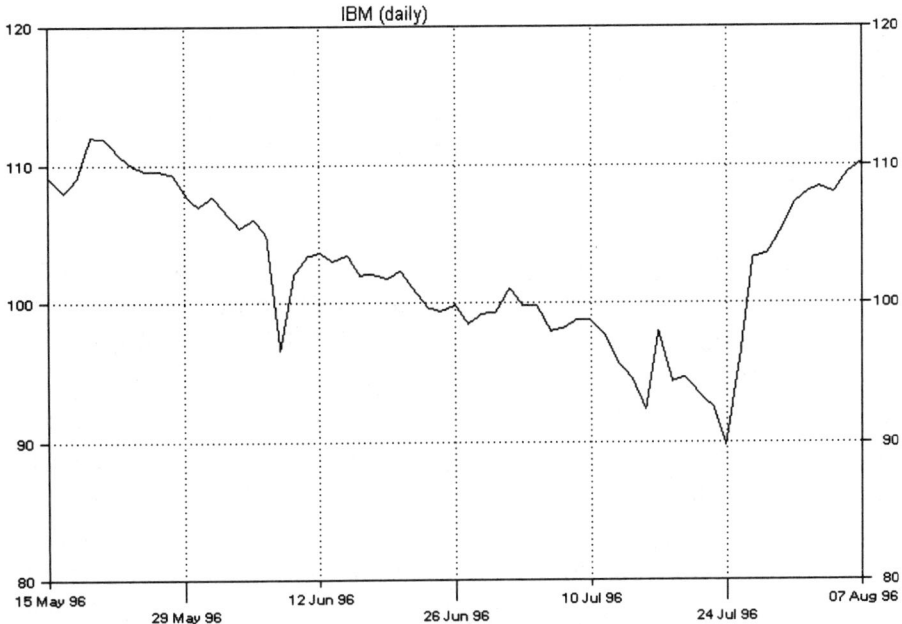

Figure 3.5. *A period of falling price in **IBM** stock.*

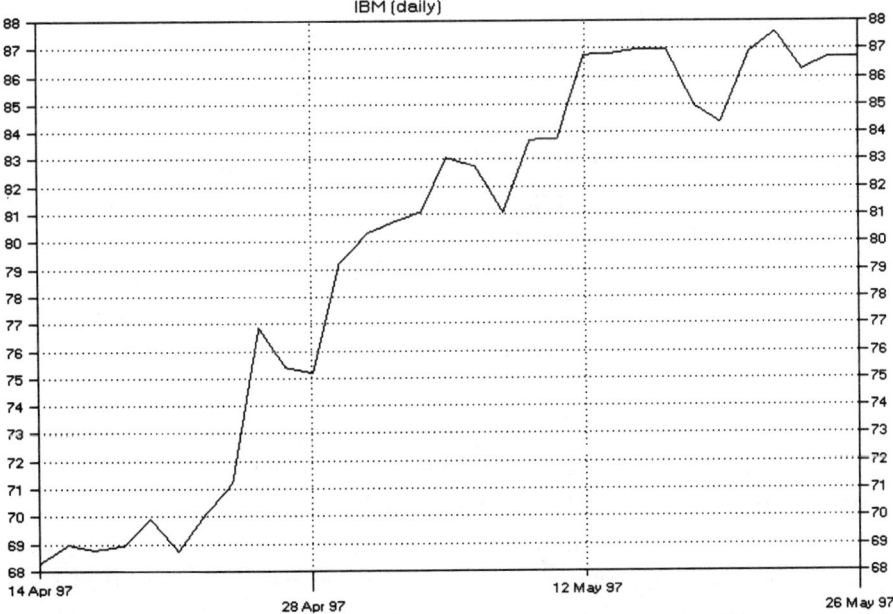

Figure 3.6. *In a period of rising prices there are usually more rises than falls. In this example from **IBM** there are 19 daily rises, 9 daily falls and 1 no change.*

You can see that during the sustained rise there were more than twice the number of rises than falls, with the average daily rise being higher than the average daily fall. Similarly, during the sustained fall there were nearly twice as many falls as rises, with the average daily fall being greater than the average daily rise.

We can now see that although the daily rises during a prolonged rise become larger than the norm, as do the daily falls during a prolonged fall, **it is the imbalance between the number of daily rises and the number of daily falls which is the prime cause of the overall rise or fall during a period.** This is illustrated in Figure 3.6. During the period covered by the chart there were 19 rises in price, 9 falls in price and 1 no change. This behavior is not restricted to **IBM** stock, but is universal, and applies to all stocks in all markets, as well as currencies and commodities. Of course, a sufficiently long data history must be used to establish the overall values for the average daily rise and fall, and a number of rising and falling periods have to be studied. This is because there may be a few occasions when there is hardly any imbalance between the number of rises and falls exists, but where the overall rise or fall is caused by a greater change in the individual rises or falls.

If, during a period in which there is an overall increase in the stock price there are more rises than falls, then it follows that there is an increased chance of sequences of successive daily rises compared with the number to be expected over the total history of the stock. Conversely, for periods where there are more falls than rises, there will be an increased chance of sequences of successive daily falls.

In order to simplify the discussion, we need a term to describe these sequences of successive rises or falls. Since these sequences are the building blocks from which longer term trends will be built upon, the term 'block' is appropriate. The minimum dimension of a block is two days (two successive rises or falls). In theory there is no upper limit to the number of successive daily rises or falls, but in practice a run of 10 successive rises or falls is almost unheard of. We can therefore take the maximum dimension of a block as being around 10 days. It should also be noted that it is possible to have a sequence of no changes in stock price, and of course with an inactive stock, this might run to many days. Such a sequence can still be considered a block, but neutral in its effect. We will see more of this type of block in the following chapter.

Over a long history of stock price movement, we will find that for sequences of two or more successive rises or falls, there are more of these than would be statistically predicted. In terms of blocks, this means that there are more blocks of a particular size than would be expected on the basis of a random distribution of daily changes. In other words, blocks tend to be bigger than the predicted size. From this we can deduce that stock price movement is not totally random.

It is difficult to come to an arithmetical value on the amount of random behavior present in stock prices, but it appears to be around 50%, so that about 50% of price movement is not random. This is not a constant amount, since there is a variation in random behavior. Stocks go through periods when their behavior is very random, and other periods when their behavior is much less so. In the latter case the price seems to meander with no apparent direction. Stocks that move in this fashion are of no use to investors. On the other hand, stocks that show strong trends are the ones that generate good profits for us.

INTERVALS OTHER THAN DAYS

The interesting point about the exercise we have just gone through is that we will arrive at the same conclusion irrespective of the time interval used. The only difference is the random content of price movement increases as we shorten the interval. Thus intra-day trading on hours or ticks is more difficult than trading on daily closing prices. On the other hand, we will see in later chapters there is an advantage in moving to longer intervals. For example using weekly data in addition to daily data.

Daily Ranges

It is also worth pointing out that the intervals used must be constant, since the theory of cycles developed later in this book demands that sampling occurs at fixed intervals. This puts us in difficulty when drawing cycles and channels on the typical stock market chart showing daily ranges. The two extremes of the daily range occur at random points of the day, although one extreme might be at the day's close. The policy adopted in this book is to use many charts that display the daily or weekly closing prices in order to achieve absolute clarity in presenting the concepts of cycles and channels. Where charts are shown with the vertical bars showing daily or weekly ranges. If channels are drawn they will use the closing prices, that may or may not be at the extremities of the bars. More often, the daily range will be used simply to find out if the stock was rising or falling towards the end of the day, with a view of anticipating the price trend at the beginning of the next business day.

We shall see in the following chapters that by using the technique of channel analysis we will be able to filter out the random behavior and concentrate on the predictable element of price movement. This will quickly show us those stocks that will provide us with healthy profits and those that will not.

We will be able to predict the start and end of price trends with reasonable success by using the idea of '*prediction boxes*'. These boxes are target areas into which we expect the current trend to take the price in the future before the trend comes to an end and the price reverses. The horizontal width of the box represents the uncertainty as to the time the price trend will reverse direction. The vertical height of the box represents the uncertainty the stock price at the time the trend reverses direction. Sometimes these prediction boxes will be quite large, but at other times they will be remarkably small, giving an astonishingly accurate prediction of the end of the current trend in terms of price and time.

Naturally, the further into the future we try to predict, the less accurate our prediction will be. We do not need to determine the price more than 50 to 100 days into the future. This is because we saw in chapter 2 that a trading interval of 50 to 100 days provides the optimum return.

CHAPTER 4

Trends within Trends

Before entering a discussion of trends in stock prices, we need to define what we mean by **'trend.'** The dictionary defines it as *'general direction and tendency.'* If after a period of time a stock price is higher than it was at the beginning, then we can argue the general direction and tendency is up. However, if we take a situation such as that shown in Figure 4.1, when the price showed a sustained, gentle decline followed by a rapid movement that took the price higher than at the start, then we are in some difficulty. If anything, we can argue the general tendency is down, since this was the direction of the price movement for the majority of the time. Quite obviously, the dictionary definition of 'trend' is far too vague for our purposes. We need a much clearer view of what constitutes a stock market trend.

From the last chapter we saw that price movement, using the day as the unit of time, consists of random day-to-day movement plus sequences of successive daily rises or falls, that are much less random. We called these blocks. The minimum duration of rising and falling blocks is 2 days, and a practical maximum is about 10 days. In addition there are neutral blocks in which the price remains unchanged for a number of days. These neutral blocks also have a minimum duration of 2 days but may have a much longer duration than 10 days in an inactive stock.

If the unit of time is a week, then price movement consists of random week-to-week movement plus sequences of successive weekly rises or falls that are much less random. These weekly blocks have the minimum duration of two weeks, and again the practical maximum seems to be around 10 weeks. We can of course have time units of minutes, hours, months or even years.

Our very restricted definition of a random movement is therefore a movement that lasts for one unit of time, and whose direction is not the same as that of the block or random movement that precedes it. This allows us to have a run of random movements where the movement over each unit of time is different from that over the previous unit of time.

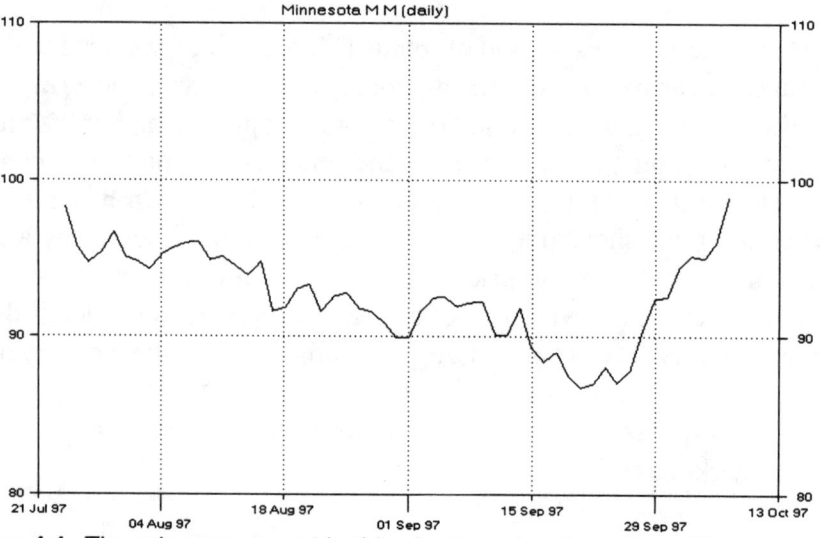

Figure 4.1. *The price movement in this chart can be viewed as either a down trend since the price was falling for most of the period, or an up trend since the price was higher at the end than at the start.*

UNINTERRUPTED TRENDS

We can start with a definition of a trend as *a series of price movements that takes the price higher or lower than it was at the start of the movement.* A neutral trend is one where the price ended up exactly the same as at the start.

An uninterrupted trend is obviously *a trend where all the price movements are in the same direction*, in other words, a block according to our definition. If we ignore neutral trends, then the shortest uninterrupted trend is therefore a 2-day (or 2-week) block. The longest is a block of about 10 days (or 10 weeks) duration. We can now use the terms 'block' and 'uninterrupted trend' interchangeably and qualify blocks further as rising blocks, falling blocks and neutral blocks.

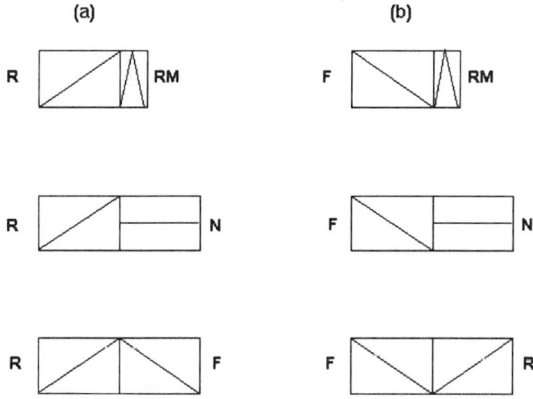

Figure 4.2. *(a) rising blocks (R) can be terminated by either a random movement (RM), a neutral block (N) or a falling block(F) (b) falling blocks can be terminated by either a random movement, a neutral block or a rising block. In this context blocks are sequences of rises, falls or sideways movements that last for more than one unit of time. A random movement is one that lasts for just one unit of time and is in a different direction from the movement in the previous unit of time. Units of time can be ticks, hours, days, weeks, etc.*

A block becomes terminated either by a random one day (or one week) movement or by another block operating in a different direction. Since we are principally concerned with either rising or falling trends, a neutral block can be viewed in the same light as a one day (or one week) random movement in that it will terminate a rising or falling block. Thus:

- Rising blocks are terminated by either a random daily (or weekly) movement, a neutral block or a falling block.
- Falling blocks are terminated by either a random daily (or weekly) movement, a neutral block or a rising block.

These concepts are shown in Figure 4.2.

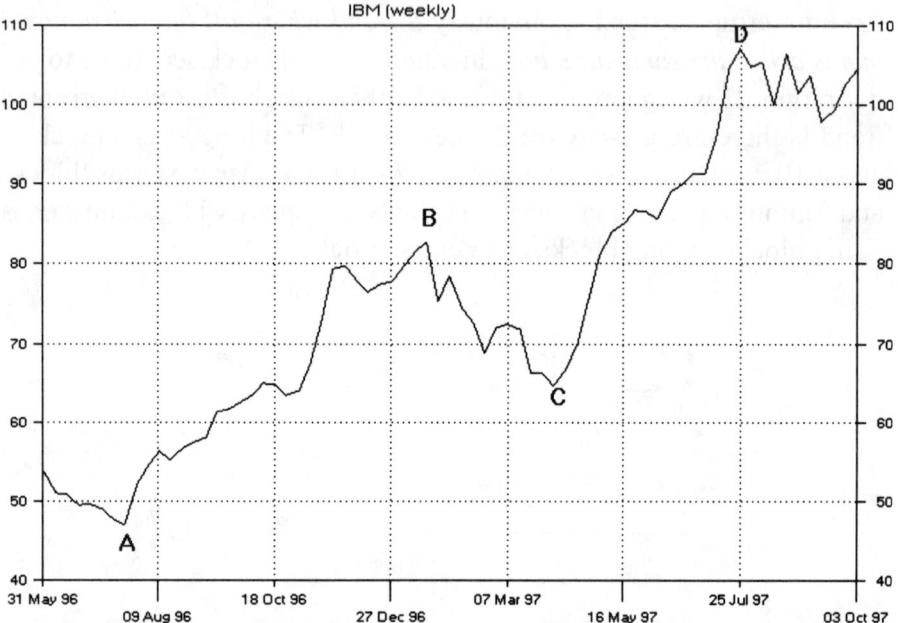

Figure 4.3. *A section of IBM weekly closing prices. The one year trend from point A (July 19, 1996) to D (July 25, 1997) lasted 53 weeks. This can be broken down into three shorter term trends, A to B (26 weeks), B to C (11 weeks) and C to D (16 weeks). These can be broken down into blocks, the longest block being one of seven successive rises from point C. The end of this block was caused by a random sideways movement. Note the sequence of seven random movements that followed point D.*

INTERRUPTED TRENDS

In Chapter 2 we discussed the trends for the Dow 30 stocks over various periods of time, looking at various rising trend lengths up to 101 days. Since we have seen that the longest uninterrupted trend is about 10 days, then to achieve a trend of 101 days means that such trends cannot be uninterrupted. These longer-term trends are therefore composed of varying numbers of blocks. These will be a mixture of rising and falling blocks and there may also be neutral blocks present during the lifetime of the trend.

TRENDS ARE ADDITIVE

Once we look at a long-term trend which is composed of a considerable number of blocks, then it will be obvious that shorter sections of it, composed of just a few blocks, will themselves constitute trends. We will be able to split a long-term trend into a number of shorter-term trends, and each of these shorter-term trends into a number of even shorter-term trends until we reach the smallest component, one block. The block can be based on daily, weekly or even intraday movements. This is shown in Figure 4.3. **This view of trends as being additive is one of the most important concepts of this book.**

Thus:

• Blocks build into very short-term trends

• Very short-term trends build into short-term trends

• Short-term trends build into medium term trends
  and so on.

Since we have applied the terms 'very short term,' 'short term' and 'medium term' to these trends, we can see that trends must have a time scale attached to them. This means that the term 'up trend' in isolation has no real meaning unless the rest of the sentence is describing the time frame over which the trend is operating. We will see shortly that trends are derived from cyclical movement that must have a time base.

As an example, we can assume the presence of a short term trend which causes a stock price to rise by say $2 over a period of four weeks, and fall by $2 over the next four week period. At the same time that this trend is in existence, we can assume there is a longer term trend coexisting such that it causes the price to rise by say $8 over a period of say 40 weeks. Such a trend is shown in the lower left of Figure 4.4.

When we combine the two, the net result is the composite trend shown in the right of Figure 4.4. When viewing a chart, it is this net result we will see. Although we will also be able to see the net result is due to some short term trends and a longer term trend coexisting, we will not be able to deduce the exact profile of any of these component trends by simply viewing the chart.

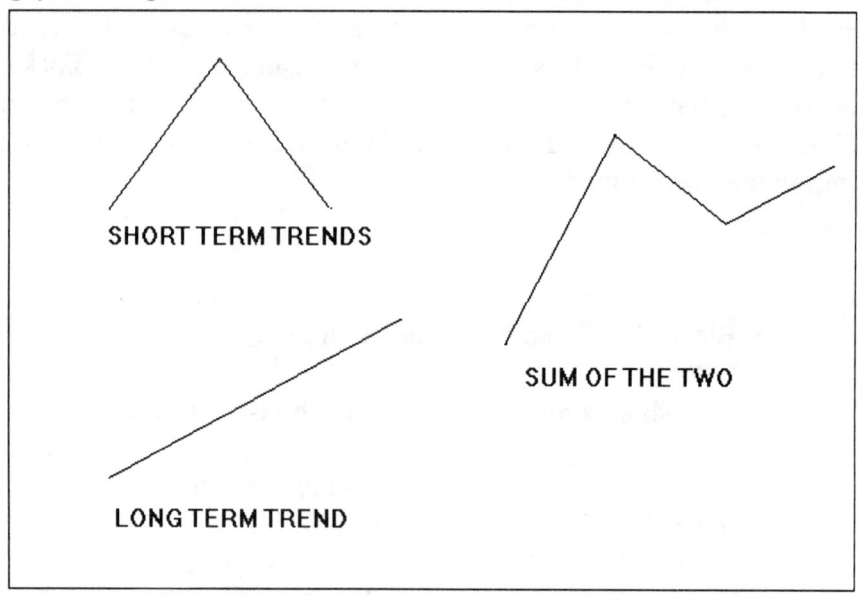

Figure 4.4. *If the short term trends shown on the upper left exists at the same time as the long term rising trend shown on the lower left, then the investor will actually see the combined trend seen on the right, which is the sum of the two components. The initial leg rises even faster than the rise in the component trends.*

The arithmetic of combining the two trends is simple. It is a matter of deciding how much the long-term trend contributes for each leg of the short-term trends. Thus over the first four weeks, the short-term trend results in a rise in price of $2. Since the long-term trend rises by $8 in 40 weeks, this is equivalent to a rise of 80 cents in four weeks. If we add this to the rise due to the short-term trend, we see that the total effect of the two trends is to cause a rise in price of $2.80. The following four weeks the long-term trend again adds 80 cents to the price, but the short-term trend is causing a fall of $2. Thus the net effect is for a fall of $1.20. For the final four weeks there is no short term trend, so that we see the unchanged long trend.

When looking at the chart itself, we see a rise of $2.80 followed by a fall of $1.20. If we are unaware of the existence of the long-term trend, we come to the conclusion that we have a short term up trend giving a rise of $2.80 followed by a short term down trend giving a fall of $1.20.

It is this effect of exaggerating short term rises relative to short termfalls when there is an underlying longer term rise that is partly responsible for the results we obtained in chapter 3, when we saw that the average daily rises were slightly large than the average daily fallsduring a price rise, with the opposite applying during a price fall.

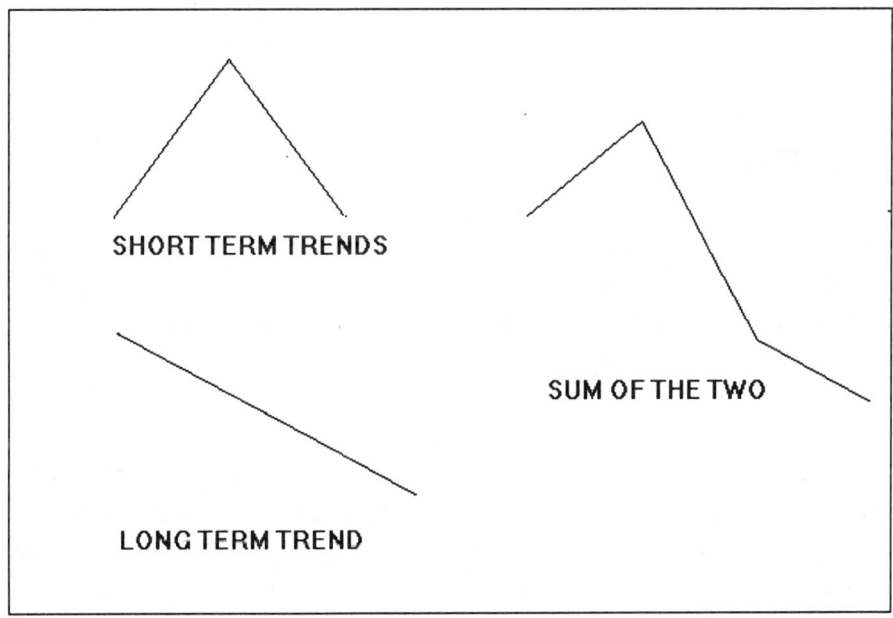

Figure 4.5. *If the short term trends shown on the upper left exists at the same time as the long term falling trend shown on the lower left, then the investor will actually see the combined trend seen on the right, which is the sum of the two components. The middle falling leg of the combined trend falls even faster than the comparable legs of the component trends.*

For the sake of completeness, it is worth looking at the effect of adding a long term down trend to the same short-term trends as in the previous example. In this case we can take the long term down trend as causing a fall of $8 over a 40-week period. The net effect of adding these trends is shown in Figure 4.5. The arithmetic is now different. Over the first four weeks the long-term trend causes a fall of 80 cents, while the short-term trend causes a rise of $2. The net effect is for a rise of $1.20. Over the next four weeks the long-term trend still causes a fall of 80 cents, but the short-term trend causes a fall of $2. The net effect is a fall of $2.80. Finally, for the last four weeks there is no short term trend, so that we see the unchanged long term trend.

When looking at the chart, we see a rise of $1.20 followed by a fall of $2.80. If we are unaware of the existence of the long-term trend, we come to the conclusion that we have a short term up trend giving a rise of $1.20 followed by a short term down trend giving a fall of $2.80.

DISTRIBUTION OF TRENDS IN STOCK PRICES

It is possible to analyze stock price movement for the numbers of trends that fall into various time categories. As an example, such an analysis for the weekly closing prices of **Eastman Kodak** stock over a 10-year period gave the following results:

Long term trends. There were six rising trends with an average persistence of 76 weeks, the maximum length being 147 weeks and the minimum 32 weeks. There were also six falling trends with an average persistence of 31 weeks. The maximum length of trends was 46 weeks and the minimum 11 weeks.

Shorter term trends. There were 31 rising trends with an average persistence of 13 weeks, the maximum being 31 weeks and the minimum 3 weeks. There were also 31 falling trends with an average persistence of 11 weeks, the maximum being 27 and the minimum being 3 weeks.

This distribution will vary from one stock to another. Obviously stocks that have shown a long climb will have very few individual trends, and these will mostly be of the long-term variety. Other stocks will have oscillated quite rapidly over their history and will have a predominance of short-term trends. Even so, it is extremely useful to have an indication of the distribution of trends for an individual stock of interest. The persistence of these trends is a useful piece of information, giving an indication of how long a new trend might be expected to last.

THE SHAPE OF TRENDS

In Figures 4.4 and 4.5 we drew trends as straight lines. This was done for clarity in illustration the point that trends were additive. We will show through the many examples in this book that trends are cyclical in nature. This means they have low points (troughs) and high points (peaks) that recur at intervals. Perfect cycles are *sine waves*, and their peaks and troughs recur at exactly the same intervals in time. They also have identical vertical displacements. Because of the random content of stock price movement, cycles in the stock market are subject to a variation in the position of their peaks and troughs in time and their vertical displacement can vary.

Sine Waves

A perfect sine wave is shown in Figure 4.6. A radio wave would be a good example of such a wave. We can describe this sine wave exactly by three quantities:

- Wavelength (or frequency)
- Magnitude (or amplitude)
- Phase

The **wavelength** is the distance between successive troughs or successive peaks. For radio waves in the broadcast spectrum, this distance is measured in meters. In radar the distance is in centimeters or less. As far as the stock market is concerned the units depend on the rate at which price data is sampled. Thus we could have wavelengths of minutes, hours, days, weeks, months or even years.

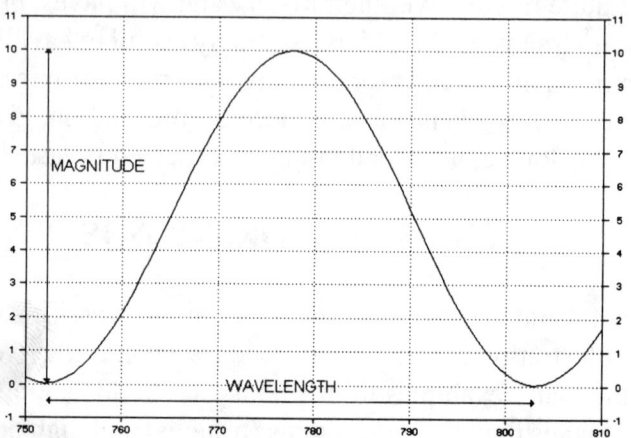

Figure 4.6. *A sine wave. The wavelength is the distance between two successive peaks or troughs. The magnitude is the vertical distance between a trough and the next peak (or a peak and the next trough).*

Radio waves can also be specified by frequency such as kilocycles and megacycles, where frequency is an inverse of wavelength. If we have a stock market sine wave with a wavelength of two weeks, then its frequency would be 52/2, *i.e.* 26 cycles/year.

There is confusion over the meaning of the term 'amplitude' when applied to sine waves. Many take it to mean the complete vertical distance covered in rising from a trough to the next peak. However, mathematical calculations to produce sine waves use a value for amplitude that is one half of this. To avoid ambiguity, we will use the term 'magnitude' rather than 'amplitude.' Thus the **magnitude** of a sine wave is *the vertical distance from trough to peak.* For stock market waves the magnitude would be in a currency such as dollars, pounds, etc. and for currencies it would be in the form of ratio measurements. For a market index such as the Dow it is of course measured in points. The amplitude is one half of the magnitude and is therefore the vertical distance from the horizontal centerline of the wave-form to a peak or trough.

The **phase** of a sine wave is a measure, in degrees or radians; of how far along from some arbitrary stating point the wave has traveled. If two sine waves of the same wavelength and magnitude are exactly in phase, then they can be exactly superimposed on each other. If they are 180 degrees out of phase, then the trough of one is exactly lined up with the peak of the other.

It is not necessary to go into any more depth about the mathematical aspect of sine waves. However, the term 'cycle' may cause confusion, since it is loosely used to describe a repetitive sine wave, or may be used for just a section of a sine wave which takes the price from say a trough to the next trough. In this book we will use, for example '10 week cycle' to mean a repetitive sine wave of wavelength equal to 10 weeks, and use the phrase 'one complete wave of the 10 week cycle' to signify just the section from one point to the next identical point. This latter form will be used quite frequently because it enables us to predict the next peak or trough in a stock market cycle and therefore determine whether the current trend due to that cycle is rising or falling.

RELATIONSHIP BETWEEN TRENDS AND CYCLES

An up trend is simply the rising half of a sine wave and a down trend the falling half. If a sine wave has a wavelength of say 10 weeks, then the rising half will take 5 weeks to move from the trough to the following peak, and the falling half the same time to move from the peak to the following trough. We can now see why trends have to have a time scale attached to them. Taking two different stock market cycles of wavelength 40 days and 400 weeks, we show the up trends of both of these in Figure 4.7. The trends are obviously quite different, and they are different in two ways. Firstly, one-trend takes ten times as long as the other to run its course, while secondly, the price rise caused by the 20-week wave is larger than that caused by the 10 week wave.

This latter effect is a general one and of great importance—the greater the wavelength, the greater the magnitude. It leads the investor to focus on long term trends as well as short term ones.

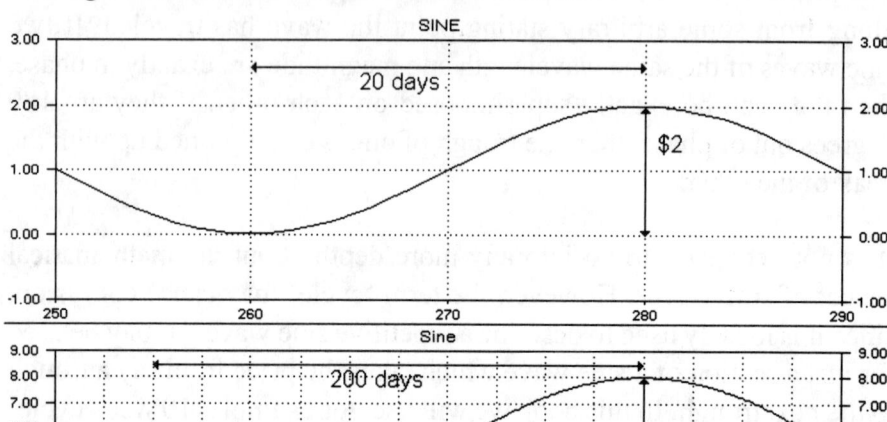

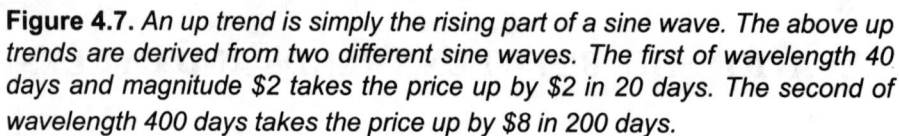

Figure 4.7. *An up trend is simply the rising part of a sine wave. The above up trends are derived from two different sine waves. The first of wavelength 40 days and magnitude $2 takes the price up by $2 in 20 days. The second of wavelength 400 days takes the price up by $8 in 200 days.*

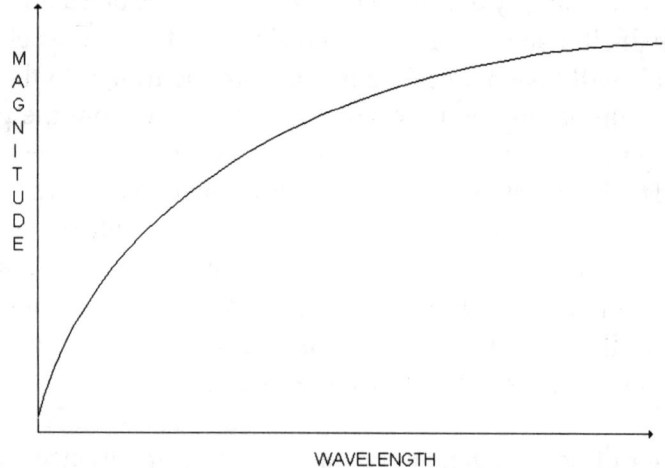

Figure 4.8. *The approximate relationship between cycle magnitude and wavelength in stock prices.*

It is generally considered that the important cycles present in stock market data have wavelengths of: 18 years, 9 years, 3 to 4 years, 18 months, 12 months, 26 week, 13 week, 6.5 weeks and 3.25 weeks. The general form of the relationship between the wavelength of the various cycles present in stock price data and their magnitude is shown in Figure 4.8. The magnitude increases rapidly with increasing wavelength until wavelengths of over four years are reached; at which point the magnitude increases only slowly.

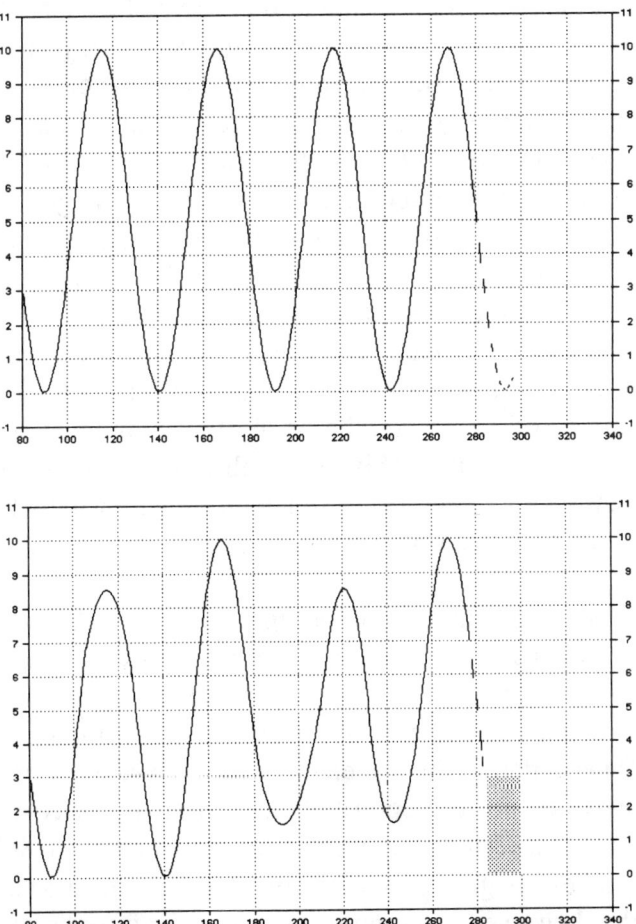

Figure 4.9. *Upper panel: The next turning point in a perfectly regular sine wave can be predicted accurately into the future. Lower panel: If there is a fluctuation in magnitude and wavelength then a 'prediction box' (hatched area) must be drawn which takes into account the smallest and largest changes in either.*

Fluctuation over time

The relationship shown in Figure 4.8 is only approximate, for the reason that each of the three components of a stock market cycle, disguised wavelength, magnitude and phase, are fluctuating with time. The fluctuation in wavelength is not large, but because it exists we use the term 'nominal wavelength' to describe a cycle in the data. Thus a nominal one-year (52-week) cycle can change between limits of about 45 and 60 weeks. Fluctuation in phase is difficult to observe clearly, as it appears to manifest itself as a fluctuation in wavelength, since the position of the next peak or trough will be shifted. However, the shape of the cycle will remain the same, since only a sideways movement in time is occurring, whereas a change in wavelength also changes the shape. The fluctuation in magnitude is much more important, because it can change within very wide limits over the course of time. This can mean that a particular nominal cycle can disappear from the data for a time because its magnitude has effectively dropped to zero. It is this fact that makes stock markets, currency markets and commodity markets moderately predictable rather than being highly predictable over the long term. In practice, we are faced with periods of time when the price of an individual stock, currency or commodity is quite highly predictable, and other periods when it is almost totally unpredictable. Fortunately, we will usually be able to predict which of these two states is paramount at any particular time.

The effect of these fluctuations on the degree of predictability of cycles is shown in Figure 4.9. The upper trace is a perfect cycle of exact peak-to-peak wavelength of 52 weeks. For the purposes of the example we will take the magnitude as being $10. The rising portion of this cycle (the up trend) takes half of the wavelength. *i.e.* 26 weeks for completion will therefore make a positive contribution of $10 to the price movement of the stock over this period of 26 weeks, while of course the falling part of this cycle makes a negative contribution of $10 for the next 26 weeks. We can see that because it is completely regular its future movement is known exactly. If we determine that the trend is currently down, then we would be interested in knowing when it will change direction. The point where it will bottom out, *i.e.* the trough, will be exactly 52 weeks on from the previous low point, and exactly 26 weeks on from the previous peak. In terms of the vertical position of this trough, it will be identical with that of the previous trough.

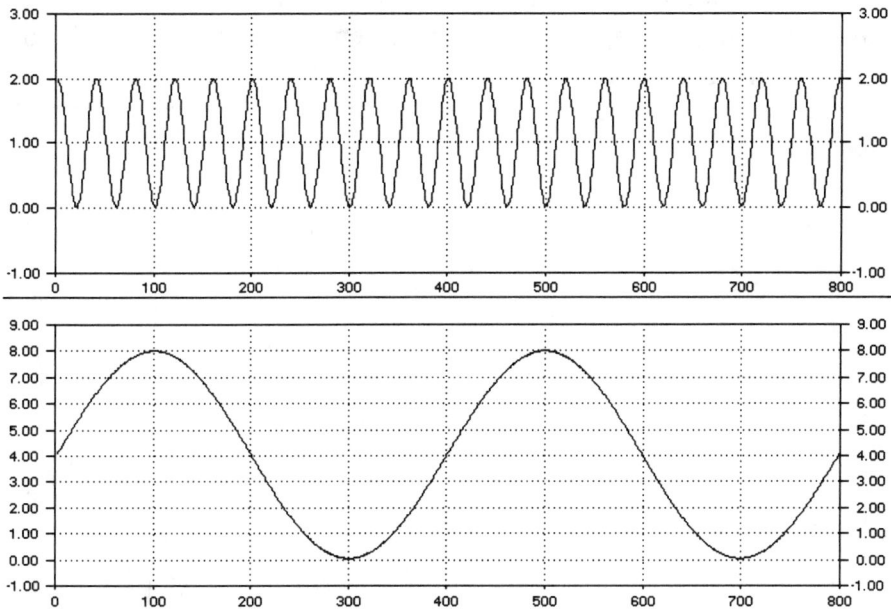

Figure 4.10. *Upper panel: a cycle with wavelength 40 days and magnitude $2. Lower panel: a cycle with wavelength 400 days and magnitude $8.*

In the lower trace, we have taken a cycle with the same nominal wavelength of 52 weeks, but where the wavelength is subject to a moderate but unpredictable variation, as is the magnitude. Because of the variation in wavelength we can no longer say that the next trough will occur exactly 52 weeks after the previous trough or 26 weeks after the previous peak. Our best estimate is that it will occur at a point 26 weeks on from the previous peak, plus or minus a number of weeks. We can get an idea of this range by looking at the previous variations of the wavelength as given by the past peak to peak distances. An even better way is to split these into half wavelengths, measuring the distances in time between peaks and the next trough and troughs and the next peak. This gives us twice as many measurements upon which to base the estimate.

Although the best estimate from these measurements would be given by a statistical calculation of mean and standard deviation, this is overkill in the context of what we are trying to achieve. It is enough to take the shortest value, for example 21 weeks, and the longest value, for example 30 weeks and use these. Applying these particular values means we can expect the trough to appear somewhere between 21 weeks and 30 on from the previous peak.

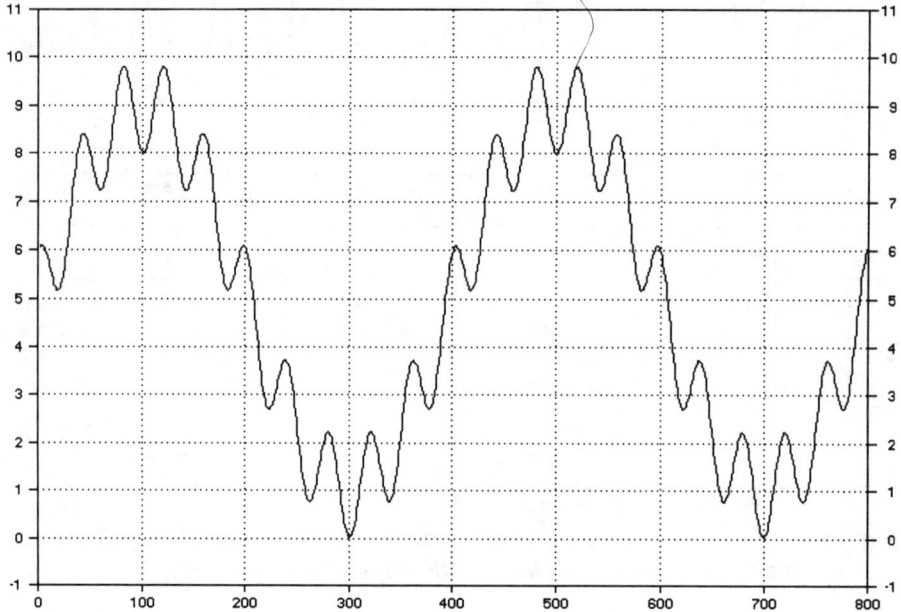

Figure 4.11. *This is the result of adding together the two cycles shown in Figure 4.10.*

Since the magnitude is also varying, we can use a similar approach. This time we take measurements of the rises from troughs to the next peak and the falls from peaks to the next trough. This might give, for example, the shortest rise/fall being $7 and the largest $10. Applying these particular values means we can expect the fall from the most recent peak to be between $7 and $10.

Applying both the wavelength estimation and the magnitude estimation from the position of the last peak gives us a window in which we expect the next trough to appear. The window, or prediction box, has a height of $3 and a width of 10 weeks.

We have situations where the variation in both wavelength and magnitude is so high that although we could draw a prediction box by the same method as just discussed, its size is so large that its usefulness in determining the future movement is virtually zero.

CYCLES ARE ADDITIVE

Since trends are additive, and a trend is one half of a cycle, it follows that the cycles themselves are additive. Thus, what we see in stock price movement is the sum of all of the cycles present, taking into account the fact they are fluctuating from their nominal wavelength from time to time and that their magnitude and phase is also changing. In addition to the sum of these, there is also grafted on to this total picture an amount of random day-to-day movement.

We have discussed the addition of short-term trends to a long-term trend to give a composite trend, as shown previously in Figures 4.4 and 4.5. In

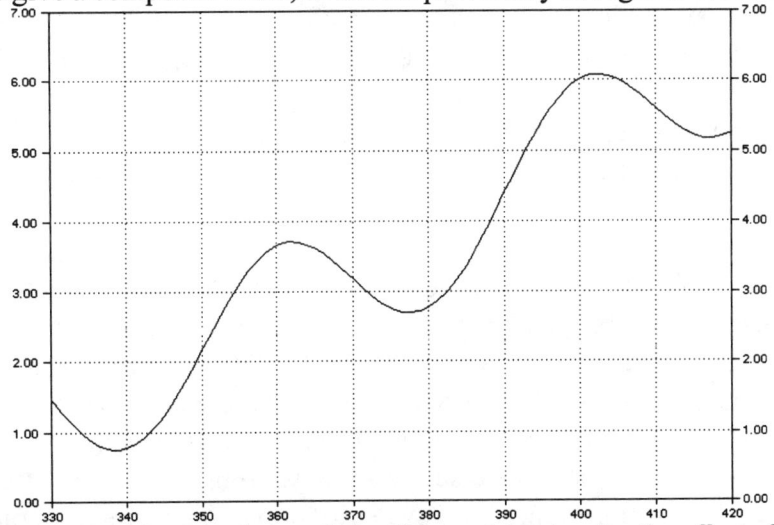

Figure 4.12. *A expanded section of Figure 4.11 showing the effect of a rising long wavelength cycle.*

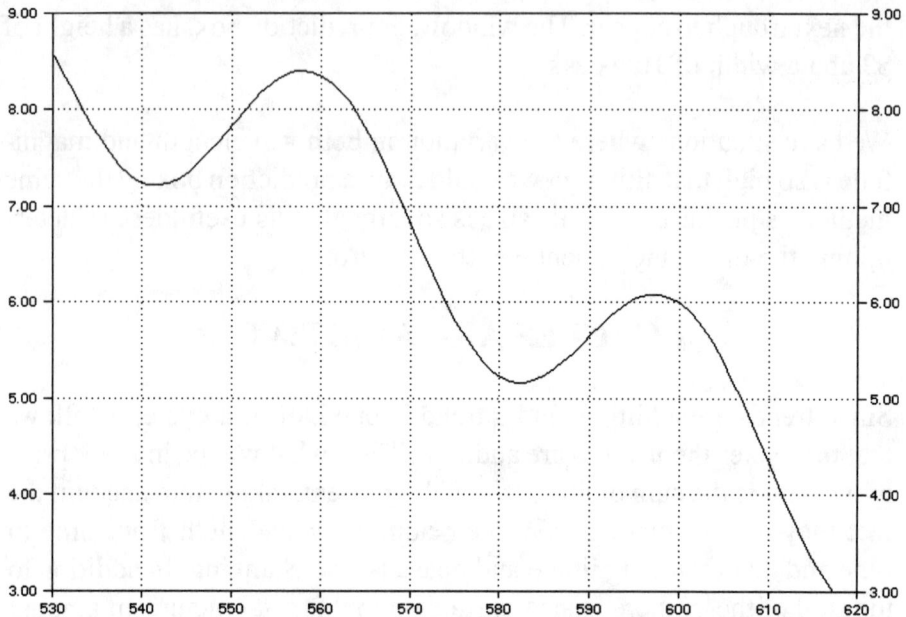

Figure 4.13. *A expanded section of Figure 4.11 showing the effect of a falling long wavelength cycle.*

those examples the long-term trend caused a price rise of $8 over a period of 40 weeks. In terms of cycles, this trend can be represented by the rising half of a cycle of wavelength 80 weeks (or 400 days) and magnitude $8. The short term trends caused rises and falls of $2 in four weeks, and was represented by a cycle of wavelength 8 weeks (or 40 days) and magnitude $2.

These two cycles, based on daily data, are shown in the two panels in Figure 4.10. The upper panel contains the cycle of wavelength 40 days and magnitude $2 and the lower one the cycle of wavelength 400 days and magnitude $8. These values can be checked by reference to the peak-to-peak and peak-to-trough distances in each case, since the vertical scales are in dollars and the horizontal scales are days from an arbitrary starting point. The addition of these two cycles to form a composite is simple. It is only necessary to take the readings off the vertical scales for each cycle at the same point in time and add these together to produce a value that can be plotted at this same point. At point 600, for example, the reading of the upper cycle is $2 and of the lower cycle is $4. This gives a composite value of $6 that can be plotted at point 600. This process is repeated for all of the daily points available. The resulting plot is shown in Figure 4.11.

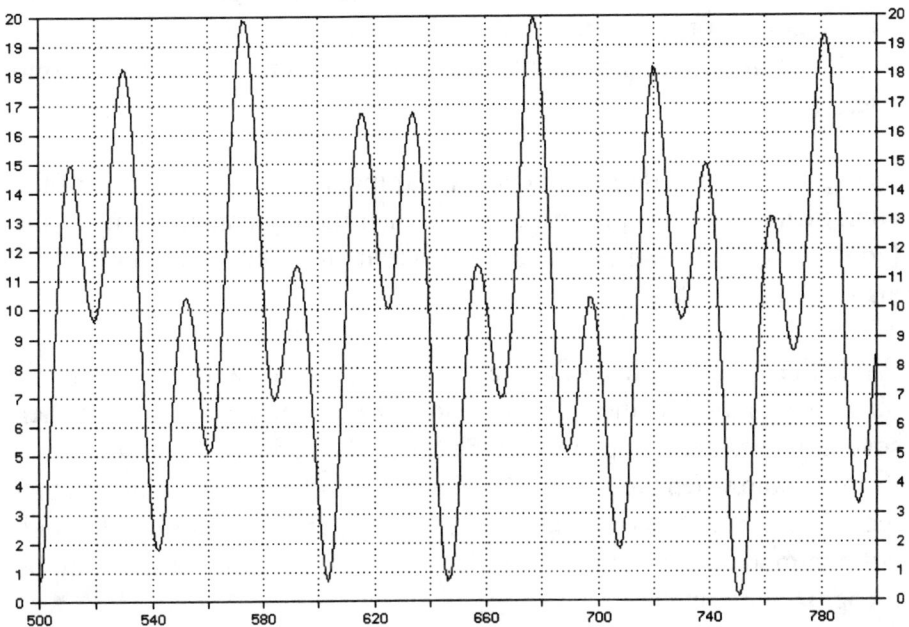

Figure 4.14. *The combination of a cycle of wavelength 21 weeks with one of wavelength 52 weeks.*

Of rather more interest is an expanded view of sections of this plot. The first, shown in Figure 4.12, shows the position between days 330 and 420. This is the section in which the long term cycle is rising. We can see quite clearly the relationship to the composite trends given in Figure 4.4. The rising legs increase the price about twice as much as the falling legs decrease it.

On the other hand, a different section is shown in Figure 4.13 where the increase in price of the rising legs is about half of the decrease caused by the falling legs.

The important point about any pattern is that the cycle with the longer wavelength and largest magnitude dominates the movement and provides the major underlying trend. This cycle is the major cycle. The second cycle, the minor one, causes a fluctuation in the major trend. Thus in Figure 4.12 the major cycle is rising, and the rising part of the combined cycle rises at a faster rate than the equivalent part of the long wavelength, dominant cycle, because at this point the minor cycle is also rising. Since the cycles are additive, the net effect is to cause a more rapid rise.

In Figure 4.13, the dominant cycle is falling, and the falling part of the combined cycle falls at a greater rate than the equivalent point in the long wavelength, dominant cycle because at this point the minor cycle is also falling.

While the additive effect of two cycles that are rising at the same time is obviously favorable, there are occasions in stock price movement when several cycles are rising at the same time. The additive effect will be at its maximum when the group of cycles has coincident low points, so that they all rise from this position simultaneously. These situations, although not common, provide an outstanding potential for profit if they can be recognized in time.

CHART PATTERNS FROM CYCLES

Chartists place a great deal of emphasis on patterns in stock price movement. In general they look for the start of a recognizable pattern and then make the assumption that the probability is that it will complete its move in the previous way. The patterns they look for include support and resistance lines, double tops, double bottoms, head and shoulders and inverse head and shoulders, triangles, flags and so on. It is perfectly possible to explain each of these as being formed by a certain combination of cycles that are present in the stock movement at that particular time.

In Figure 4.11 we showed the result of adding two cycles together of

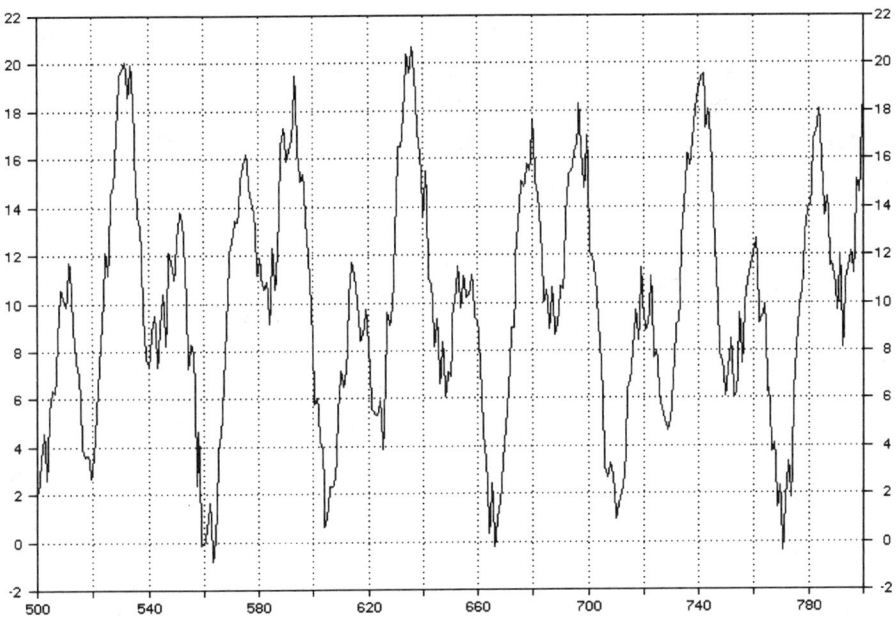

Figure 4.15. *The combination of a cycle of wavelength 21 weeks with one of wavelength 52 weeks with an added amount of random movement.*

wavelengths 40 and 400 days. It should be noted that there is a repeating pattern in the plot. For every point in the plot, there is an identical point 400 days, *i.e.* one complete wavelength of the major cycle further on. These repetitions separated by exactly one wavelength of the major cycle always happen when the two cycles that have been added together have wavelengths that are related by multiples of two. The reason is because if we start with the two peaks exactly aligned, then the minor cycle will always arrive at a peak at the same time as the major cycle, even though the minor cycle will have gone through at least one other peak in between the major cycle peaks.

Mathematically, the point when two cycles arrive at exactly the same relationship to each other as they were on a previous occasion is at a point that is the lowest common multiple of the wavelengths further on in time. Thus, if we have a cycle with wavelength 2 years and another with wavelength 3 years, the lowest common multiple is 6 years. Thus, every six years we will find that these two cycles pass through the same relationship to each other. Because of this, the combination of the two cycles will give patterns that are repeated at six-yearly intervals. If we have two cycles of 30 weeks and 40 weeks wavelengths then the repeats would be every 120 weeks.

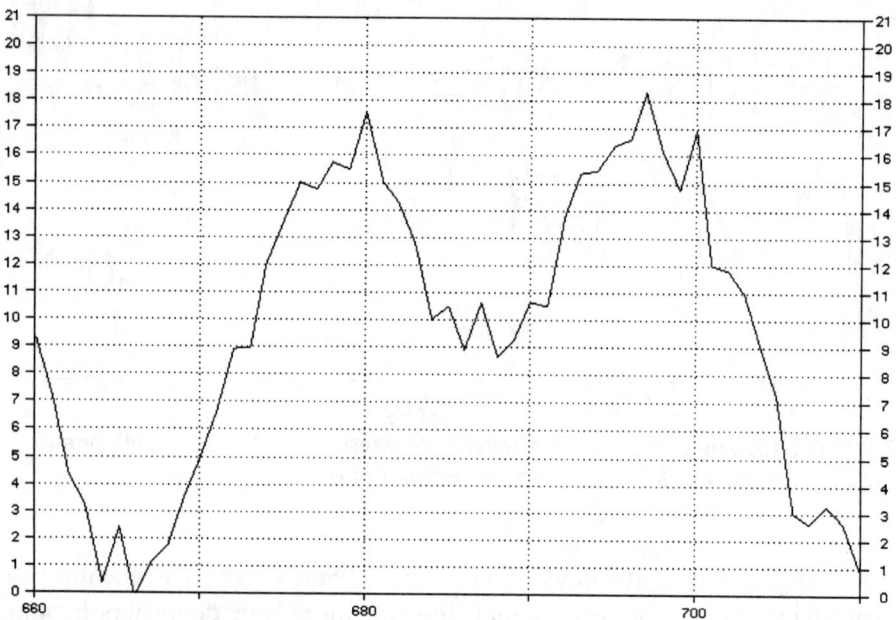

Figure 4.16. *A section from Figure 4.15 enlarged to show a double top formation.*

Figure 4.14 shows the result of combining two cycles, of 21 and 52 weeks respectively. Because of the limited span of the time axis, there are no repetitions of the visible pattern.

It is perfectly possible to add a random movement to the combination of cycles by the same additive process as was used earlier for two cycles. The result of doing this is shown in Figure 4.15. The interesting aspect of this Figure is that there are patterns present that the chartist will recognize. In order to see these more clearly sections of the plot are enlarged in Figures 4.16 and 4.17.

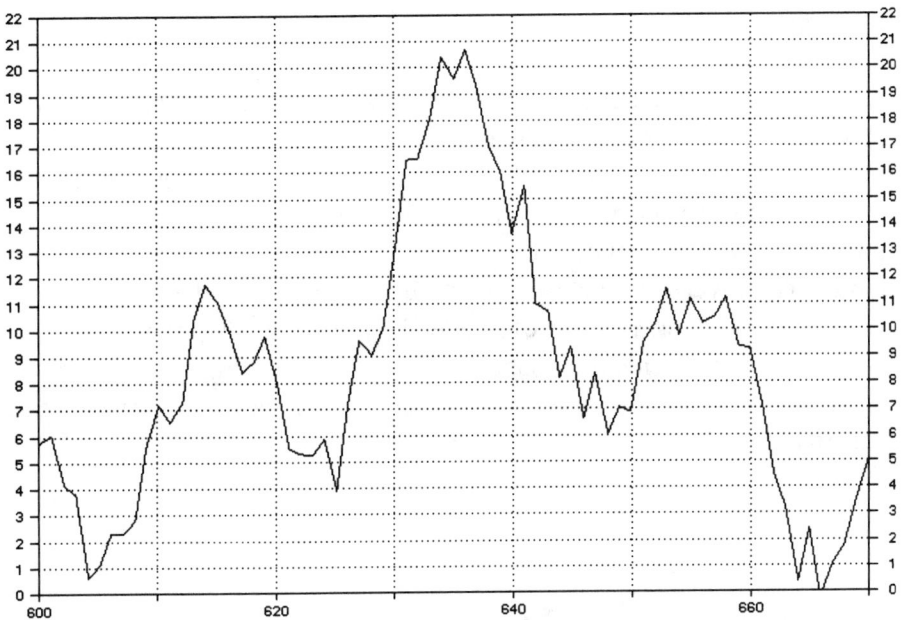

Figure 4.17. *A section from Figure 4.15 enlarged to show a head and shoulders formation.*

In Figure 4.16 we show how a double top formation occurs as the result of combining two cycles such as those used here. The addition of the random movement gives a better approximation to the patterns we see in charts of stock prices. The reason for the double top is that while the dominant cycle is passing through its maximum, the minor cycle is initially on the way down from its maximum. Once the minimum point of the minor cycle is reached, it rises again to its second maximum, giving the pattern shown. As the two cycles become less synchronized, one of the two peaks will become less prominent, until eventually the pattern vanishes altogether.

In Figure 4.17 we see a head and shoulders formation. The major cycle is just passing through its peak, and the most symmetrical version of the head and shoulders forms when a peak in the minor cycle coincides with the peak in the major cycle. Once we move away from the coincidence of the peaks, the pattern will become distorted so that one shoulder is higher than the other.

Although in these theoretical combinations, we have looked at the question of pattern repetition, in the case of real stock prices the chance of a pattern being repeated after an interval of time is low because of the variation in wavelength and magnitude. By the time two cycles are subject to such variation we arrive at the same position relative to each other as on a previous occasion, the variation in wavelength makes the relative positions quite different. Chartists concentrate more on a pattern of a general type as it develops and have a set of rules to help to decide if the pattern will become meaningful. It is the variation in wavelength and magnitude of the constituent cycles of a pattern that can cause it to fail.

CHAPTER 5

Graphical Channel Analysis—The Basics

Even though stock price movement is a complex mixture of trends, there are methods for isolating trends so they can be used as the basis for investment decisions. Investors who wish to place money for the longer term will be able to select a long term trend and time entry into this trend for the maximum profit, while short term traders will be able to choose short term trends to suit their quite different time scale. In this chapter, we will be using an approach where all we need is a chart of a stock price over a number of years, a pencil, a ruler and perhaps one of those flexible curves that enable you to draw curves of any shape. Although in the next chapter we will use calculators and computers to determine trends, starting with a graphical estimation will help build a better understanding of the various components of stock price movement and how they can be separated. The progress we make with a quite simple method will also be surprising.

In chapter 4, we explored the idea that different cycles can be combined together with random movement. This produced a composite movement similar to that shown by charts of stock prices. It was necessary to develop this theme in order to demonstrate that cycles are fundamental to how stock prices move over a period of time.

Of course, as investors, we want to do the opposite of this. First, we want to remove the random movement from our stock price data so we are left with predictable data, even though this will still be composed of a mixture of trends. Second, we want to separate this mixture of trends into its component parts. The least we want to see is a separation to the broad categories of very short term, short term, medium term and long term trends. Although these might have different meanings for different investors, in this context we can take long term trends to mean those that take a year or more to complete, medium term trends, those that take about three months to a year to complete, short term trends, those that take a few weeks to a few months to complete, and very short term trends, that only take a matter of days to complete.

Once we have categorized the trends as being in the present, we can estimate where they are in their development and how long they are likely to continue. This will give us a handle on how they should affect the stock price in the near future so that we can make a decision of when to buy and when to sell. Since there is a varying amount of random behavior in the market, we need to find ways of removing this so we can study the cycles present.

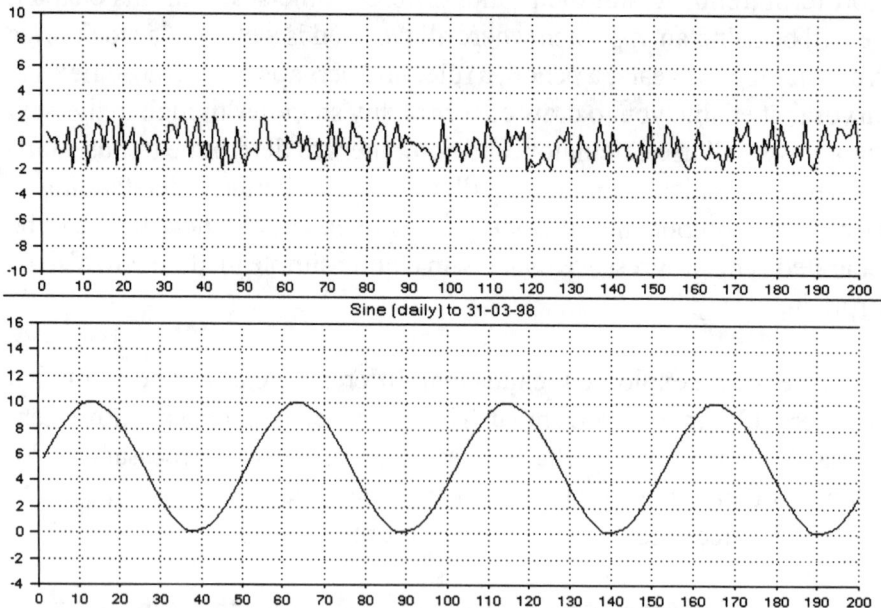

Figure 5.1. *Upper panel: random movement with a range of -$2 to +$2. Lower panel: a cycle with wavelength 52 weeks and magnitude $10.*

Rather than start with actual stock market data, the principles are easier to understand if we use artificial data. This is because we know the wavelengths and magnitudes of the cycles in the data and will be able to verify that our methods give acceptable results. Once we are comfortable with the methods, we can then apply them to stock prices with the *proviso* that we know that the cycles will be subject to a variation in their wavelengths and magnitudes and that the amount of random content will also vary.

ONE CYCLE PLUS RANDOM MOVEMENT

A good place to start is with a simple combination of one cycle and some random data, using the additive method discussed in Chapter 4. The two components are a cycle of 52 weeks wavelength and magnitude of $10 and a random movement that ranges from +$2 to -$2. The two separate components that are being combined are shown in Figure 5.1. The result of combining these two is shown in the upper trace of Figure 5.2.

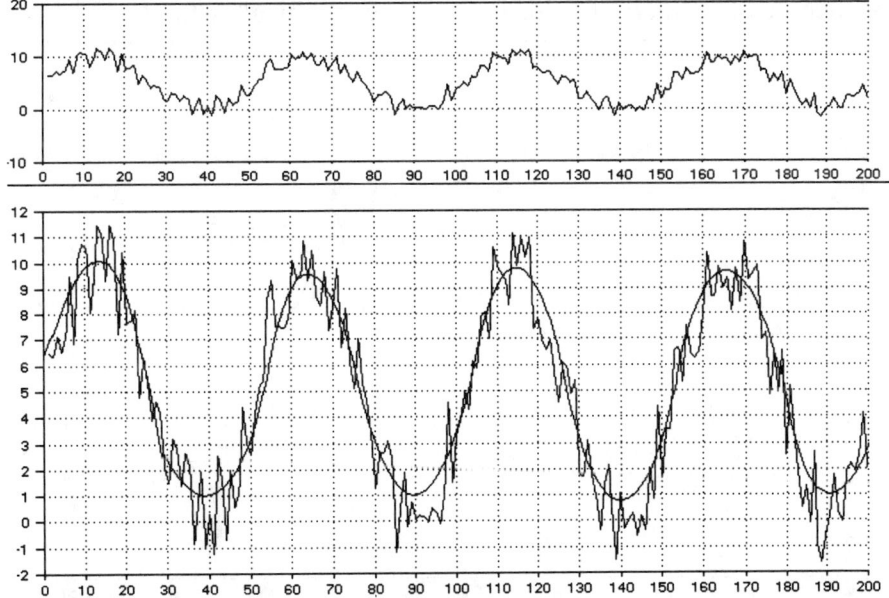

Figure 5.2. *Upper panel: the combination of the random and cyclic components. Lower panel: with the vertical scale expanded, it can be seen that a line drawn through the center of the fluctuations is close in shape to the original cyclic component.*

Finding the Cycle

If we now draw the best line we can so as to pass through the center of the short term fluctuations, we get the result shown in the lower trace of Figure 5.2. The line can either be drawn freehand or with the flexible curve. In the latter case it might be necessary to draw sections at a time. It is obvious that our line is a good approximation to a cycle, and if we examine it more closely we will find that the peaks are about 52 weeks apart, as are the troughs. Thus we can conclude we have a cycle of wavelength around 52 weeks. This is of course the wavelength used in constructing the combination in the first place, so that this simple method of drawing a line through the center of the noise has given us this vital information about the underlying wave form. Not only that, but if we examine the vertical distances between a peak and the next trough or a trough and the next peak we find they represent a value of about $10. So, not only have we extracted the wavelength, but also the magnitude with a reasonable degree of accuracy, by this very simple graphical method.

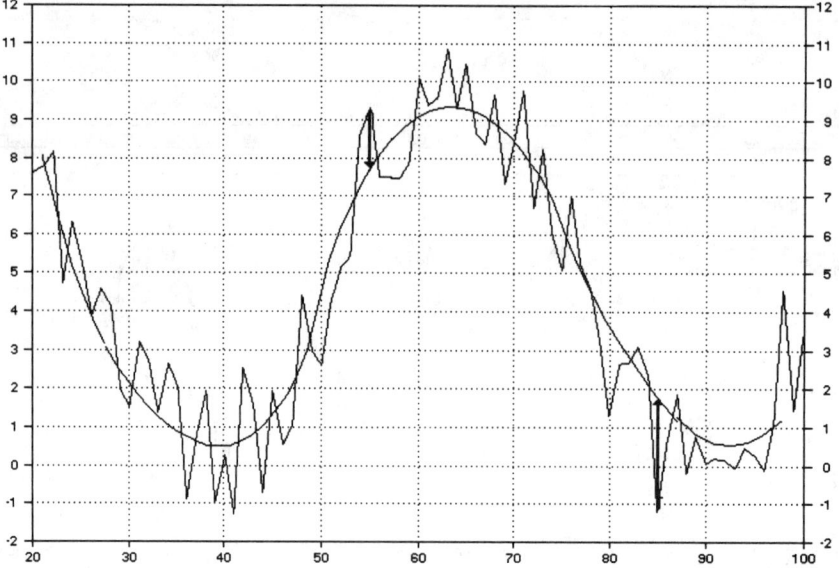

Figure 5.3. *The random movement is the difference between the line drawn through the center and the value of the data at each point across the plot. The differences at weeks 55 and 85, for example, are shown by the vertical arrows. Data below the line will have a negative sign, and those above a positive sign.*

Finding the Random Content

Since we have been able to find the cycle present in the data, the next step is to ask if we can estimate the amount of random movement incorporated into the data. The answer is yes, we can, because:

combined data = cyclic data + random data

Therefore:

random data = combined data - cyclic data

We can therefore find the random data by taking the difference between the combined data and the cyclic data that we have now isolated by the line we have drawn. This is done at each point in time as we move from left to right of the chart. This process is illustrated in Figure 5.3. The main reason for doing this is to show it is perfectly possible by this simple graphical method to determine the random movement at every point in the synthesized data. In practice there is not much value in doing this at this level of detail. This is because when dealing with random behavior it is not the individual random contributions in the past that are of interest. Such individual contributions, being random, will be unpredictable in the future. What is important is to gain an overall view of how much random content is present in the movement. Mathematically, if we know the mean and standard deviation of the random movement, we will be able to calculate the probable contribution of this random movement at any point in the future. Graphically, determining the maximum contribution of random behavior, will be extremely valuable.

A Simple Channel

We can see that in Figure 5.2 the fluctuations in the composite cycles are limited in their extent. We can emphasize this limited range by drawing a channel to contain the fluctuations. This must be done quite carefully and certain rules must be followed:

•The upper and lower boundaries of the channel must be at a
  constant vertical distance apart.
• The boundaries should be drawn so as to contain as much of the
  movement as possible.
• It is permissible to allow a few movements to penetrate the bound
  aries if this aids the drawing of smooth lines, but the penetrations should not be extensive.

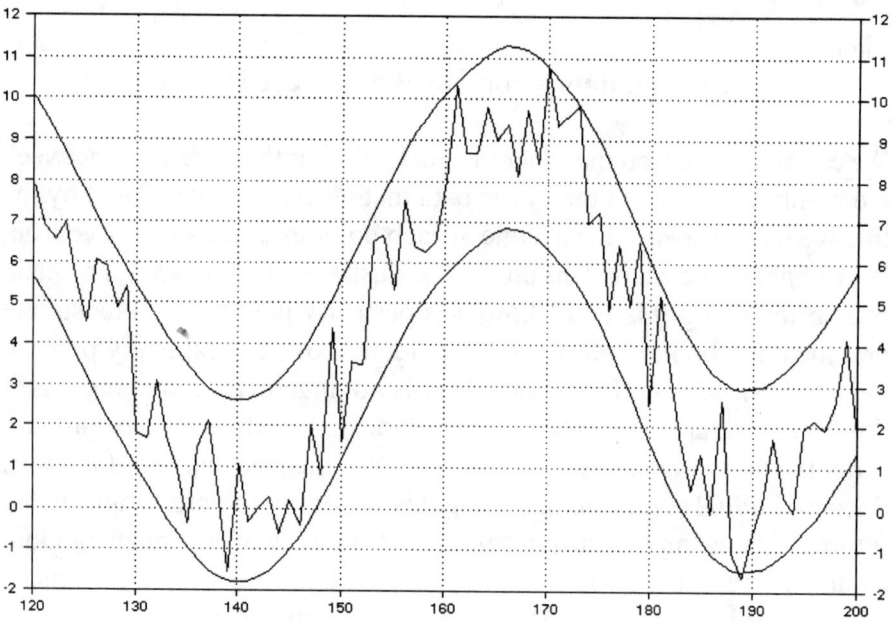

Figure 5.4. *A channel, of constant vertical depth, can be drawn so as to enclose the random fluctuations.*

Using these rules, two boundaries have been drawn to produce the channel shown in Figure 5.4. We can get a great deal of information from this
channel. First, the peaks and troughs in the channel are regular, and tell us
that there is a regular cycle in the data. The distance between two successive peaks or troughs is 52 weeks. This gives us the wavelength of this
cycle directly. Second, the short-term fluctuations are contained in the
channel. The vertical depth of this channel is close to $4, so we can say
these short-term movements give a maximum excursion of $4. This is

close to the random value used in constructing the composite cycle in the first place (from -$2 to + $2). If we look at Figure 5.1 again, we will see that the extreme movement of $4 is rarely seen. The bulk of the random movement occurs in a band that is about $3.5 in height. So, by this simple exercise we have isolated the random movement and established the wavelength of the cycle as 52 weeks.

It is only necessary now to see if we can establish the magnitude of the cycle itself and we will have achieved a complete analysis of the data in the simplest possible way. The overall magnitude is given by the vertical height between a trough in the lower boundary and the next successive peak in the upper boundary. This is about $12.5. The magnitude of the 52-week cycle is the difference between these two, since the overall height includes the depth of the channel due to random movement. Thus, the magnitude of the 52 week cycle is $12.5 - $3.5 = $9.

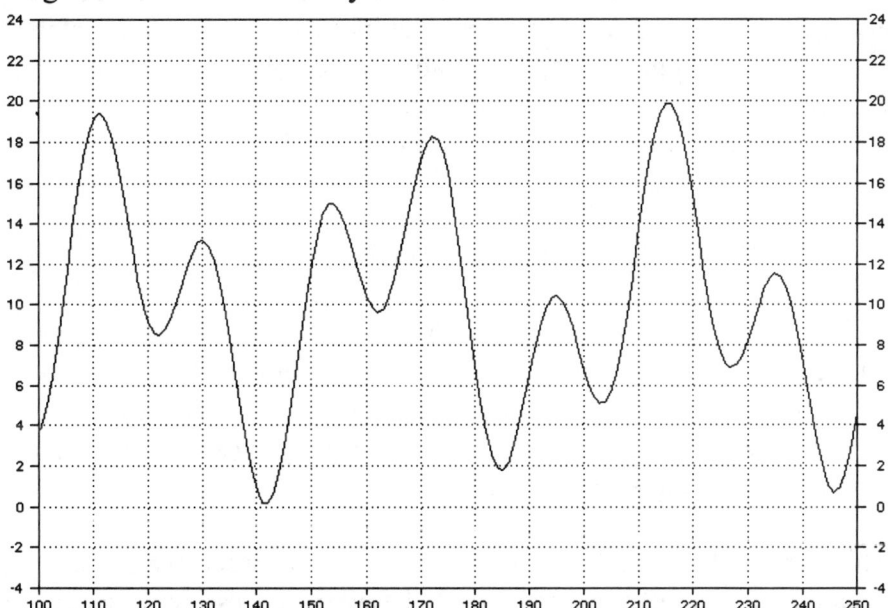

Figure 5.5. *The result of adding together two cycles of wavelength 21 weeks and 52 weeks.*

An alternative way to find the magnitude is to draw a line down the center of the channel. This line will be very close in shape to the one drawn earlier in Figure 5.2. This line is a truer representation of the original cycle, since it now has a minimum at about $0.5 and a maximum at about $9.5, giving an overall magnitude of $9. This is very close to the actual value of $10 that was used in constructing the composite waveform in the first place.

This simple example gives us a flavor for technique of channel analysis and how powerful it can be for isolating trends and random behavior in share prices. We can now move on to rather more complex sets of artificial data before applying the technique to real stock market data.

TWO CYCLES

Having seen that it is fairly simple to extract both the random movement and the cyclic movement from a mixture of the two, it is now of interest to see if we can apply the same technique to a combination of two different cycles. In Figure 5.5, we see the result of adding a cycle (cycle 2) of wavelength 21 weeks and magnitude $10 to our 52 week cycle (cycle 1) which also has magnitude $10.

Finding Cycle 1

In Figure 5.6 we show the result of drawing a channel of constant depth on the chart of these combined cycles to allow only the extreme movements to touch the upper and lower channel boundaries. The result shown in Figure 5.6 is the best compromise between keeping a constant channel depth, and drawing a smooth channel.

This exercise has resulted in the isolation of the 52-week cycle (cycle 1), because we can measure the distance between successive peaks in our channel and find they are approximately 52 weeks apart. Just as in the previous example the channel depth shows the extent of the random movement, then in the current example the channel depth represents the extent of the component of shorter wavelength (cycle 2). This channel depth is around $10, the magnitude of this component. The magnitude of the longer-term component can be found by difference. The lower channel boundary has a minimum at around $0 and the upper boundary a maximum at around $20. Thus the amplitude of the 52 week component is $20 - $10 = $10.

Finding Cycle 2

We have already noted that the depth of the channel is due entirely to the cycle 2, and that its magnitude is about $10. The only other quantity we need is its wavelength. Noting the points where the extremes of cycle 2 touched the channel easily does this. These of course alternate between the upper and lower channel boundaries. Using the numbers on the time axis as a guide (Figure 5.6) the touching points or nearly touching places are at points 111, 122, 130, 142, 154, 163, 173, 185, 195, 216, 227, 235 and 246. These give distances in weeks of 11, 8, 8, 12, 9, 10, 12, 10, 11, 11, 8 and 11. Note that these are a constant distance apart. Although they are due to cycle 2, they are distorted slightly by the presence of cycle 1.

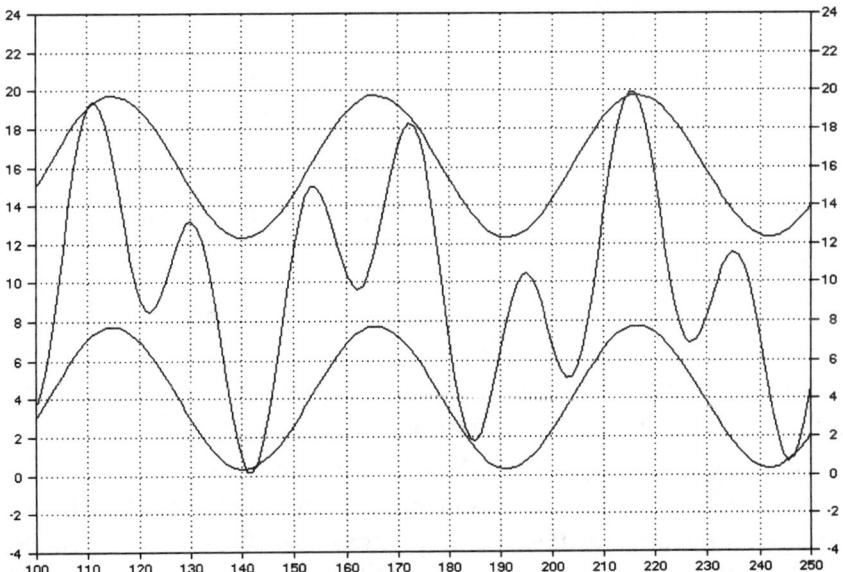

Figure 5.6. *A channel of constant depth is drawn so as to enclose only the extremities of the movement.*

The way to find the wavelength is to take a mean of all of these distances. The total is 121 for the 12 measurements, giving a mean value of just over 10 weeks. Since this value is the mean distance between successive peaks and troughs, it represents one half of the wavelength, which is therefore just over 20 weeks. This is an excellent result for the graphical method since the actual wavelength used in constructing the mixture of two cycles was 21 weeks.

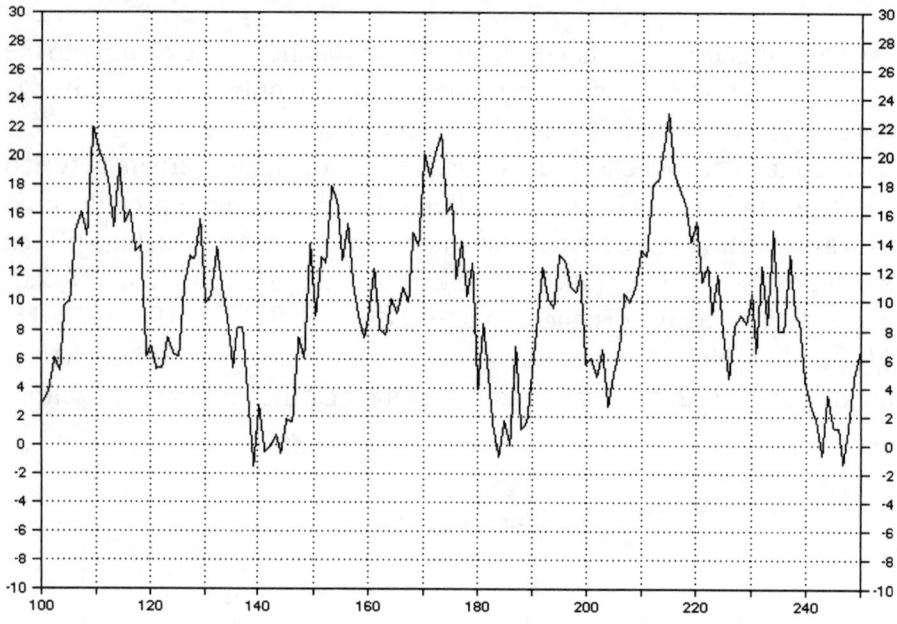

Figure 5.7. *Some random content has now been added to the combined cycles from Figure 5.5.*

Two Cycles Plus Random Movement

While we could analyze a large number of composite cycles to demonstrate the ease with which this graphical analysis can be carried out, it is only necessary to use as a final example the previous mixture of two cycles of 51 and 21 week wavelength and similar magnitude of $10 with some random movement added. Since we now have two cycles, the range of values of the random movement should be doubled from its previous of -$2 to +$2 to a new range of -$4 to +$4. This is done in order to preserve the proportion of random movement in the total. This new composite waveform is shown in Figure 5.7.

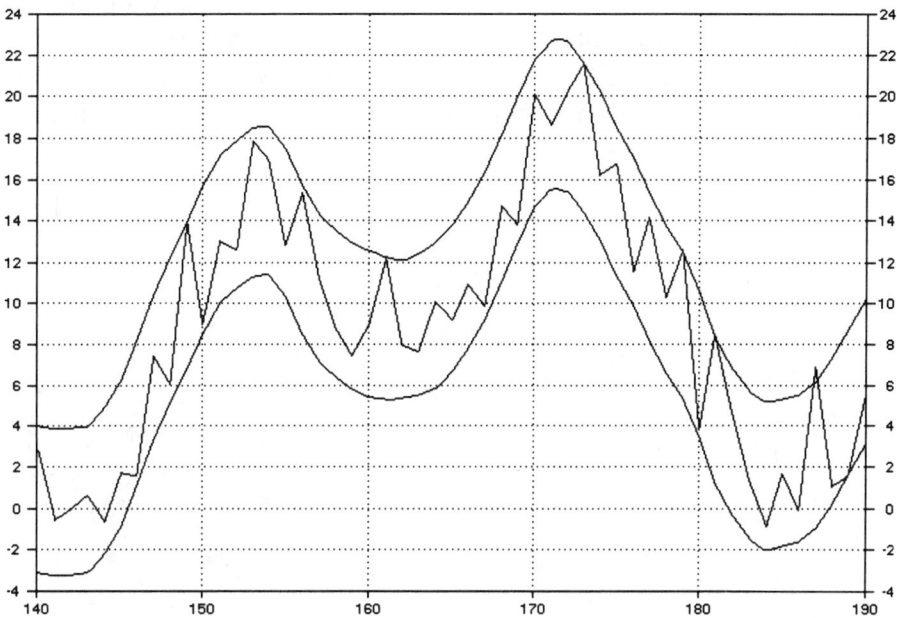

Figure 5.8. *A channel can now be drawn so as to enclose the minor fluctuations which are due to random movement.*

Finding the Random Content

In order to show the innermost channel that can be constructed; a section of the plot is enlarged in Figure 5.8. A smooth channel is drawn to keep to the rules of channel analysis. Note it is impossible to have all of the troughs on the lower boundary and all of the peaks on the upper boundary. A compromise must be made in order to keep a smooth channel of constant depth. By this means, we will see that about seven or eight peaks are close to the upper boundary, and a similar number of troughs lie close to the lower boundary.

This channel of course encloses the random movement within its boundaries. Since the random movement is not cyclical, the only property of it we can determine is the extent of the random excursions. This is given by the channel depth, about $6.5. Although we used a maximum range of $8 for the random content when building the composite wave form, the nature of random movements are very few values at these extremes of -$4 and +$4. The vast majority of the random movement lies within the range of -$3 to +$3. Thus this deduction of a range of $6.5 is therefore excellent.

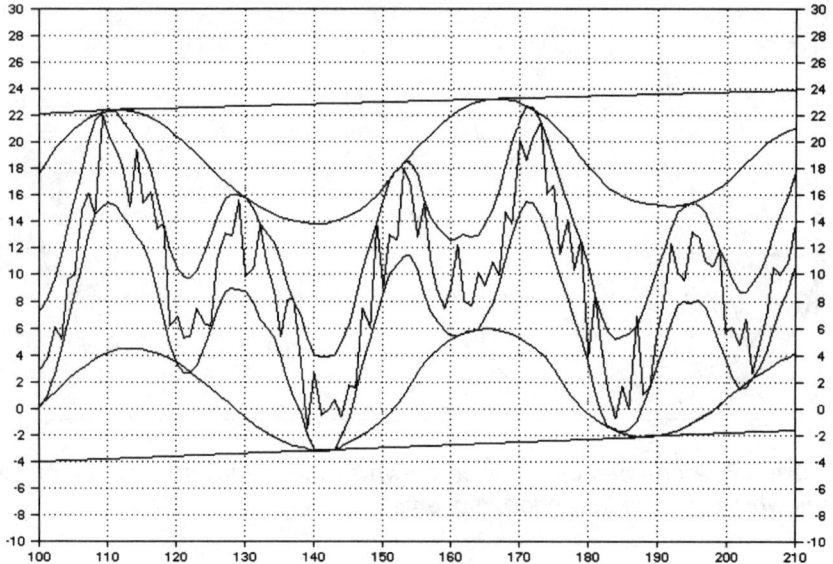

Figure 5.9. *Once the inner channel has been drawn, an middle one can be constructed of constant depth so as to enclose most of the peaks and troughs in the inner channel, and an outer one to enclose the peaks and troughs in the middle one.*

Nesting of Channels

In the previous example where we had combined two cycles without any random content, we were able to deduce the magnitudes and wavelengths of both cycles by drawing just one channel. Strictly speaking, we should have drawn another channel so as to touch the extremes of the first channel. This will be done in the present example. The idea of nesting of channels is that successive channels enclose cycles of successively longer wavelengths. Working from the inside out, we keep drawing channels so as to touch the extremities of the next innermost channel until we no longer have enough extremities to draw a valid channel. This is shown in Figure 5.9. We have already drawn the innermost channel as shown in Figure 5.8. The next (second) channel outside of this one is drawn to touch as many extremities of this first channel as possible, keeping to the rules about smoothness and the maintenance of constant depth. Once we have this second channel in place, we draw a third channel outside of this, again keeping to the rules of channel analysis. This channel is more or less horizontal, because there is no third cycle present to modify its envelope. If we had had quite a number of different cycles in our composite waveform, then we would be able to draw even more such channels, and indeed, this will normally be the case when we deal with long runs of actual stock market data.

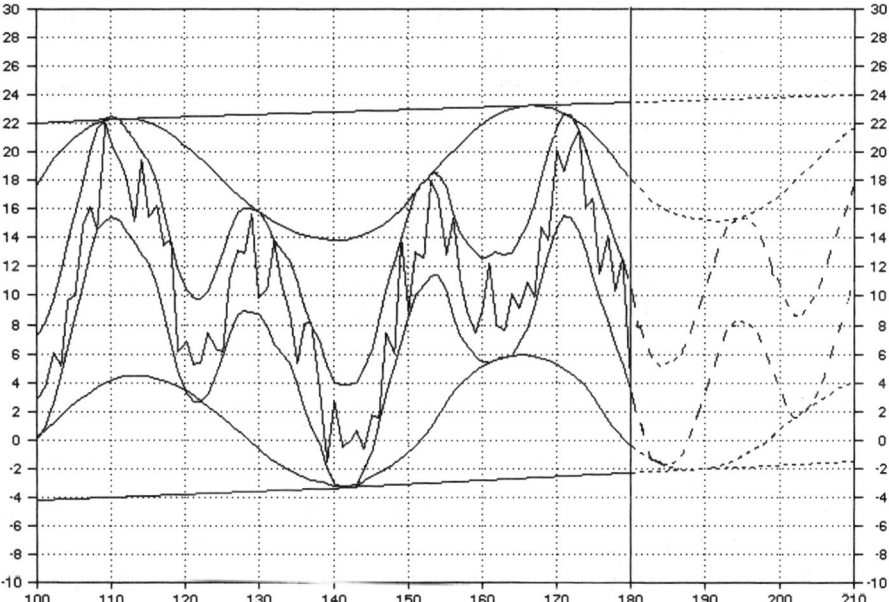

Figure 5.10. *It is possible to project channels into the future from the last available data at point 180 if the extrapolation proceeds from the outermost channel inwards.*

Finding the Magnitudes

Now that we have three channels, we will be able to find the magnitudes of the various components by difference. The principle of this is each channel encloses all those movements with the same or lesser wavelength (including the random movement) than the nominal wavelength of the channel. The channel depth is therefore the sum of the magnitudes of all of these movements. Thus, the inner channel contains only random movement and has a depth of about $6.5. The next channel contains random movement plus the movement of the shorter wavelength cycle. This channel depth is about $16. Therefore the magnitude of the shorter wavelength cycle is the difference between the two, *i.e.* about $9.5.

The outermost channel contains the movement of all the components, and has a depth of $26. The magnitude of the longer wavelength cycle is therefore the difference between its depth and the depth of the next inner channel. This gives $26 - $16 = $10.

We now have the magnitudes of the components as:

> longer wavelength cycle = $10 (actual = $10)
> shorter wavelength cycle = $10 (actual = $10)
> random movement = $6.5 (actual = $6 to $8)

Finding the Wavelengths

The longer wavelength is found by noting the distance between the points where the middle channel touches the outermost channel. The upper boundary is touched at points 115 and 167, while the lower boundary is touched at points 141 and 191. This gives two measurements, by difference, of the wavelength: 52 weeks and 50 weeks. The mean of these is 51 weeks, which is a very close estimate to the actual value of 52 weeks.

The shorter wavelength is found by noting the distance between the points where the inner channel touches the middle channel. The upper boundary is touched at 110, 130, 154, 172 and 195, giving values of 20, 24, 18 and 23 weeks. The lower boundary is touched at 121, 142, 162, 185 and 203, giving values of 21, 20, 23 and 18 weeks. The mean of these eight measurements is 20.9 weeks, or 21 weeks to the nearest whole number. This is exactly the wavelength used in constructing the composite waveform. The analysis is now complete, and from a very simple exercise we have been able to determine from the complex waveform that there are three components—one random and two cyclical ones. We have been able to determine the magnitudes of all three components and the wavelength of each of the cyclic components with remarkable accuracy. This can only be done by strictly applying the rules of channel analysis. These rules can be restated as:

•Start with the channel that will enclose the minor fluctuations in the data.

•A smooth channel, whose upper and lower boundaries are a constant vertical distance apart, is drawn to enclose the minor fluctuations.

•The depth should be adjusted so that as many peaks as possible are close to or touching the upper boundary, with the same consideration for troughs and the lower boundary.

•In the case of very irregular data, it is acceptable to have one or two troughs or peaks penetrating the boundaries slightly. Boundaries can be adjusted inwards or outwards to achieve this aim.

•Once the inner channel is drawn, draw a channel outside of this to enclose the fluctuations in the inner channel. Keep a constant vertical depth and adjust this so as many peaks and troughs in the inner channel are close to or touching the boundaries. In the case where there are many

peaks and troughs in the inner channel it is acceptable to
have one or two peaks or troughs penetrating the boundaries slightly.

•As long as there are sufficient peaks and troughs in the
current outermost channel, it is acceptable to draw further channels outside of these.

One important point must be stated about the charts used in channel analysis. **These must be linear, not logarithmic.** The use of a logarithmic
vertical price axis means that a channel of constant price depth would
become narrower as we move towards the top of the chart. This makes
the drawing of channels virtually impossible.

On a linear scale, because of the requirement of constant vertical depth,
one gets the illusion that the channel is deeper where it runs horizontally,
and narrower where it is rising steeply. This is just an illusion, but until
the investor gets used to the way that channels should be drawn, it can
cause a little difficulty.

There are several technical analysis methods that draw bands or channels
on stock price data. Some of these are based on standard deviations,
some on percentage rises or falls in the data, and so on. **Only constant
depth channels satisfy the mathematical requirements to enable cycles
to be extracted from the data in the way we have seen.**

Predicting the Future

In the following chapter, we will see how to apply the channel analysis
technique to real stock market data. For the present we can show the
steps followed using the synthetic data. We will assume that the actual
data ends at point 180 on the horizontal time scale, as shown in Figure
5.10. Obviously, the key to predicting the movement of the price data in
the near future is to make as accurate a projection as possible of the
channels. The innermost channel is the one closest to the movement of

the actual data because it encloses the random movement. However, the smoothest channel, and hence the one easiest to project into the future is the outermost. **Because of this fact, the procedure to follow is the reverse of that used to produce the channels in the first place, where we started with the innermost and worked outwards.** Now, we start with the outermost and work inwards. When a channel reaches a boundary of the next outer channel, then by the rules of channel analysis, either zero or limited penetration is allowed. Thus, the channel must reverse direction to avoid this. When projecting channels forward in time, this reversal of direction must be converted into a smooth, rounded maximum or minimum, depending upon whether an upper or lower boundary is being reached.

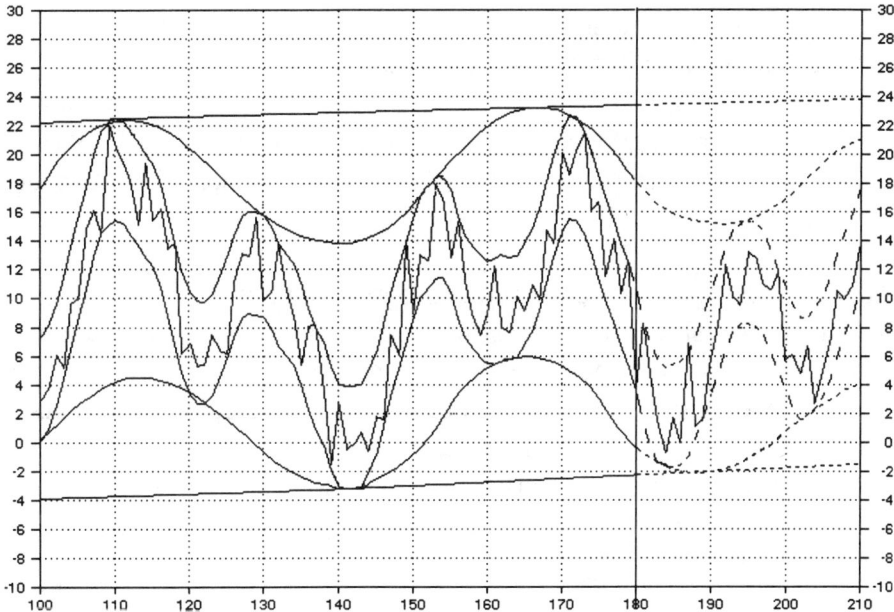

Figure 5.11. *The actual course of the data shows how accurate the prediction of channels (dashed lines) was.*

The outermost channel is running virtually horizontal, and its smooth projection from point 180 onwards is shown in Figure 5.10. We can project the next innermost channel, bearing in mind that we have established the wavelength of this channel is around 51 weeks. Because of this, we expect it to pass through a minimum. Its projection downwards from its present position will cause it to hit the lower boundary of the outermost channel at around week 188, so this is the natural point at which to make this middle channel bounce up again. As a further check, the minimum in this channel should occur at around week 188, since this is half a wavelength, 26 weeks on from the last maximum that was at point 172. Since these two facts agree, we can make the middle channel bend up again in a smooth transition from falling to rising to give a minimum at point 188. It will then keep rising for half a wavelength before peaking out again somewhere around point 214 (188 + 26). Following this line of reasoning the channel boundaries are shown as dashed lines in Figure 5.10.

The inner channel when projected forwards in the downwards direction is headed at point 180, will strike the middle channel at about point 184, and then reverse direction to rise. With the middle channel projection as shown in Figure 5.10, the inner channel will top out around point 195 and fall again towards the lower boundary of the inner channel, where it should arrive at about point 205.

In Figure 5.11 we can see the actual progress of the data from point 180 forwards. This shows that our estimate of the future course of the innermost channel was a good one. It must be pointed out of course, this estimate was based on an analysis of regular data created from regular cycles. It will be shown in the next chapter that since cycles in stock market data are subject to variation, it will not be quite as easy as the current exercise. Even so, we will see remarkable predictions achieved by this simple technique.

The further rules of channel analysis that enable us to project into the future once we have drawn channels up to the current position are:

- Work from the outside to the inside.

- Draw the outermost channel forwards in time, in a smooth

continuation of its current position at the last data point. **This is the control channel, since it determines the direction of all other channels** (Note: this is not the same as J.M. Hursts' 'control channel').

• Inner channels are drawn in a smooth continuation until they meet the boundary of the next outer channel. This causes a reversal of direction. It is important that the reversal is similar to reversals in the historical data, *i.e.* they are very smooth and rounded maxima or minima.

• We will never be able to draw the actual predicted price movement itself because of the existence of random behavior. The best we will achieve is a narrow channel within which the majority of this random behavior will be contained.

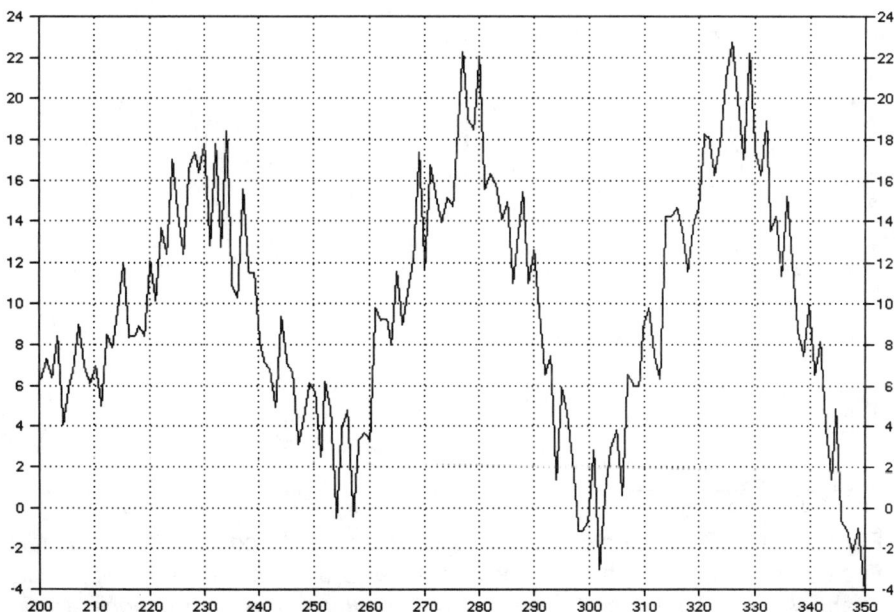

Figure 5.12. *The combination of a cycle of wavelength 45 weeks, a cycle of wavelength 52 weeks and random movement.*

Cycle Resolution

It is important to point out that the more channels we are able to draw, the better our prediction will be of future movement in the data provided the channels are quite distinct in shape. We saw with the simple example that it was possible to draw a channel to enclose each component, so that with the mixture of random movement and two different cycles we could draw three channels. From these three channels we were able to derive a great deal of information about the nature of each of the three components, but the main reason for the ease with which we could do this was because the cycles were quite widely separated in wavelength. **As a general rule, the greater the difference between the wavelengths, the easier will it be to resolve them.**

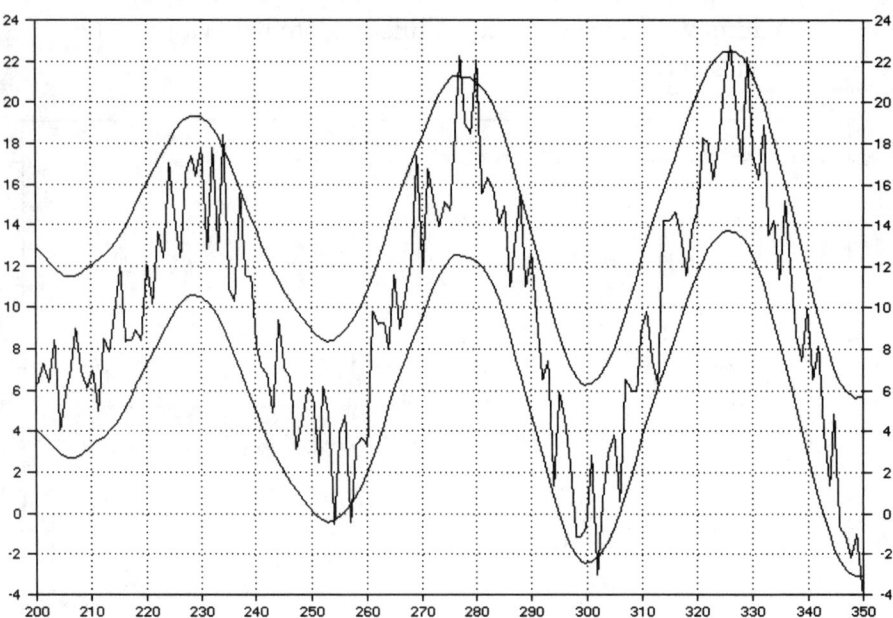

Figure 5.13. *One inner channel has been drawn to contain the short term fluctuations. The fact that it is not possible to draw a constant depth outer channel to touch each of the maxima and minima in the inner channel implies the existence of more than one cycle in the data.*

The difficulty we run into when the wavelengths of the two cycles are close together is illustrated by Figure 5.12. Here we have used the same level of random movement and the same 52-week cycle, but have replaced the 21-week cycle by one with a wavelength of 45 weeks. While it appears at first that there is only one cycle present with wavelength of about 50 to 52 weeks, it can be seen that its magnitude is changing as we move from point 200 to point 350. This change in magnitude is not caused by the random element, since that can be contained quite tightly in a channel, as can be seen from Figure 5.13. Thus, we conclude that there is at least one other cycle present. Although it is not immediately obvious, we find that the distance between successive peaks and troughs is not constant, but gives values, for example, of 22, 26, 23, 23 and 25 weeks. Since the wavelength is twice these distances, we can see that the apparent wavelength runs through the successive values of 44, 52, 46, 46 and 50 weeks. Taking the two extreme values, will lead us to the conclusion that we have two cycles present with wavelengths of around 44 weeks and 52 weeks. What is not possible to do is to gain any indication of the relative magnitudes of these two.

Figure 5.14. *The combination of a cycle of wavelength 40 weeks, a cycle of wavelength 52 weeks and random movement.*

If we separate the two cycles rather more in wavelength, say to 40 and 52, we get the situation shown in Figure 5.14. The center part is now distorted, giving us the much firmer impression that we are dealing with at least two cycles. We are just about at the smallest amount of separation of the cycles that will allow us to derive the magnitude of each component by graphical channel analysis. The graphics are shown in Figure 5.15. It is easy to draw the innermost channel to contain as tightly as possible the short-term movement caused by the random component. It is the next channel outward that requires some explanation. The only way in which the large vertical change in the inner channel between point 330 and 350 can be accommodated at the same time that the small changes in the inner channel in the central part of the plot is by having three peaks and two troughs in the upper boundary with coincidental peaks and troughs in the lower boundary. Finally, the outermost, third channel should be drawn so that its upper boundary is touched by the two peaks in the upper boundary of the middle channel. There are many ways in which this can be done, the two extreme positions being an upper boundary with a mini-

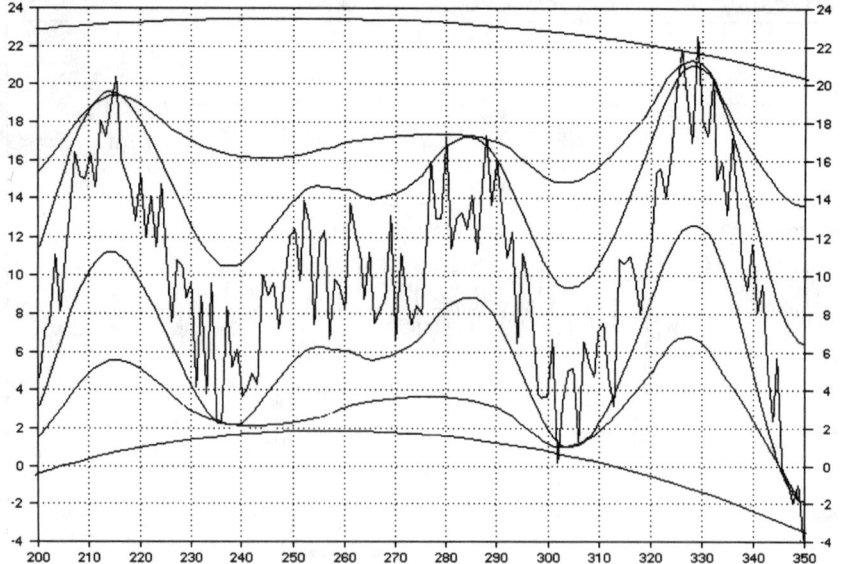

Figure 5.15. *One inner channel has been drawn to contain the short term fluctuations. The way in which the middle and outer channels can be drawn is explained in the text.*

mum in it at around point 250, or a maximum at around point 250. This is where the requirement for constant depth comes into play. The lower boundary can be drawn to accommodate the major trough at point 350 only if the channel has a maximum at point 250.

The reader should go through this exercise using tracing paper over the chart in Figure 5.15, because this practice of checking alternate boundaries constantly as we move from left to right, *i.e.* from the past to the present is essential to the correct positioning of the boundaries. The constant vertical depth requirement will usually mean that any ambiguity in positioning the channel will be resolved as we move to the next feature in the alternate boundary. If, for example the major trough at point 350 had been higher than the previous trough at point 304, then we would decide that the outer boundary had a minimum at point 250 rather than a maximum. This would lead to a completely different forward projection of the channel. Hence future predictions of the movement would not only be wrong, but wildly so. It is imperative the first drawing of channels is always considered to be a rough estimate of their position. The investor should check very carefully, making adjustments as necessary before finalizing the position.

Now that we are comfortable with the channel positions, we need to analyze the result to determine the wavelengths and magnitudes of the components.

Magnitudes

We will be able to find the magnitudes of the various components by difference, as in the earlier example. The inner channel contains only random movement and has a depth of about $8. The next channel contains random movement plus the movement of the shorter wavelength cycle. This channel depth is about $15. Therefore the magnitude of the shorter wavelength cycle is the difference between the two, *i.e.* about $7.

The outermost channel contains the movement of all the components, and has a depth of about $24. The magnitude of the longer wavelength cycle is therefore the difference between its depth and the depth of the next inner channel. This gives $24 - $15 = $9.

We now have the magnitudes of the components as:

longer wavelength = $9   (actual = $10)
shorter wavelength = $7   (actual = $10)
random movement = $8   (actual = $6 to $8)

Once again, this is an excellent result for a method where the analysis is totally carried out by visual estimation.

Wavelengths

The longer wavelength is found by noting the distance between the points where the middle channel touches the outermost channel. There are not many such points. We are looking for touching of alternate boundaries successively by peaks and troughs if possible. The best such occurrences are at points 304 and 329, giving a half wavelength of 25 weeks, *i.e.* **a wavelength of 50 weeks for the longest cycle.** Since we are looking at half wavelengths, it follows that an error of one week in placement will double the error in the wavelength. So that in arriving at this value of 50 weeks compared with the actual value of 52 weeks, we have been accurate to within a week in our estimation.

The shorter wavelength is found by noting the distance between the points where the inner channel touches the middle channel. We note successive touches at points 214, 236, 254, 270, 285, 304 and 329. The successive distances, which represent half wavelengths, are 22, 18, 16, 15, 19 and 25. This gives an average value of 19, which means **our estimation of the shorter wavelength is 38.** Since we know the actual value was 40 weeks, we have made an error of just one-week in our estimation of the channel touching points which of course will depend entirely on how we have drawn the channels.

The reader will find in practicing on charts such as those shown in this chapter, the graphical method is surprisingly robust, tolerating quite a latitude in the placement of the various channels. This robustness will be very welcome when we come to deal with real stockmarket data.

CHAPTER 6

Graphical Channel Analysis—Applications

In this chapter we will apply the simple techniques developed in the previous chapter to actual data, starting with stock price data. Although we will be dealing with much more complex movements, we will see it will still be possible in most cases to come to some conclusion, not only about the direction of movement in the near future, but also a target area into which this movement is likely to take the stock price.

DATA FREQUENCY

We have mentioned that when trying to extract cycles from data, it is essential the data has been sampled at constant intervals of time. The interval can be one or more weeks, one or more days, one or more hours, etc. Long term trends are best analyzed using weekly data, while daily data is better for the analysis of short-term trends. We will see that we can fine-tune the decision point by using both data sets.

What does give rise to a difficulty is the use of the daily range of data. Daily closing prices are obviously separated by a fixed interval of a trading day, but the time relationship between the high and low prices on one day and the high and low prices the next day is a random one. Because of these considerations we will begin with examples of the channel analysis of weekly closings, then move on to the additional information that will be obtained when daily data is used. Finally, we will show some bar charts

that use weekly and daily ranges. You will see that the clearest pictures
are given when channels are drawn on closing prices rather than on ranges.

TYPE OF DATA

By this we mean the type of data that will give the best results when
channel analysis is applied. In the last chapter we saw there was a difficulty when two cycles were quite close in wavelength. Since it was only
the distortion of what looked like a single cycle, it drew attention to the
fact that we probably had a mixture of cycles. When it comes to the movement of stock, currencies, commodities, etc., then the data most ame-
nable to channel analysis by graphical methods will be those where there
are a number of strong cycles present and that are widely separated in
wavelength. At this point it is useful to define what is meant by short,
medium and long term as applied to cycles. Investors are more used to
the idea of short, medium and long term trends, and a generally accepted
view is that trends can be put into the following categories:

> **Long term** - trends of one year or longer
> **Medium term** - trends of three months to one year
> **Short term** - trends of 5 days to than three months
> **Very short term** - trends of less than 5 days, including
> intra-day trends

Since a trend is caused by one half of a cycle, then the cycles would have
the following wavelengths:

> **Long term cycles** - wavelengths of two years or longer
> **Medium term cycles** - wavelengths of six months to two
> years
> **Short term cycles** - wavelengths of 10 days to six months
> **Very short term cycles** - wavelengths of minutes up to
> 10 days.

Although these are very broad categories, they turn out to be useful in our analysis. We want to see a strong cycle present in each of these above categories, and preferably no more than one cycle in each. We also want to see the wavelengths of these strong cycles being around the middle of each of the short and medium term categories, *i.e.* around two to three months for short term and around one year for medium term. Since the degree of random movement increases as the wavelength decreases we want to avoid cycles of less than a few weeks wavelength. This of course represents the ideal, and we are unlikely to find it.

Visual Estimation of Cycles

In the next chapter we will be looking at numerical ways of determining which cycles are present in stock market or other data. In this chapter, we are dealing with simple graphical analysis, since we need a quick and easy way of estimating whether we have the types of cycles present that will enable us to use channel analysis successfully. In Figure 6.1 is a chart of the weekly closing prices of **Delta Airlines** since the beginning of 1980. The immediate impression is that there are many cycles of quite varied wavelength and these are quite strong because of the vertical movement caused by each one. The vertical grids are exactly 100 weeks apart, so it is easy to get an approximate value for wavelengths of the various cycles present. This is done by looking at low points, that can be taken at the start and end points of a cycle, does this. The start and end points of long-term cycles are marked by lows that are much lower in value than those caused by cycles of shorter wavelength. It is also usual to see some short-term cycles also start at the same point as a longer-term cycle.

As an example of a quick analysis for long term cycles, the points marked A, B, C, D and E on Figure 6.1 designate the start and end points of such cycles. Very approximately, since the grids are 100 weeks apart, the distances can be estimated as:

A to B, cycle of wavelength 100 weeks

B to C, cycle of wavelength 120 weeks

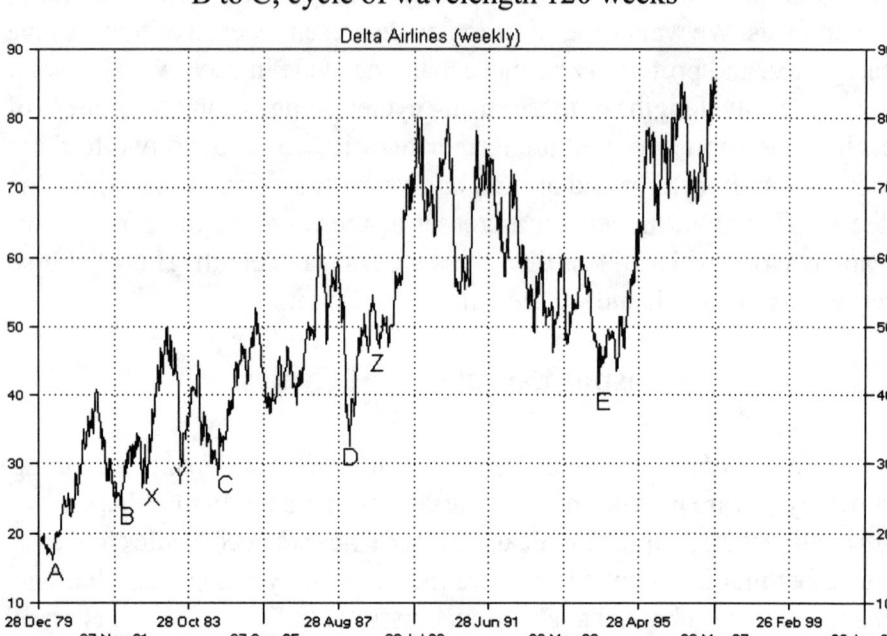

Figure 6.1. *A chart of the weekly closing prices of Delta Airlines since 1980 (see text for explanation of marked points)*

C to D, cycle of wavelength 160 weeks
D to E, cycle of wavelength 320 weeks

The distance between B and C can also be seen to contain three medium wavelength cycles:

B to X, cycle of wavelength 40 weeks
X to Y, cycle of wavelength 60 weeks
Y to C, cycle of wavelength 50 weeks

Point B is therefore the start of a medium term cycle of wavelength about 40 weeks as well as a long-term cycle of wavelength 120 weeks. A number of even shorter wavelength cycles can also be seen in the weekly data, for example the group at point Z.

In general, where a low point is particularly low in terms of historical low

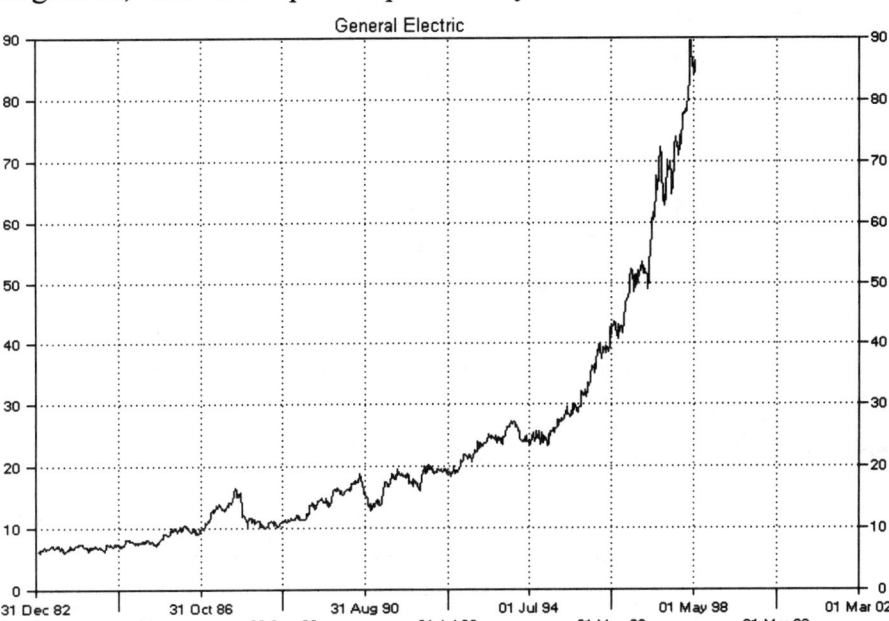

Figure 6.2. *Except for a very long term cycle, strong cycles appear to be absent in this chart of weekly closing prices of General Electric since 1983*

points, this is because a number of different cycles are all bottoming out at the same time. The opposite is true for high points that are particularly high. In later chapters we will see points in time in the near future where it can be anticipated that a number of cycles will reach their low points simultaneously are prime investment points, leading to a rapid and extensive rise in the stock price. Such points are rare, but can often be predicted. Similar predictions that a number of cycles are going to reach their high points simultaneously sound a warning that the stock should be exited speedily.

It is not necessary to spend a great deal of time on this exercise of visual estimation, and after a modest amount of practice you will be able to decide almost at a glance whether a chart is worthy of further consideration or should be discarded because there are either too few cycles or they are too weak.

Thus, a glance of **General Electric** in May 1998 (Figure 6.2) leads to the conclusion that there are not enough dissimilar cycles and that the chart is dominated by one very long wavelength that is probably coming to an end soon. Thus the criteria for a good analysis is not present and the investor should move on to another stock.

CHANNEL ANALYSIS OF DELTA AIRLINES

Now, we have seen that the **Delta Airlines** chart is a good candidate for graphical channel analysis. It is interesting to see what we can make of the position at around point E, since the stock made a very useful gain from that point onwards.

December 1994

In Figure 6.3 we see the chart as it appeared on the December 9, 1994. Three channels are drawn, and although it is rather difficult to see the

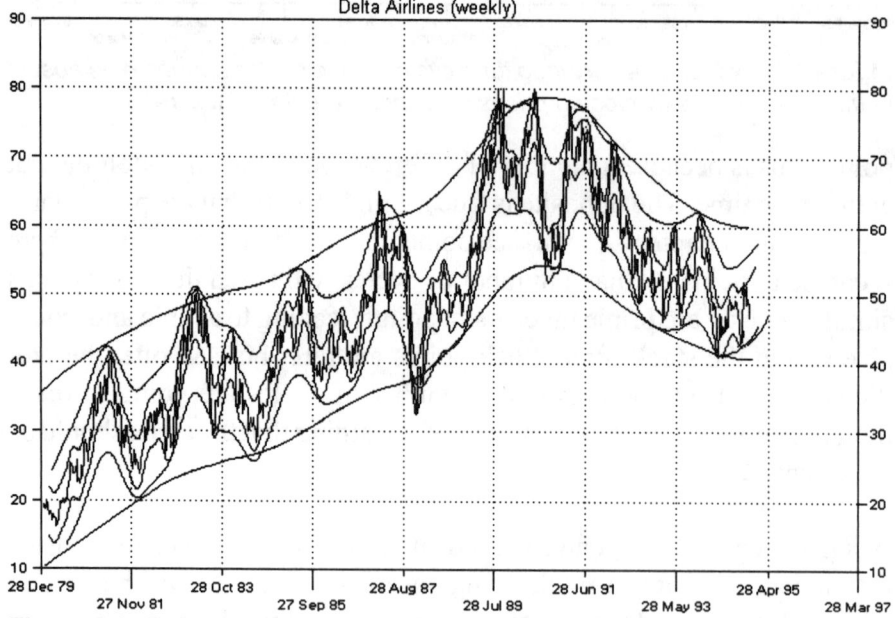

Figure 6.3. *Delta Airlines as at December 9,1994.Three channels have been drawn. The inner and middle channels are rising, and the rate of descent of the outer channel is slowing.*

detail of the price movement within the inner channel, we are more concerned with the middle and outer channel shapes. This will give us an indication of the medium term outlook for the stock. The most recent trough in the inner channel is at a higher level than the previous trough in this channel. Because of this, we can draw the middle channel as having changed direction at the place where the penultimate trough occurred in the inner channel, so that the middle channel is now rising. Thus the medium term trend is now upwards. Normally, this would be an indication that we could consider buying the stock with a view to making a short to medium term profit. However, the contra-indication is that the actual stock price has fallen from its value the previous week, or, in other words the very short-term trend is downward. An investor should never buy until the very short-term trend has turned up, so it is necessary to wait for a rise in price before the stock can be bought.

As far as the long-term trend is concerned, we have just the beginnings of an indication the downward fall of the outer channel is beginning to come to an end. Thus the position on December 9 was:

*long term trend (outer channel) - **falling**, but expected to reverse soon*
*medium term trend (middle channel) - **rising***
*short term tend (inner channel) - **rising***
*very short term trend (current price versus previous value) - **falling***

Now everything is poised quite nicely for an imminent buying signal. This will be given when the very short-term trend changes direction. When this happens we can buy the stock, but with the reservation that if the long term trend is still down, there is much greater risk involved than if it is rising. The investor with a longer time scale would wait for a rise in the outer channel. The shorter-term investor would buy even if the outer channel is falling, but should exit the stock via a stop-loss at the first sign of a reversal of the middle channel.

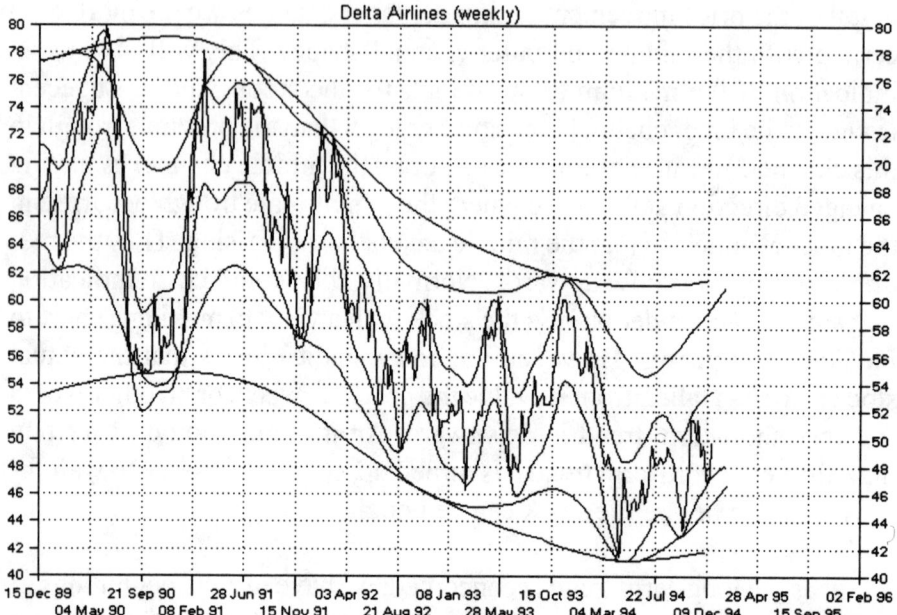

Figure 6.4. *The position in **Delta Airlines** two weeks later on December 23, 1994. The outer channel has now probably begun to rise and since the price has risen since the from that of the previous week it is time to consider buying the stock.*

In Figure 6.4 we see the position two weeks later on December 23. It took these two weeks before the very short-term trend changed direction; *i.e.* there was a rise in price from that of the previous week. This extra two weeks were also invaluable in clarifying the outer channel had probably changed direction, and was now rising. Thus the position on December 23 was:

long term trend (outer channel) - ***probably rising***
medium term trend (middle channel) - ***rising***
short term tend (inner channel) - ***rising***
very short term trend (current price versus previous value) ***rising***

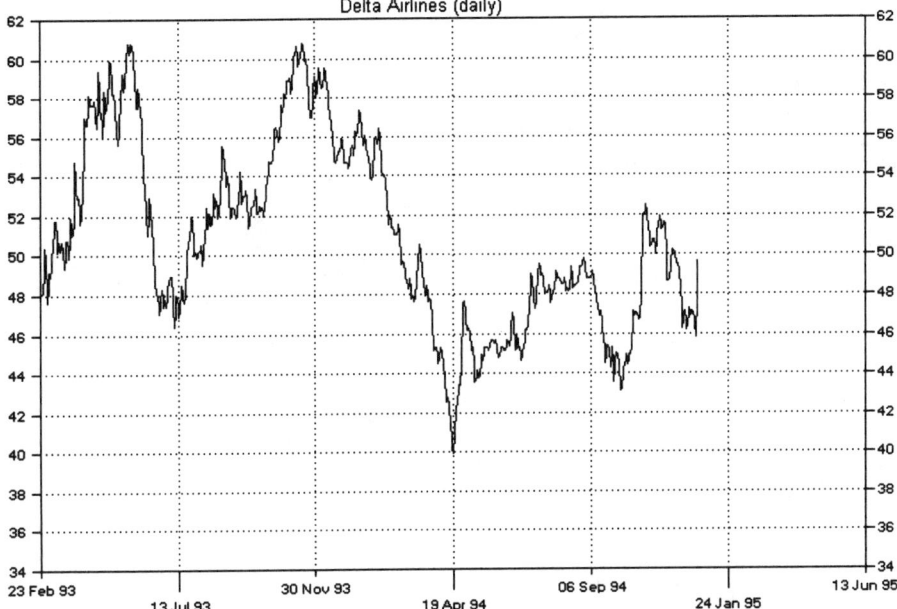

Figure 6.5. *The position in* **Delta Airlines** *on December 23, 1994 when daily data is plotted. There was a large jump in price from December 22.*

All signals are now at go. However, it is very useful to view the position with daily data as soon as we reach this point, because daily data will show up very short-term trends and short term trends that were not visible in the weekly data. This gives us an advantage in the situation where a short-term trend is still falling on the December 23. In such a case, waiting for this to change direction gives us a better buying price than jumping in immediately. Figure 6.5 shows the daily data chart for December 23. We can see that the stock price hovered in a band between $46 and $47 for a few days, but then made a large jump to just below $50 in a day. If we leave out the channel that would enclose the day to day fluctuations, then the two obvious channels that we can draw are shown in Figure 6.6. We can now see that there have been three fairly major low points in the recent history, on April 19, 1994 (39^7/_8$), October 6, 1994 ($43$^1/_8$) and December 22, 1994 (45^3/_4$). The fact that these are successively higher will force a bend in the outer channel around the April low point, so that the outer channel is obviously rising. The inner channel had

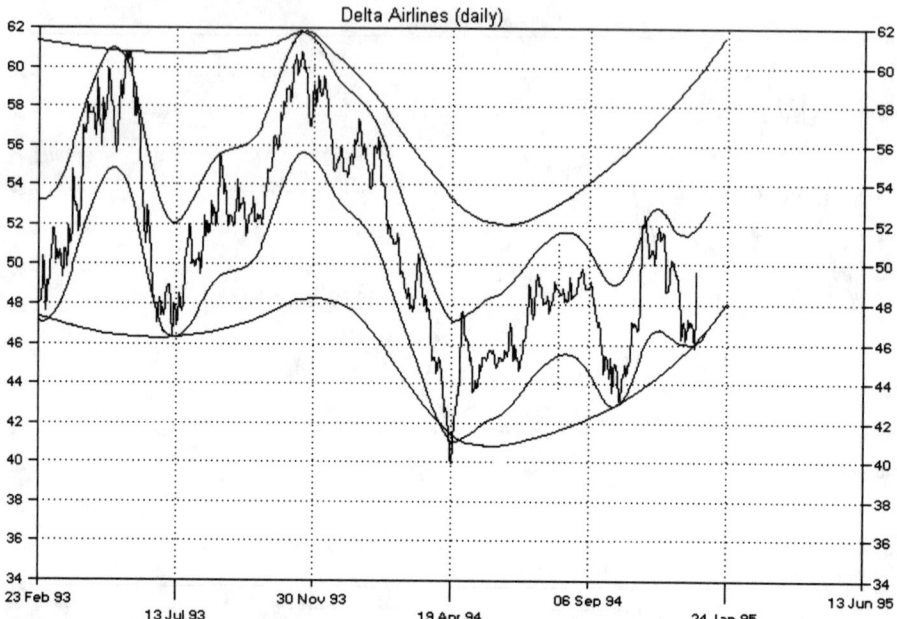

Figure 6.6. *Channels have now been drawn on the data from Figure 6.5. The outer channel can be seen to have turned up near the low point of April 1994, and the inner channel which was falling for most of December must therefore have bounced up from the lower boundary of this rising channel.*

a peak in it to coincide with the high point in the stock price of \$52½ on November 2, 1994. This channel will now have arrived at the lower boundary of the outer channel, and therefore must be made to bounce back up.

Thus the daily data confirms fully the position seen in the weekly data, and the very short-term trend not visible in the weekly data is also rising. It therefore appears to be time to buy the stock.

We can fine-tune the buying decision more if we move to a chart of the daily ranges in **Delta Airlines** as shown in Figure 6.7. The only additional information in this chart that helps with our analysis is the behavior of the stock on the day we are making our decision, *i.e.* on the December 23. The stock opened at \$45⅞, its low point for the day, and made an intermediate high of \$49⅞ before closing at \$49⅝. Thus, the very short-term intra-day trend is essentially rising, with a very small correction at the

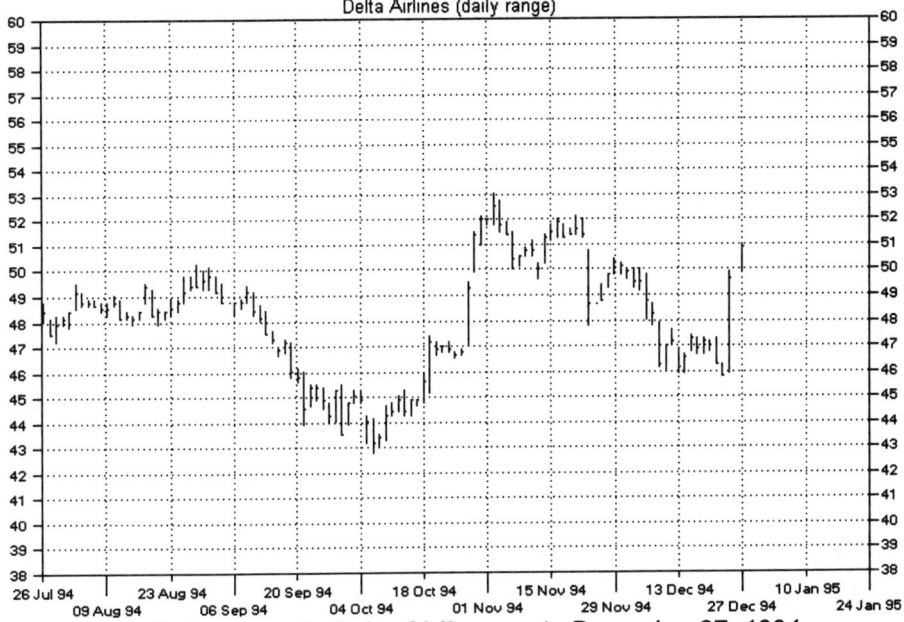

Figure 6.7. *Daily ranges in **Delta Airlines** up to December 27, 1994.*

close. Since this very short-term trend is also in our favor we would now be seeking to buy **Delta Airlines** the next trading day, which was the December 27. The stock opened at 49\frac{7}{8}$ and rose throughout the day to a high of $51 before closing down slightly at 50\frac{7}{8}$. The investor would have bought early in the day as soon as it was apparent the price was rising from its opening value.

This simple approach to daily ranges is to be much preferred to the estimation of the following day's trading range by means of the pivot point. This is taken to be the average of the three values of high, low and close for a day. Thus, by the close of business on the December 23 we will add 49\frac{7}{8}$, 45\frac{7}{8}$ and 49\frac{5}{8}$ and divide by three to give a pivot point of 47\frac{3}{4}$.

The next day's predicted low is then given by taking the value of the day's high from twice the value of the pivot point, *i.e.* 2 x 47\frac{3}{4}$ - 49\frac{7}{8}$ = 45\frac{5}{8}$.

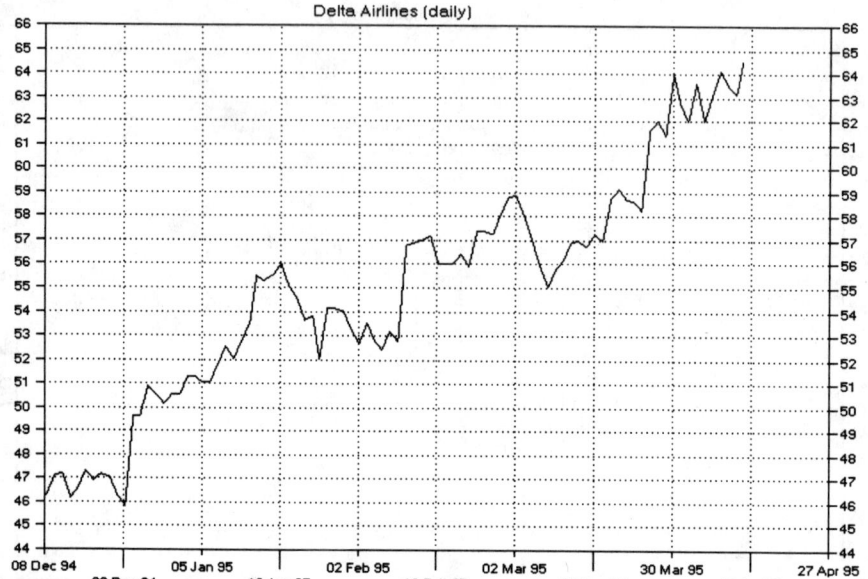

Figure 6.8. *The subsequent movement of **Delta Airlines** stock since buying in December 1994.*

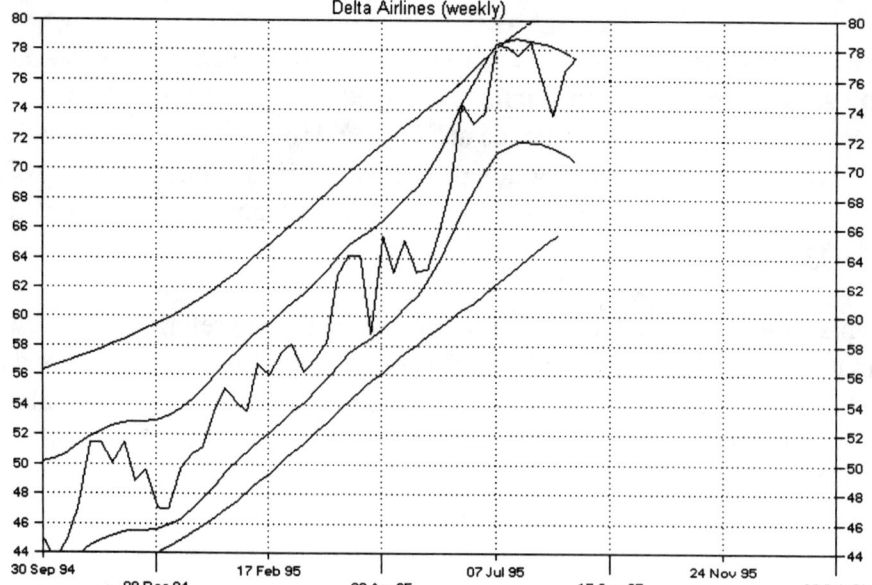

Figure 6.9. *The position in Delta Airlines in August 1995 with weekly data. The inner channel must be made to bend downwards in order to accommodate the peaks in July and August.*

The next day's predicted high is then given by taking the value of the day's low from twice the value of the pivot point, *i.e.* 2 x $47³/₄ - $45⁷/₈ =$49⁵/₈.

This gives an estimated range for the following day of $4. As can be seen from the values given for trading on the next business day, the December 27, these estimates were not very good in this particular case, and the simple method of trying to determine the trend on the next day gives much more consistent results.

The development of the price on the daily chart over the next few months is shown in Figure 6.8. In the short term the price rose to $56 by January 19, 1995 and to $64 by March 30, 1995. The latter represents a gain of 29% in three months. Although this is not spectacular, the gain is being achieved at a rate of over 100% per annum, and by any standards is very acceptable. If other stocks which displayed similar gains in similar time periods were available to move into, then we would make a compound gain of around 175% in a year!

August 1995

By late August 1995 the weekly chart of **Delta Airlines** appeared as shown in Figure 6.9. The stock made a useful advance throughout the year, and although the outer channel appears to be still rising, the investor should be concerned because the inner channel would now have to be made to turn downwards in order to accommodate the series of peaks and troughs between July 1995 and late August. In order to clarify the position, attention now turns to a chart of the daily data, as shown in Figure 6.10. This shows that because the vertical excursions between peaks and troughs in the data are much greater than the channel depth, the channel must have passed its peak position for the time being. The expanded section shown in Figure 6.11 helps to clarify exactly how the inner channel would be drawn.

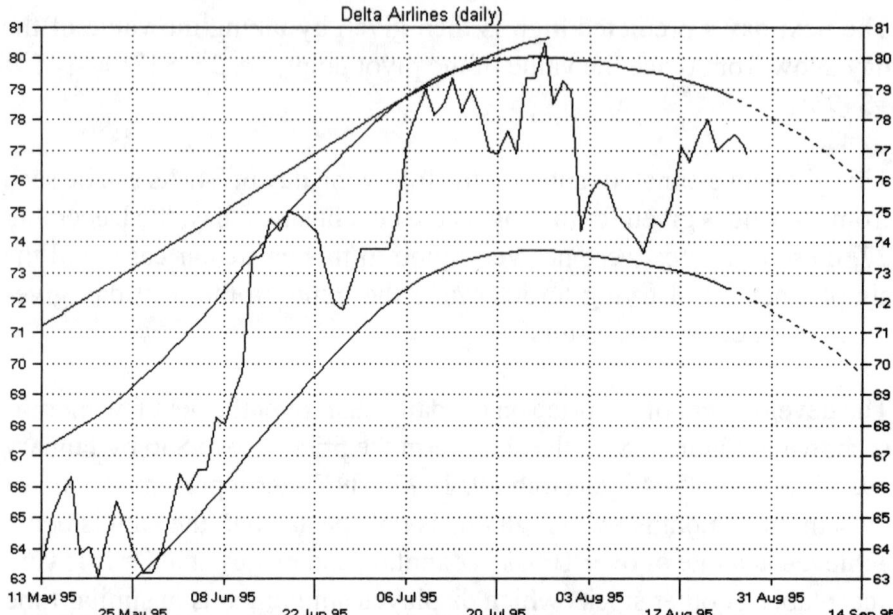

Figure 6.10. *Attention now turns to daily data in order to decide on the course of action in August 1995. The arrangement of peaks and troughs in July and August confirm that the inner channel must have topped out.*

The key features that lead the investor to the conclusion that the inner channel had topped out were the peak at 80^{1/2}$ on July 27 and the vertical fall to 74^{3/8}$ by August 2. The price rose from this to $76, so the investor draws the lower boundary through the trough formed by this rise. While in this position the channel is still rising, its rate of increase is decreasing. The price then fell from the value of $76 to 73^{5/8}$ on August 11. It is this lower trough that is crucial, because it forces the lower boundary even lower. Because of the previous high peak on July 27, this means that the inner boundary is now definitely falling. This is a danger signal, and the investor would now be ready to sell at the best opportunity.

Since the trough has already been formed at the lower boundary, a bounce up from this position is to be expected, and the investor would probably wish to take advantage of this before selling the share. This bounce takes the price up to $78 on August 22 before falling back to $77. At this point in time the estimate of the position of the upper boundary puts it at about

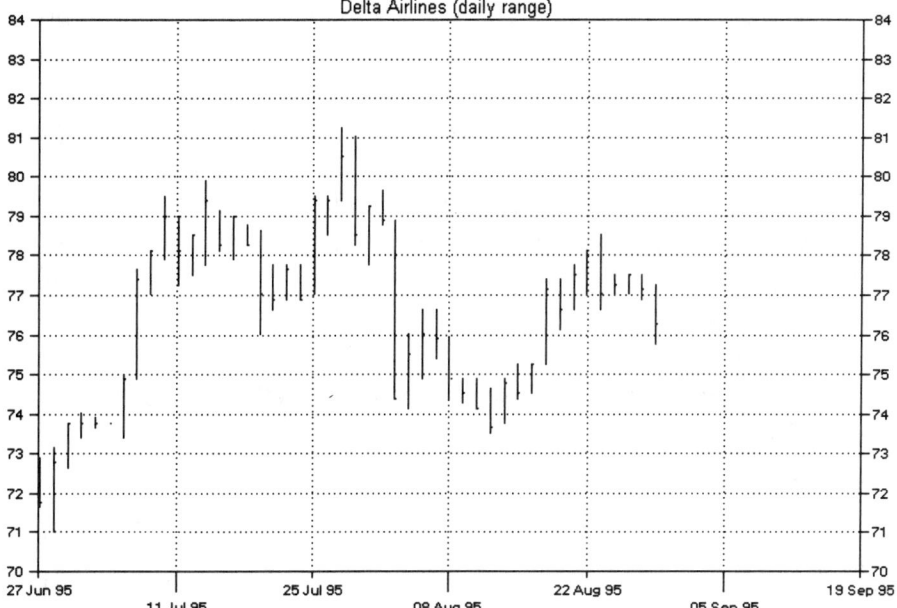

Figure 6.11. *The daily ranges in **Delta Airlines**. The last plotted bar is on August 29, 1995. A cautious investor would have sold on August 23.*

$79. Thus the rise has taken the price to a level at which the probability of a fall is increasing rapidly, and the investor will realize that the selling point is imminent. The next rise from this trough peters out at 77\frac{1}{2}$ since there was a fall back to 77\frac{1}{8}$ in the next day, August 28. Because of this failure of the very short-term trend to rise to a higher level than the previous short term high, the investor must sell. The price closed at 76\frac{1}{4}$ on August 29.

A chart of the daily ranges for **Delta Airlines** is shown in Figure 6.11. The crucial period is between August 22 and 29. We noted that the close of $78 on August 22 took the price within about one point of the upper boundary. The high for that day was 78\frac{1}{4}$, so that the close was only marginally lower. The next day the stock opened at 77\frac{3}{4}$. The cautious investor would sell at this point on August 23 since, with an open lower than the previous close, the very short-term trend is down. The less cautious investor would be hoping for a closer approach to the upper boundary than $78 and would stay with the stock. During the 23rd the price reached a high of 78^{1}/_{2}$ before falling back. This was the highest level reached by the price for a couple of weeks, and the investor selling at this point would have been quite pleased. The investor who held on hoping for even better would see that the stock failed to rise above daily highs of 77^{1}/_{2}$ on three successive days, while on the 29th the stock failed to reach even this level. Even the most optimistic investor would exit the stock at this point.

Thus we have seen a range of selling prices from around $77 for the investor who followed daily closes and came out at the start of trading on August 29, to between $77 and 78^{1}/_{2}$ for the investor who followed intra-day movements closely.

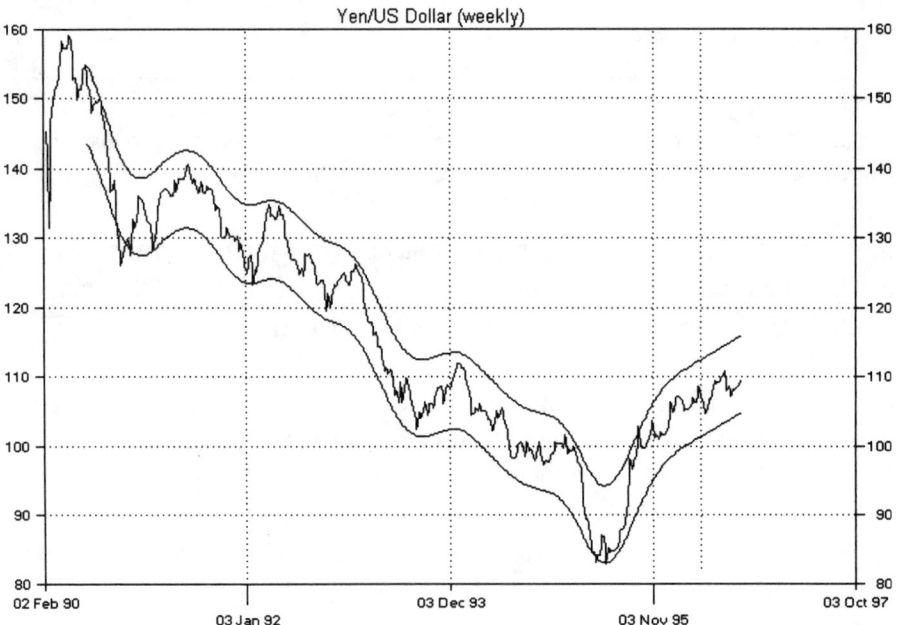

Figure 6.12. *Weekly closings of the Japanese yen versus the US dollar. One channel is drawn to show the difficulty of taking a decision in 1995 based solely on weekly data.*

CHANNEL ANALYSIS OF JAPANESE YEN IN 1995

A weekly chart of the yen versus the US dollar is shown in Figure 6.12. The prime question is whether an investor could have used channel analysis to take early advantage of the profit potential during the period May to June 1995, when the yen was trading in the 80-90 band. Clearly we can draw a channel as shown in the figure, but the rapid weekly rise and fall during the second two weeks in May would make it rather difficult to take an early decision. The first point where we would be quite satisfied that the channel was rising and the yen/dollar ratio was at the lower boundary and hence ready for a rise would be in September 1995. At this point (28th) the yen was trading at above 100 to the dollar once again, and the large move from the April low would have been missed.

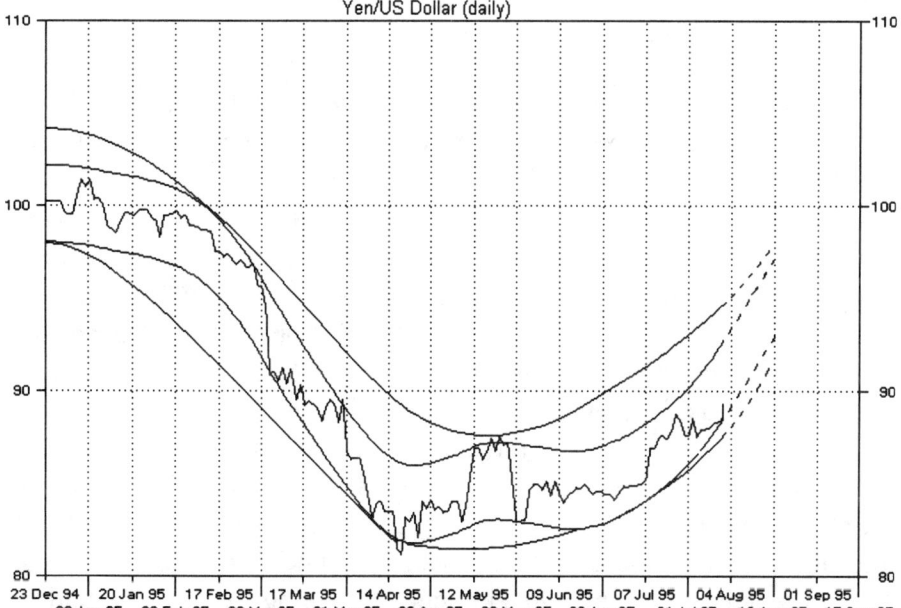

Figure 6.13. *When daily values are used the investor could take a positive view on August 2, that the dollar was strengthening since both channels appeared to be rising and the yen had just bounced up from the predicted lower boundary of the inner channel. A rise towards the 100 level by September could be anticipated.*

When daily data is used, the position would have crystallized much sooner. The center of Figure 6.13 shows the position in mid-May 1995. The yen/dollar ratio had risen slightly from its low point in April, and a trough was formed on May 9 at 82.895 because of the rise the next day to 83.84. At this point, the investor would consider the channel to be still falling, although the yen/dollar ratio is now towards the top of this channel. The rapid rise to 86.95 by May 12 took the yen/dollar ratio well above the estimated upper boundary of the channel, so that an adjustment was necessary to accommodate this new level. The adjustment would entail bending the channel upwards so that its low point was more or less coincident with the April low. Since the yen was now running along the top of the channel, the investor would have to wait for a fall to the lower boundary and then a bounce upwards to provide a trough to validate the lower boundary before any action could be taken.

The fall to 85.1 by May 25 took the yen/dollar ratio down to the estimated position of the now rising channel, but the next day a further fall to 82.875 took it well below the boundary. This would mean an adjustment to the boundary to make it turn down again. By the time the trough was formed on May 26, the channel was clearly established in a downward direction, leaving the investor on the sidelines for the time being. As time elapsed, the ratio ran along the middle of this channel, but then made a slight rise in July, culminating in a peak at 88.735 on the 18th. Turning the channel upwards once again, as shown in Figure 6.13 could only accommodate this peak. The investor is now in the same position as in May, with the yen/dollar ratio near the upper boundary of a rising channel. It was not until the August 2, with the yen at 88.305 that the investor judged the ratio to be near the lower boundary. It arrived there not by a fall, but by a sideways movement which allowed the boundary to catch up with it. At this point the investor could take action by selling the yen at around 88 to 89, and would have been very pleased by the very useful rise in the yen/dollar ratio to 104 by September 20.

CHANNEL ANALYSIS OF GOLD IN 1993

The movement of gold between December 1992 and February 1994 is shown in Figure 6.14. The most significant feature is of course the large rise in the price of gold between March and August 1993, moving from $326.4 on March 10, to $407.05 on July 30. Almost as significant is the subsequent fall back to $343.875 by September 13, 1993.

This rapid rise and fall provides a stiff test for channel analysis, since the investor would naturally have liked to have participated in this rapid rise, but would also have wished to have been warned about the equally rapid fall.

Figure 6.14. *Daily values for gold between August 1990 and June 1994.*

In Figure 6.15 the position on April 22, 1993, of gold at $340.65, has risen from $339.1 of the previous day. The two features that would encourage us to believe the inner channel is now rising are the trough at

March 10th and the peak at $340.35 on April 2nd. The only way we can accommodate both of these is by causing the inner channel to bend up-

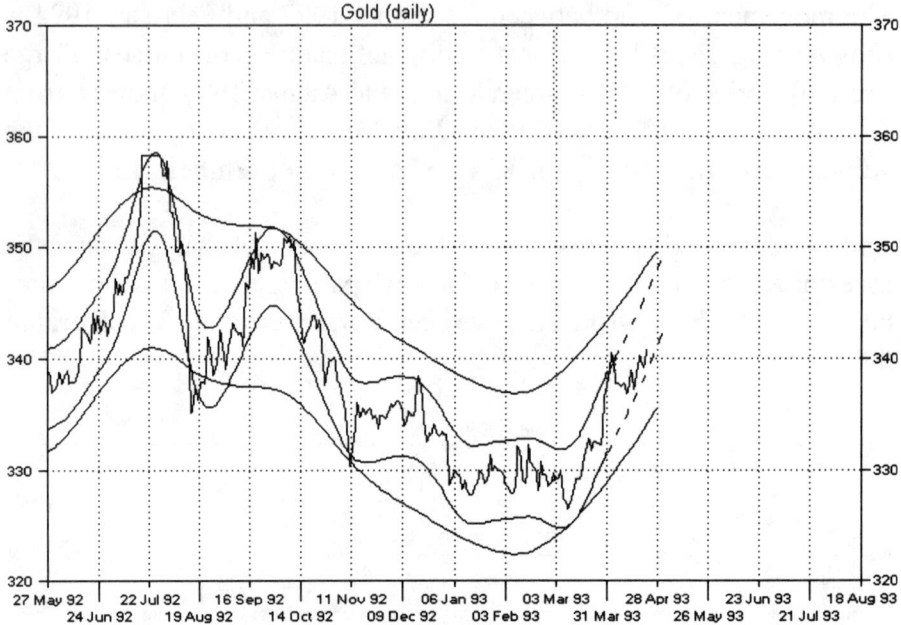

Figure 6.15. *Channel analysis of gold on April 23, 1993. The prime features that decide the current direction of both inner and outer channels are the trough on March 10 and the peak on April 2. These force bends in the channels so that they are both currently rising. This gives a positive outlook for gold in the medium term with a target of around $360 if the channels are extrapolated.*

wards with the trough on March 10 as the turning point. Once we have drawn the channel in this way, it becomes apparent that the latest trough on April 21 is at or very close to the lower boundary of the channel. Thus we can anticipate a rise of the gold price within this inner channel.

Our attention would now shift to an estimate of the position of the outer channel. At this point in time there is nothing to suggest this is not still falling. We are therefore in the position of having a medium term channel rising, and the long-term channel falling. We would therefore accept that there is a potential for profit, but that the falling outer channel will limit the probable rise in the gold price. A further point, which will be developed later, is that the inner channel is about halfway up the outer channel. These mid-channel points usually see the most rapid increase in price,

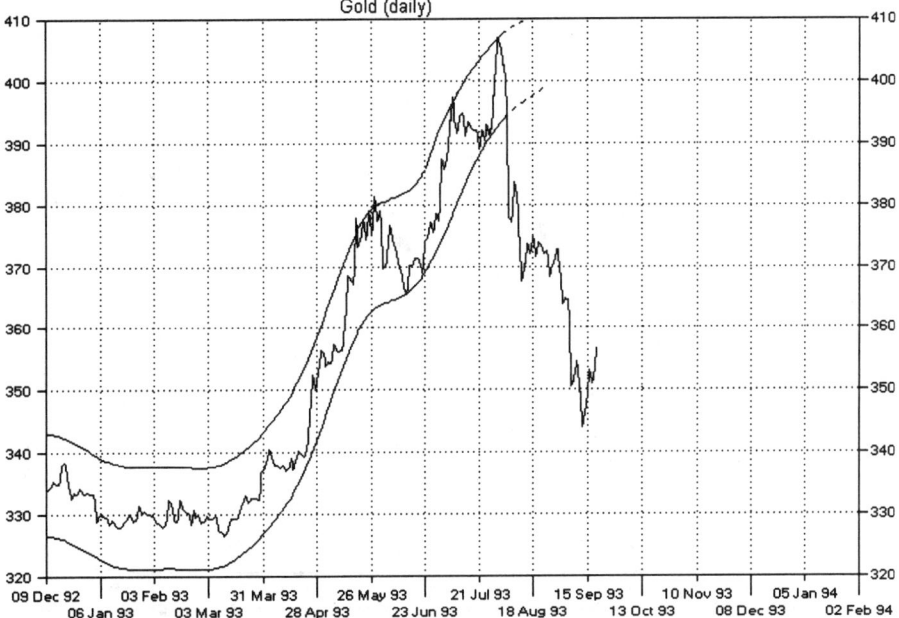

Figure 6.16. *The position in gold in early August 1993. The estimated future boundaries of the channels are shown as dashed lines. The fall through the estimated position of the lower boundary on August 5, was an indication that gold should be sold. The actual price movement until September 1993 is plotted to show that this decision would have been correct.*

and so we would expect a quick profit to be available from an investment in gold at this point. Although the subsequent rise to around $355 is in line with the predicted short-term target area, what is unexpected is the further rapid rise to just over $380. The investor who sold in late May 1993 could have gotten back in during June at a better price and benefited from a further rise to around $405 in early August.

The position on August 5, following the climb to the peak price of $407.05 on July 30 is shown in Figure 6.16. The group of minor troughs between July 21 and 27 would help to define the lower boundary of the channel as having a slight curve with its rate of climb now starting to decrease. The position of the peak on July 30 is also consistent with this decrease. By

the next day the future channel direction could be estimated as shown by
the dotted line in Figure 6.16.

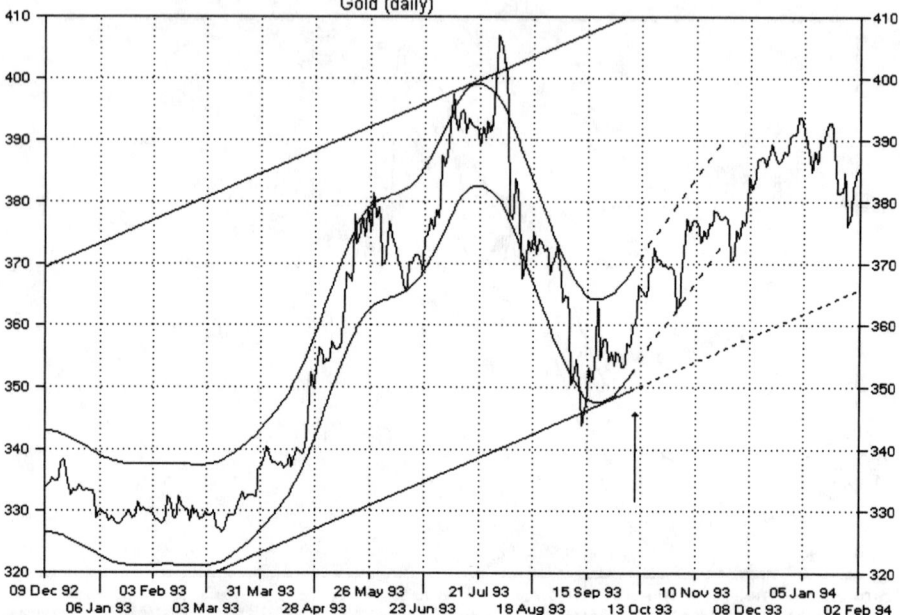

Figure 6.17. *The position in gold in early October 1993 (shown by arrow). The
estimated future boundaries of the channels are shown as dashed lines. The
actual price movement until February 1994 is plotted to show how good the
estimation was in the near term.*

By August 4 the price had fallen over the previous few days in a series of
small steps to $400.1. Since the channel depth is around $17, this brings
the gold price to around mid-channel and falling. Since the lower boundary is now estimated around $392 (at the peak of $407 it was at $390, but
it is predicted to be still climbing), the investor would probably decide
that a further fall of $8 or so could be tolerated because of the expected
bounce back up from the lower boundary once the latter was reached.
However, the next day the gold price fell rapidly to $377.75, well below
the position of the estimated lower boundary. Once a lower boundary is
violated in this way, it is time to exit, since position of the boundary, and
hence the channel, must be adjusted downwards to accommodate the
new price level. This puts the direction of the inner channel firmly headed
downwards, and it is time to exit gold with no ifs or buts. That this was

the correct decision can be seen from the subsequent behavior of the gold price in Figure 6.16, which fell to $343.875 by September 13.

A much clearer buying opportunity occurred once again in gold in October 1993 following its fall from the August peak to a low point of $343.875 on September 13, 1993. The position just a few weeks later is shown in Figure 6.17. As with the other turning points we have discussed, the rise from this low point to the high of $363.7 on September 21 would force us to incorporate a bend upwards in the channel, with the trough on September 13 as its turning point. From September 21 onwards we would be waiting for the gold price to arrive near the lower boundary, at which point we could buy. This happened in early October when the price fell to $353.2 before making a slight rise to $352.25. We have now formed a trough that we estimate at the lower boundary of the inner channel that is rising. We can now buy gold with the reasonable confidence that there will be a rise from this point. As Figure 6.17 shows, the price subsequently rose to a peak of $393.6 on January 1, 1994.

CHANNEL ANALYSIS OF GEC
(LONDON MARKET)

The chart of the weekly closing prices of **GEC** on May 8, 1998, is shown in Figure 6.18. Before moving to the analysis of this stock, it is interesting to note the general shape of the inner channel. The magnitude of the cycles represented by the inner channel is increasing as we move from 1983 to the present time, the peak-to-peak, *i.e.* the wavelength, distance has also increased. It is also apparent that in general, the turning points in the inner channel are fairly symmetrical, *i.e.* the sections on either side of a vertical line drawn through an exact peak or trough would be almost mirror images of each other. While exact mirror images are rare (for an example see chapter 9, Figure 9.17), the channels do not deviate substantially from this relationship for some distance on either side of the turning point. This is true for channels in all markets. This fact can be used when the investor is uncertain of how to draw a channel that has just changed direction. If the new leg of the channel appears to be rising (or falling) at a rate that is grossly different from its rate of change prior to the turning point, then the channel should be adjusted to a more symmetrical position until new additional data clarifies the position.

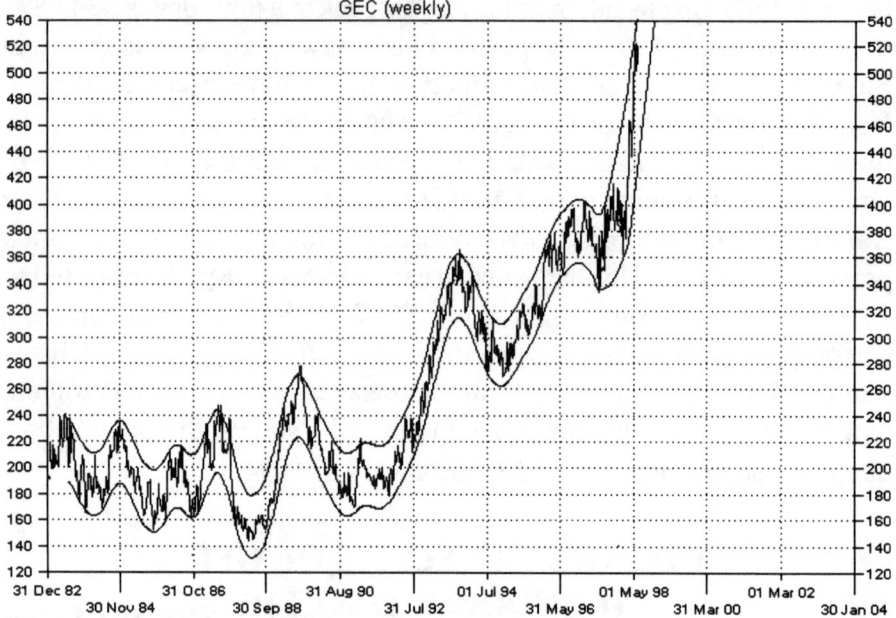

Figure 6.18. *A chart of **GEC** on May 8, 1998. Only one channel is drawn, but the purpose is to highlight the increasing magnitude of the cycles present. It is also apparent that the current rate of ascent of the channel cannot be sustained for very much longer.*

As far as **GEC** is concerned, it is interesting to see how channel analysis would have captured the rise from around 180p in December 1991 to just over 360p by late 1993, a rise of 100%. While not a rapid rate of rise, most investors would be very pleased to have doubled their money in two years.

The position in **GEC** on December 6, 1991, is shown in Figure 6.19. While the channel was obviously falling from the peak in March 1991, the two recent peaks of 199p on September 6 and 198p on October 4 are in such a relationship to each other they force the upper boundary to follow

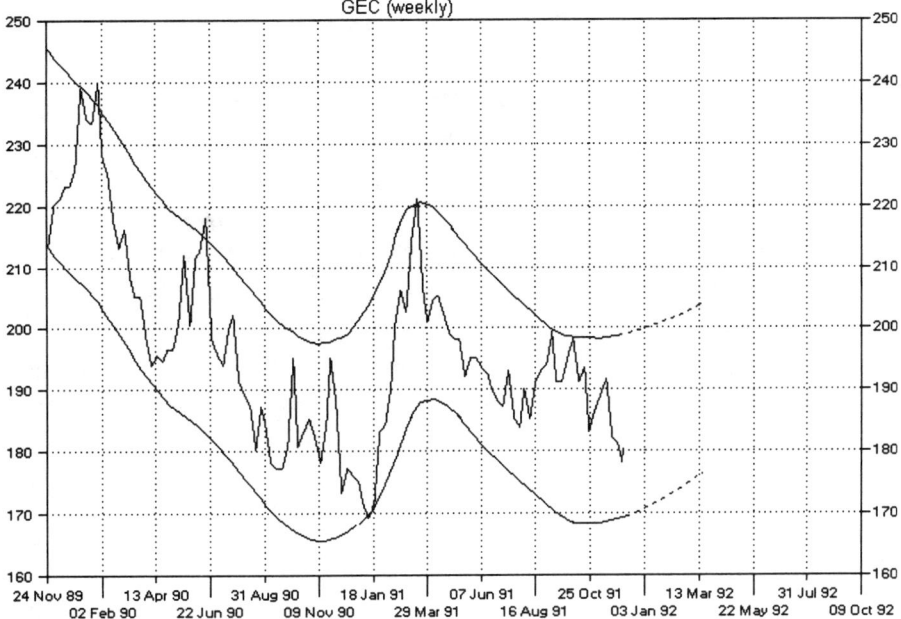

Figure 6.19. *The position in **GEC** with weekly data on December 6, 1991. The two recent peaks lead to the conclusion that the channel has now stopped falling. Because the price is rapidly approaching the lower boundary which is probably now rising, it is time to view daily data to clarify the position.*

a curve that will soon reach a minimum and start rising. The price, at 178p is therefore approaching a boundary that by this time is probably rising, and the investor will need to view daily data in order to see more clearly what is happening. The daily chart is shown in Figure 6.20. There was a trough in the data a few days earlier on December 3 at 177p. The investor is now hoping for a rise from 178p, since this would form a second trough at a higher level than the one at 177p, thus indicating a rising lower boundary. The next business day (December 9) the price did move up to 185p, so that the investor would now be ready to buy the stock.

WHAT CHANNELS REPRESENT

Channel boundaries represent the limits of excursion of all the cycles (and random movement) that have wavelengths shorter than the channel itself. Once a particular channel has been drawn, it is usually possible to determine whether it represents short, medium or long-term cycles simply by looking at it. However, to get an exact idea of the wavelength of the channel, we must look at the distance apart of successive peaks or successive troughs. If there is only one peak (or one trough), we can take the distance between this peak (or trough) and the next trough (or peak) and multiply it by 2 to get the wavelength. We will then be able to categorize

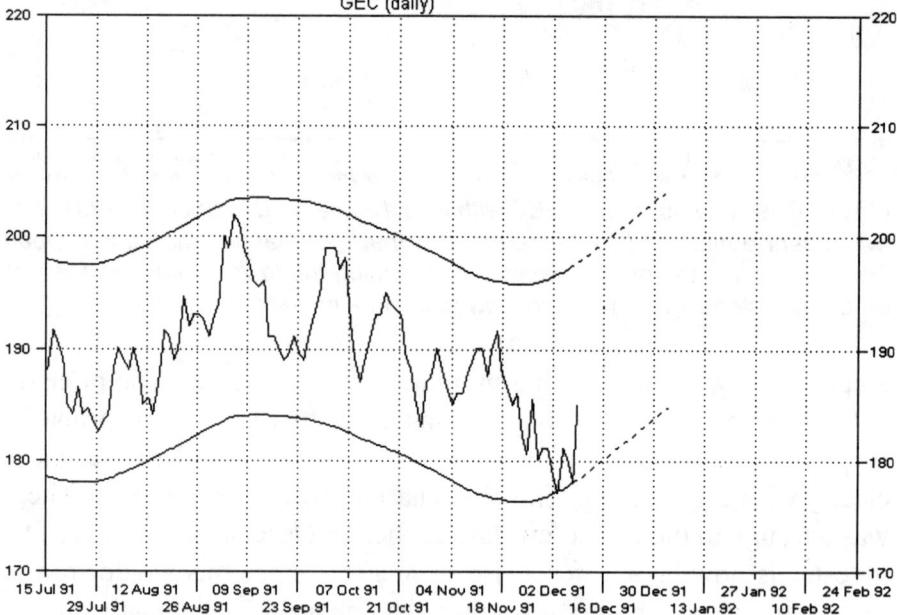

Figure 6.20. *Daily data in GEC on December 9, 1991. The price has now risen from the value of 178p on the previous business day. The trough so formed is at a higher level than the previous one, so that the lower boundary of the channel can now be estimated to be rising. The investor may now buy.*

a channel as being long, medium, short or very short term. An ideal channel analysis would give us three channels - long, medium and short term. Sometimes it might not be possible to draw the long-term channel because there are not sufficient peaks and troughs in the medium term channel to be able to draw another one outside of it. This will happen when the wavelength of the channel is greater than the time span of data that is available in the chart. The longer the amount of historical data that is available to us, the more likely we are to be able to draw a long-term channel. While it is an advantage to have a long term channel present, on many occasions we will find that we can do without it since the depth of the medium term channel is sufficient to provide us with a profit irrespective of the direction of the outer channel, although this profit will be much less if the outer channel is indeed falling. This is discussed later in this chapter.

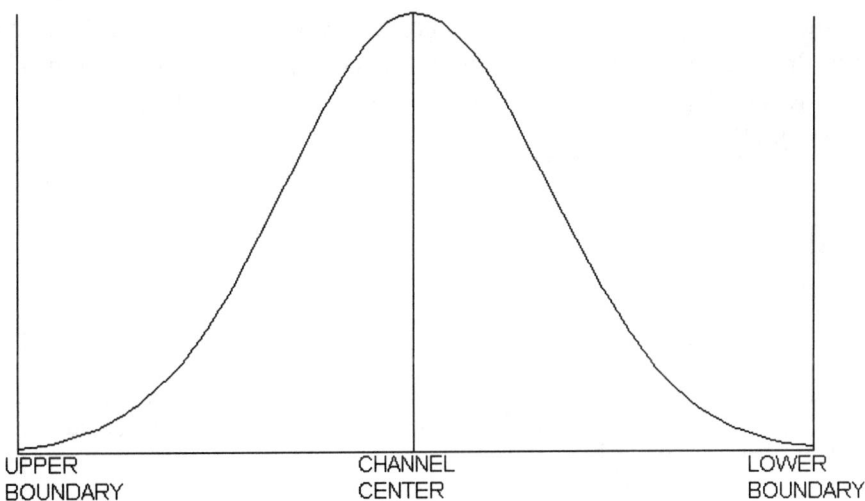

UPPER   CHANNEL   LOWER
BOUNDARY   CENTER   BOUNDARY

Figure 6.21. *The distribution of data values within a channel. The vertical axis represents the probability of the price being at the point relative to the channel boundaries as shown on the horizontal axis. Clearly the probability of the price being near a boundary is small.*

If we take an individual channel and look at how the stock price itself moves within the channel, we find that it spends very little time at the extreme boundaries. Most of the time the price is around the middle of the channel. For a very large number of observations we would get the distribution of prices shown in Figure 6.21. The vertical axis is the probability that a price will be at the position relative to the channel boundaries given by the horizontal axis. Those readers with a statistical knowledge will recognize the shape of this curve as being similar to that of the probability distribution. At this point, all we are interested in is the general shape of this curve. The probability of a price being in the center of the channel is very high, and the probability falls off rapidly as we move to either of the two boundaries. The boundaries themselves represent low probability areas. Depending upon how the channels are drawn, *i.e.* how much penetration of the boundaries by price peaks and troughs we allow when drawing them, then the boundaries represent probabilities of say 10% or less. The stock price will spend only a small proportion of its time at or close to the boundary, and will tend to move to an area of higher probability, *i.e.* towards the center. Therefore, if we know the boundary position exactly, and determine that a stock price is at the boundary, then it is almost a one-way bet that it will bounce back from this position. This is shown in Figure 6.22, with the theoretical (*i.e.* actual) boundary shown as a solid line.

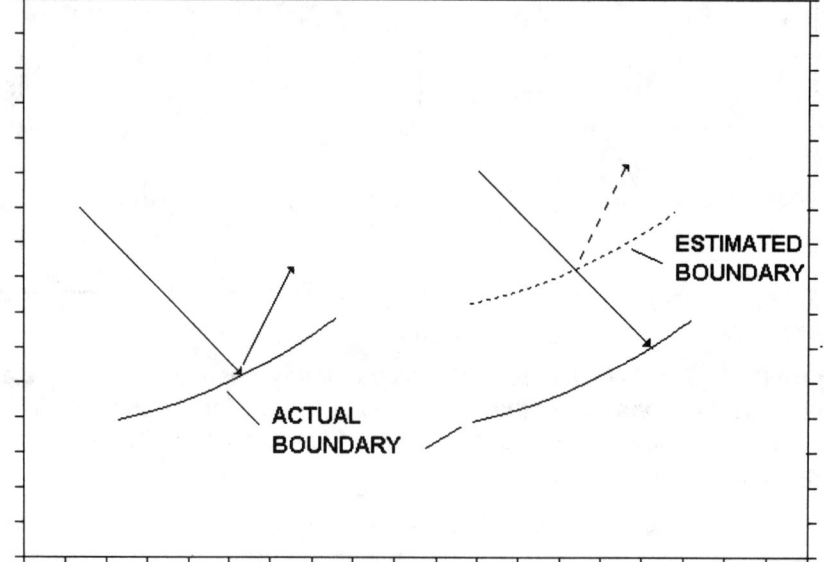

Figure 6.22. *The drawing on the left shows the actual position of a channel boundary. If, as the drawing on the right shows, we estimate the boundary to be higher than it is, then we have an incorrect expectation that the price will bounce upwards. It may well continue to fall, putting us in a losing position if we have made an investment when the price was at our estimated boundary position.*

As we will see from the many examples in this book, it is the determination of the exact position of the boundary itself that is subject to error. Such an estimate of the boundary position is shown as the dashed line in Figure 6.22.

When the stock price reaches this estimated lower boundary, we assume that the probability is now say 10% that the price will stay there, or in other words 90% that the price will bounce upwards, and take an investment decision accordingly. Of course, if we are in error, then the actual boundary is rather lower than the position we estimated on the price scale (it will not be higher because then the price would have bounced up sooner, and would not have fallen to the current level). Thus the current price is nearer to the center of the channel than we anticipated, and therefore the probability that it will reverse direction is lower than we think. The risk of being wrong about the future movement of the stock price is now very much higher.

We can see from this scenario that our prediction of future price movement depends entirely upon our estimation of the position of the channel boundary at the present point in time. Quite clearly, the more accurate we can be in the determination of boundary position, the better our trading performance will be. When we come to discuss turning points in a later chapter, we will see that it is when a channel is changing direction that our estimation of the boundary position is most likely to be in error. Unfortunately, the fact that a channel has changed direction is the most important fact we require to avoid making an incorrect investment. We therefore have to take particular care that we take into account all the peaks and troughs and their possible relationship to channel boundaries when trying to establish that a channel has changed direction.

Mid-channel Movement

One property of sine waves, important looking at the properties of channels, is the fact that the change in vertical position is greatest at the mid-point and least at the extremities. Since the channels, in their broadest sense, represent cycles, then the rate of change in the vertical position of a channel is greatest at the mid point. Translated to movement in stock prices, currencies, etc., this means that when a price is just below the mid-point of a rising inner channel we can usually expect a more rapid increase in price than when the price bounces up from a boundary. The trader who wishes to maximize the rate of return from a short term investment could therefore wait until this position is reached, rather than invest at the point at which the price has just formed a trough at the lower boundary. However, this author is of the opinion that this is taking the concept of compounding short term profits to the extreme, and a half- or full-channel profit, albeit slightly longer term, is being ignored for the sake of what might turn out to be a very truncated shorter term profit.

During the analyses of **Delta Airlines**, Gold, Japanese yen and **GEC**, several concepts have been mentioned that are now worth further explanation. These are best addressed using idealized data.

Falling outer channels

The first such concept is the question of increased risk of investing in short term trends when the outer channel which can be drawn so as to contain these trends is heading the wrong way. In Figure 6.23 we show a representation of a channel which rises to a maximum and then falls back again. Contained within the channel is a series of movements which are, by the concepts of channel analysis are due to all of those cycles of shorter wavelength than that highlighted by the channel itself.

Because of the additive nature of cycles, the result we see for the movements within the channel is the sum of the shorter-term movements plus the movement of the channel itself (*i.e.* plus the movement of the longer-term cycle). Thus we can see that during the upward sweep of the channel we have a 'two steps forward, one step back' progression, with the changes due to short term rises being about twice the changes due to short term falls. On the other hand, during the falling half of the channel, we have exactly the opposite occurring, with the effect of the falls being

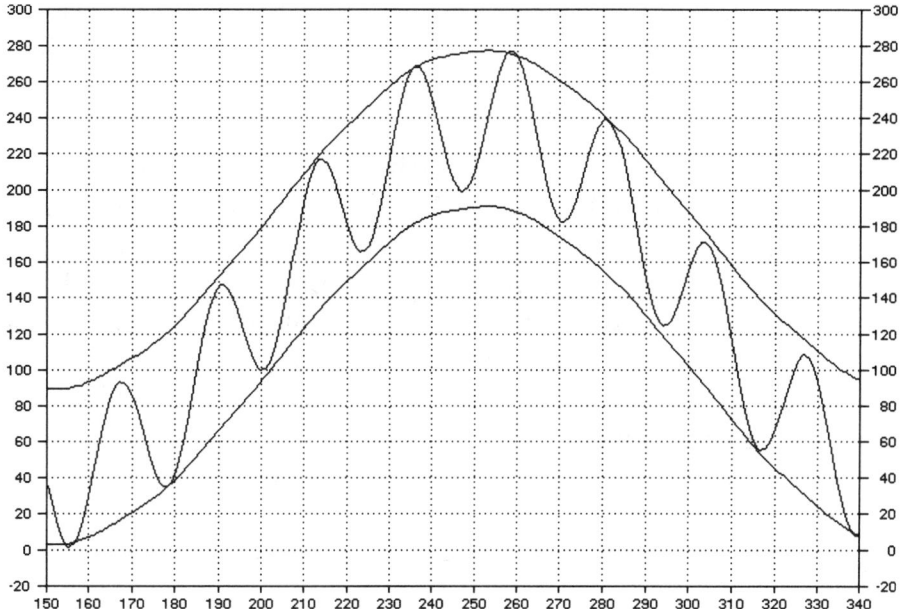

Figure 6.23. *The idealized concept of short term cycles contained within a long term channel. The additive nature of cycles means that the short term rises are enhanced relative to short term falls while the outer channel is rising. The opposite happens while the outer channel is falling.*

about twice the effect of the rises. The channels in GEC, as shown previously in Figure 6.18 showed exactly this behavior in the rise that took place from mid-1991 to the end of 1994.

Translated into risk, this means that if we invest during the upward sweep of the channel, even if our timing of entry into a short-term trend is not exact on, we will still come good quite soon. This is a manifestation of the Chinese proverb 'a rising tide lifts all boats' and means that the risk to our investment is low. If we focus on just one rise and fall of the short term trend, we can see that with perfect timing, during the upward leg of the channel, and buying at the exact minimum of a short term trend, the amount of profit we would make is about twice the amount of loss we would make if our timing was totally incorrect and we bought at the top of the short term trend. On the other hand if we buy during the downward leg of the channel, with perfect timing investing at the exact minimum of the short term trend, the amount of gain we would make is only half the amount of loss we would make if we bought at the top of the short term trend.

Thus on the upward leg of the channel, if our timing of the exact buying point is random, the odds are about 2 to 1 in our favor in this particular example, while on the downward leg of the channel, the odds are about 2 to 1 against us. In other words, in this example, the odds are around four times worse for us when we buy during the downward leg of the channel than if we buy during the upwards leg. This is why it is so important to invest when as many channels as possible are rising in order to offset any imperfections in our timing.

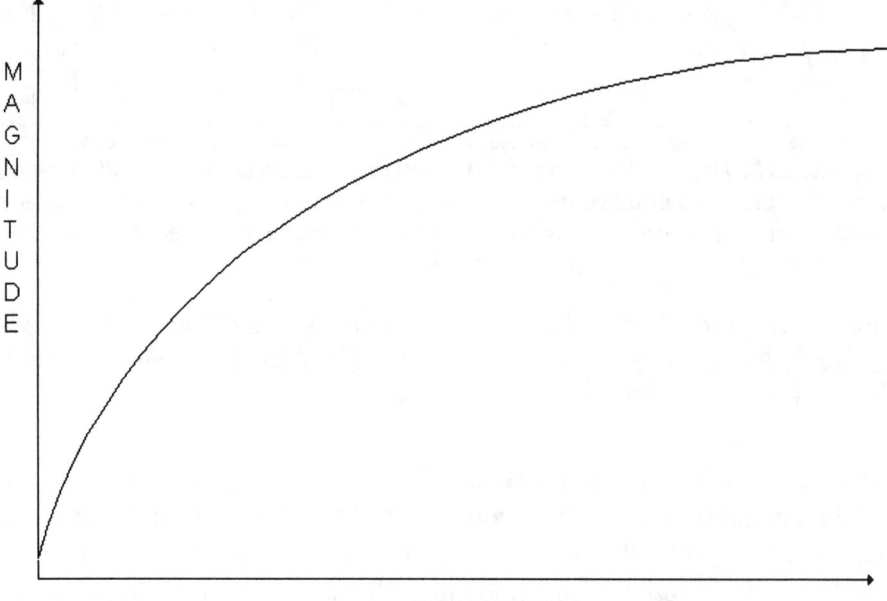

Figure 6.24. *The general form of the relationship between wavelength and magnitude of cycles. There is a minimum wavelength below which the risk in using that particular cycle as the investment vehicle becomes unacceptable.*

As our timing improves, then we can move away from the idea of risk to the question of the return that can be made. With perfect timing, we can see from Figure 6.23 that the return we would make from the short-term trend during the upward leg of the channel is twice what it would be during the downward leg of the channel.

In Figure 6.23, there was no indication of whether we were dealing with very long term, medium term or short term cycles. The principle is the same irrespective of the wavelengths of the cycles. Whether we can accept an investment if the channel is falling depends entirely on the depth of the next inner channel. It is this latter depth that determines the potential profit, and as long as this would allow us a reasonable percentage gain, then we can still buy the stock. As we move to cycles of shorter and shorter wavelength, then the channel depth decreases. This is because as mentioned in a chapter 4, the magnitude of cycles decreases with decreasing wavelength, and the rate of fall off of magnitude increases sharply as we move to shorter wavelengths. This relationship is shown again in Figure 6.24. Because of this fact we will reach a point at which the return is not worth the risk of investing as the cycle wavelength represented by the channel falls, because the trends contained within the channel have reached the critical lower limit. We will find usually that this point is reached with channels that correspond to cycles that we defined earlier as being of medium wavelength.

In the Delta Airlines examples (Figures 6.3 - 6.6) which we have used, the middle channel corresponds to the medium term cycle. If this channel is falling, then we should not invest. It is only when the outer channel, which in this case corresponds to the long term cycle, is falling and the other inner channels (*i.e.* medium and short term cycles) are rising that it might be acceptable to invest as it is appreciated that the profit will be sharply reduced. Even so, this is only to be recommended if it is not possible at the time to find a stock with much better channel characteristics.

Reversal of Channel Direction

In the charts of **Delta Airlines** shown earlier, we made the point that both the inner and outer channels had changed direction around April 19, 1994.

If we look at the enlarged section around that date as seen in Figure 6.10, then we can discuss in more detail why we considered that this was a channel turning point.

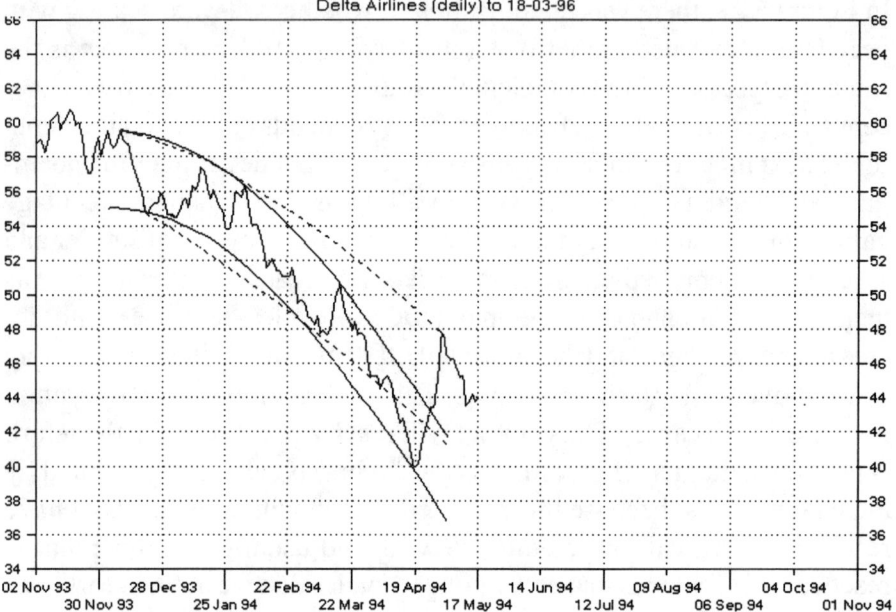

Figure 6.25. *Delta Airlines - once the trough had been formed on April 19, the channel would have been drawn as shown by the solid lines so as to accommodate this trough and the previous peak on March 10. Once the price rose above the upper boundary and eventually formed the peak shown, then the upper boundary had to be raised to the level shown by the dashed line. However, this would cause a major violation of the channel by the major trough which is not acceptable.*

Once the price rose from the low point at $39^7/_8$ on April 19, to form a trough, we would be able to draw the lower boundary of the channel so as to accommodate this trough on it. The peak of $50^1/_2$ reached some weeks previously on March 10, has also to be taken into account. The best constant depth channel that would be drawn from the data available a day or two after April 19, is shown in Figure 6.25. The channel can be extrapolated into the future as shown by the solid line, and at this point in time there is no violation of either the upper boundary or the lower boundary of the channel. The investor is therefore comfortable with this channel direction, and since it is still falling would take no buying action. However, after a few more days the price has risen quite sharply, and is soon just above the level at which we have drawn the upper boundary. At this point, we could accept this slight penetration of the upper boundary as part of the normal allowable penetration, but the price continues to rise even further, reaching a peak on May 2, 1994 at $47^5/8$. Now we are in difficulty, because if we adjust the upper boundary so as to place this peak on it, as shown by the dashed line in Figure 6.25, then the new lower boundary (also shown dashed), will be well above the lower trough, *i.e.* the trough penetrates the lower boundary by an unacceptable amount.

Thus we have two extreme positions of the channel, the upper one which gives too large a penetration of the lower boundary by the major trough, and the lower one which gives too large a penetration of the upper bound-

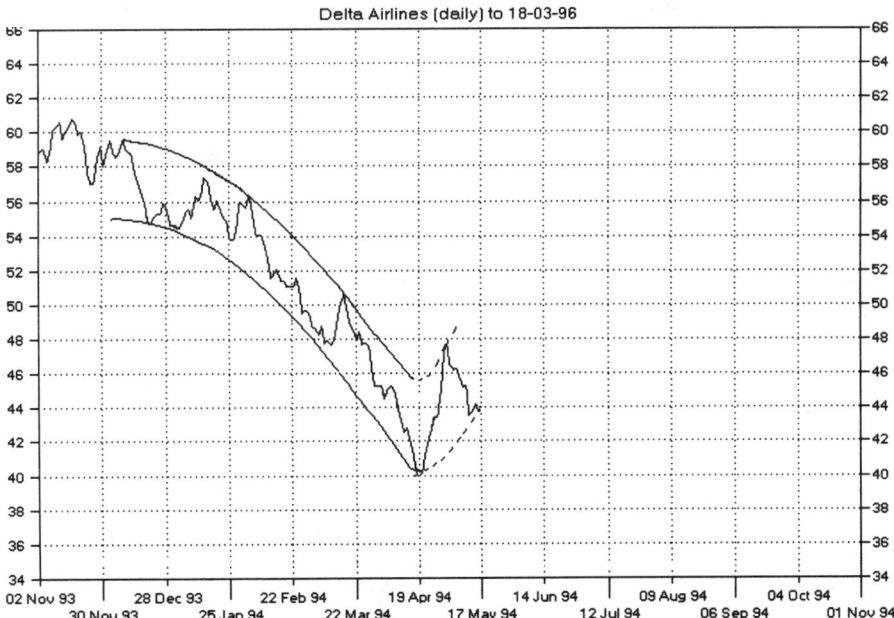

Figure 6.26. *The only way in which a constant depth channel can be drawn so as to avoid penetration above and below the channel boundaries is by causing it to bend with the trough of April 19 as the approximate turning point.*

ary by the major peak. The only way in which we can keep the vertical depth of the channel constant and reduce both boundary penetrations to an acceptable amount is by causing the channel to change direction somewhere around April 19. This is shown in Figure 6.26. In drawing the turn in the channel direction, we also keep in mind the principle of symmetry of the channel around the turning point, so that the rate of rise in the channel immediately after the turn is fairly close to the rate of fall prior to the turn.

This type of argument will be applied whenever we have to decide if a channel has changed direction. Note the very important fact that it is only well after the channel has changed direction that we are able to decide that it did. Although in retrospect the channel changed direction around April 19, it was not until May 3, some ten days later, when the price fell from its level the previous day to form the peak that we had sufficient evidence to determine that the channel must have begun to climb.

Although we will discuss channel turning points in greater detail in chapter 10, we can see that as more time elapses after the actual turning point, the probability that the turning was real also increases. Although we would like the probability to be high that our turning point has occurred, working against us is the fact that the new direction of the channel will not be maintained forever. The probability of another change in direction is increasing all of the time we are waiting for confirmation of the previous turning point. We have to take a reasoned view that we wait just long enough to be confident that the channel has turned up before making an investment.

PROCEDURE

The overall procedure that we can apply to any stock is:

1. Check the chart of as much historical weekly data as possible for strong long term, intermediate and short-term cycles

2. If these are present, draw channels on the weekly chart; other

wise move to another chart

3. If there are major violations of both upper and lower boundaries within a short time of each other, see if forcing a bend in the channel can accommodate these

4. If short term and intermediate term weekly channels are rising, fine-tune the buying decision by looking at a chart of about one year's history of daily data, other wise wait for a change in direction of the channels

5. Draw channels on the daily chart, and if the short-term trend is rising and the price has risen from previous day can buy the next trading day, otherwise wait until these two factors are positive

6. If even more fine-tuning is needed, look at the daily range to estimate the direction of the intra-day trend at the market close. If the market closes at the high for the day, then obviously the intra-day trend is up, and the probability is that it will continue in the same way the next day so that the stock can be bought. If the intra-day trend is down, then on the next trading day wait for the intra-day trend to start to rise.

As far as the improvement to investment performance over the long term is concerned, it is the initial decision based on weekly data that is the crucial factor. Investors using the fine tuning of daily charts will probably achieve a return about one tenth better than investors who buy purely on the analysis of weekly data, while investors using intra-day data will achieve a slightly better return than the investor using daily charts. For those investors who do not have access to a computer and who prepare charts themselves, then it has to be said that the additional work involved in maintaining charts of daily data is not worth the additional effort.

Although this chapter has focused mainly on buying opportunities, exactly the same logic can be applied to downward turning points, as was shown for gold in August 1993, and a similar improvement in timing will be obtained. The investor can use this information either to confirm that it is time to sell the existing holding in that security, and/or can decide to go short of that security, thereby taking advantage of down trends as well as up trends.

CHAPTER 7

Numerical Analysis—the Basics

So far we have shown how sine waves of various wavelengths and amplitudes can be combined together to produce more complex movements, and how we can build in random movement if necessary to arrive at approximations to the way in which stocks, currencies and commodities move over the course of time. We have also demonstrated how by simple graphical methods using channels, we can arrive at quite good estimations of the magnitudes and wavelengths of the various cycles.

By using artificial data, we were able to apply these methods to real data. We were able to make decisions about the turning points in trends and determine whether a trend would continue in the same direction.

Now we will adopt this same stepwise approach of developing a method, by applying it to artificial data to see how it works, and then apply it to real data. In this chapter we will show how we can analyze the numerical data to isolate the various components of the complex movements. The methods will fall into two categories— 1) those that can be carried out by simple calculations, mainly moving averages, and 2) those that require more intensive calculations, such as weighted moving averages and digital filters. The latter require a computer if they are to be carried quickly.

MOVING AVERAGES

The calculation of a moving average is quite straightforward, and the process for a 5-point average, is shown in Table 7.1. A five point average is obtained by adding five successive values and then dividing by 5. These could be daily prices, in which case the average is described as a 5-day average, or weekly data, in which case the term 5-week average would apply. It is taken for granted that the sampling interval, be it days, weeks, hours or years, is constant. It would be incorrect to use the data from week 1, week 2, week 4, week 7 and week 10, for example, adding these together and calling the result the 5-week average. Only by taking the data for weeks 1, 2, 3, 4 and 5 will we achieve a result that has any meaning when applied to investment data. The 5 used in this case is known as the span of the average, and in the stock market a variety of spans are used for averages. We will see shortly that different spans have different effects on the data to which the average is being applied.

Date	Index	Subtract	5-week total	5-week average
02/06/98	8194.72	X		
02/13/98	8340.20	X		
02/20/98	8335.72	X		
02/27/98	8545.72	X		
03/06/98	8569.38	X	41985.74	8397.148
03/13/98	8602.52	X	42393.54	8478.708
03/20/98	8906.43	X	42959.77	8591.954
03/27/98	8826.47	X	43450.52	8690.104
04/03/98	8971.20	X	43876.00	8775.2
04/10/98	8994.86	X	44301.48	8860.296
04/17/98	9167.50	X	44866.46	8973.292
04/24/98	9064.62	X	45024.65	9004.93
05/01/98	9147.07	X	45345.25	9069.05
05/08/98	9055.15	X	45429.20	9085.84
05/15/98	9096.00	X	45530.34	9106.068
05/22/98	9114.44		45477.28	9095.456
05/29/98	8970.20		45382.86	9076.572
06/05/98	9037.71		45273.50	9054.7
06/12/98	8834.94		45053.29	9010.658
06/19/98	8712.87		44670.16	8934.032

Table 7.1. *The calculation of a 5-week average for the Dow-Jones Index*

The adjective 'moving' is applied because the calculation moves through the data, taking the sum of the first five points and dividing it by 5, then the sum of the five points that start with the second data point and dividing this by 5, and then taking the sum of the five points that start with the third point, and so on until we have used up all the data.

Rather than starting each time from a point and adding up the five points, there is a short cut which simplifies the calculation, coming into its own when larger span averages are required. We keep a running total, the first value is obtained by adding the first 5 points. Dividing this by 5 gives us the first value for the average. To compute the next value of the average, it is only necessary to add in the next value of the data and subtract the value the sixth point back (for 5-point averages). This is the new running total, and when it is divided by 5 it gives us the second average point. We proceed this way, updating the running total each time and dividing it by 5.

With say a 15 point average, we would first add up the first 15 points to give the running total, then divide it by 15 to get the average. Then add in point number 16 and subtract the sixteenth point back, *i.e.* point number 1 to give us a new running total that when divided by 15 gives us the second value of the average.

While it is obvious which point is to be added in to calculate the new running total, next one in the series, the point where the process could go wrong is if the wrong point is subtracted. In order to guard against this it is sensible to keep a note of the last point that has been subtracted by means of a tick or cross in a separate column, as shown in Table 7.1.

To the majority of readers who possess computers and software to carry out such calculations, this emphasis on the calculation of moving averages might seem misplaced. However, besides the fact that it is important not to treat computers as black boxes spitting out results, but to try to understand what is going on, there is another important point that is brought out by an examination of this method of computing an average.

The change in the running total, and hence the average, is brought about not only by the value of the next data point that is being added in, but by the data point, a whole span of the average in the past, that is being subtracted (the 'drop point'). This has an important implication when it comes to the turning points in averages and channels: whether an average changes direction will depend upon the relationship of these two data points. Besides the method of checking whether it is necessary to put a bend in a channel in order to allow peaks and troughs to settle comfortably at the boundaries, the investor can check the relative values of the next data point and the drop point as an additional aid in deciding if a channel has changed direction.

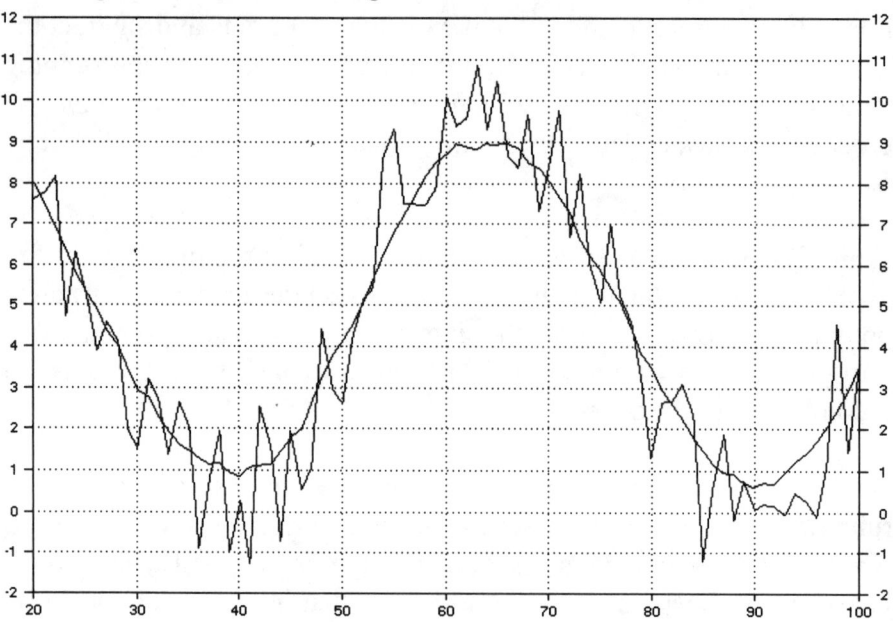

Figure 7.1. *Upper panel: a 15 point average is plotted as unlagged. Lower panel: the same average plotted as a centered average, shifted 8 points back in time.*

Unlagged and Centered Averages

In the calculation of the 5 point average in Table 7.1, the calculated running total and the average derived from it by dividing by 5 were both placed alongside the position of the latest data point that was used. When it comes to plotting such averages on a chart, we have a number of options.

An unlagged average is plotted in the same way in which the data is held in Table 7.1, *i.e.* the calculated average is plotted at the same point in time as the latest data point used in its calculation. On the other hand, a centered average is shifted back in time so that the latest calculated point is plotted at the position corresponding to the center of the set of points used in the calculation. Thus a 5-day average is plotted 3 days back in time. The amount by which it is shifted is given by the formula.

$$\textbf{shift} = \frac{\textbf{(span - 1)}}{\textbf{2}}$$

Note that with an even span, the average would be shifted back in time by an amount that caused it to be plotted in between the position of the data points. Thus, a six day average would be shifted back by 2.5 data points. Therefore in order to plot centered averages correctly, an odd span should be used. As far as the beginning of the plot is concerned, the first average point would be plotted at point 3.

The vital difference in presenting moving averages as unlagged or centered when these are plotted, is illustrated quite clearly in Figure 7.1. Here we have taken the set of data used in chapters 4 and 5, where a cycle of wavelength 52 weeks and magnitude $10 was combined with a random movement that ranged from +$2 to -$2. A 15-point average has been calculated and in the upper panel it is plotted as an unlagged average, while in the lower panel it is plotted as a centered average. The obvious feature of both plots is that the minor fluctuations have now been greatly reduced, giving a plot that is much smoother than the original data. The smoothed data can now be seen to be cyclic in nature, allowing for the fact that it is not perfectly smooth and still contains traces of the minor fluctuations.

In the upper plot the peak in the smoothed data is not aligned with the peak in the data, while in the lower plot it is. We know from chapter 5 that when we drew a line through the center of this same data (Figure 5.2), it was similar to the original sine wave of wavelength 52 weeks, in position, magnitude and wavelength. The centered average also has each of these three properties, since it is also similar to the original in position, magnitude and wavelength, while the unlagged average, while similar in magnitude and wavelength, is not in the correct position. From this, we can deduce that a centered average, when the correct span is chosen, is a very good representation of the cyclic component present. It follows, therefore, in view of the relationship between cycles and trends, that **a centered average is also a good representation of a trend.**

This is an important point, and unfortunately is ignored by most technical analysts who insist on plotting averages on their charts as unlagged. To compound the sin, they typically use averages in only two ways. One way is to have a rule that a stock is not bought if its n-day moving average is falling, where the span **n** is usually of the order of 200. Another way is to have rules such as 'buy when the x-day average rises above the y-day average,' where the spans **x** and **y** can have a number of values such as 5 and 25. The fact that the average represents a trend, be it short term, medium term or long term, is lost because the average is not plotted as centered, where the relationship would be immediately obvious.

The consequence of plotting the average as centered is that we miss points at its beginning and end. Since the average is offset by (span - 1)/2 places back from the latest point, this constitutes a gap of this much. There is also a similar gap at the beginning of the plot. Thus, for example in a 25-day average we lose 12 points at the beginning and 12 points at the end. This loss of points is the penalty we must pay for achieving a smoother plot than the original. The reason we lose points is because of the mathematics of calculating the average. For a 25-day average, we add up the first 25 points to get the first average point. We therefore have lost 24 points, and as mentioned above in the case of a centered average, these 24 points are split equally between the beginning and the end of the plot.

Since we now have come to the conclusion that a correctly chosen average will represent a trend, the fact that we are missing points at the end of the average draws attention to the fact that we do not know what the trend is doing between the last plotted point of the average and the latest data point. This question of the gap in the average will be addressed later once we have discussed the effect of using different spans for the average.

The Effect of Different Averages on Cyclic Data

We saw in Figure 7.1. that the effect of a moving average was to smooth the data to provide a 'better' estimate of the underlying trend. Since we have defined trends previously as being part of a cycle, it is necessary to investigate the effect of applying averages of various spans to cyclic data. The main properties of a moving average are:

1. A moving average will totally remove cycles of the same wavelength as the span of the average.

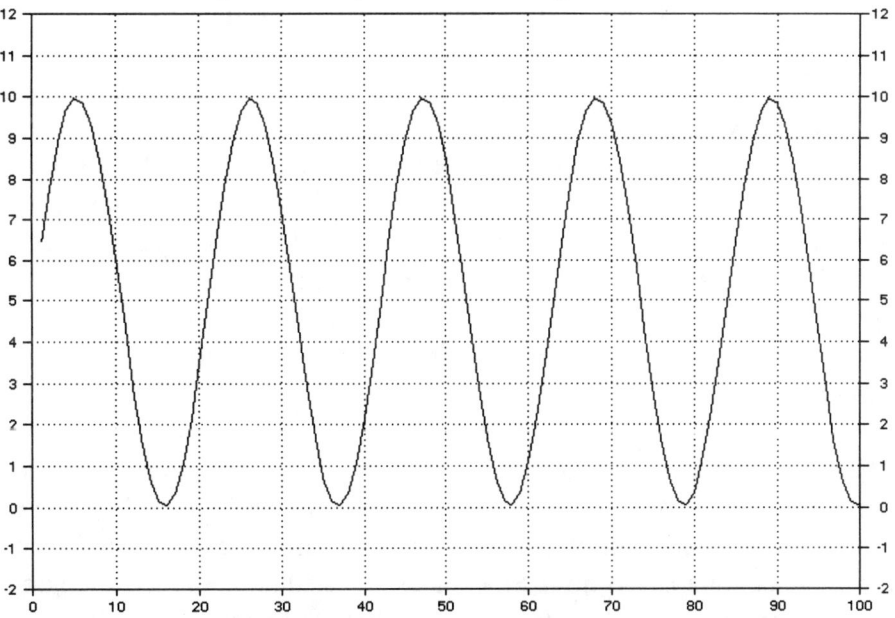

Figure 7.2. *A sine wave of magnitude $10 and wavelength 21 weeks.*

2.   Cycles of longer wavelength than the span of the average
        will be reduced in amplitude. The smaller the span of the
        average relative to the cycle wavelength, the smaller the
        reduction in magnitude.

3.   Cycles of shorter wavelength than the span of the average
        will be reduced in magnitude, and may sometimes be off
        set by half a wavelength from the original cycles, depend
        ing on the relationship between the span and the wave
        length. The greater the span of the average relative to the
        cycle wavelength, the greater the reduction in magnitude.

As an example, we will start off with a sine wave of wavelength 21 weeks
and magnitude $10. The first 100 points of this wave are shown in Figure
7.2. As expected, the peaks are 21 weeks apart and the troughs are also
separated by the same amount. The wave swings from a value of zero up
to $10.

Span equal to the cycle wavelength

The first rule pointed out that cycles of wavelength equal to the span of
the average would be completely eliminated. This can be seen in Figure
7.3, where an average of span 21 weeks is applied to the cycle of wavelength 21 weeks. The original cycle is shown, while the result of applying
the average is the horizontal line at the $5 level. Thus the cycle has been
totally removed from the data. Note the first point of the smoothed data
appears at point 11. This is because we have a centered average and 10
points are missing at the beginning of the average calculation, as explained
earlier.

The reason for the constant value of $5 for the average is to be found in
the running total calculation and the properties of sine waves. In a wave
such as the present example, every point is repeated at exact distances of
the wavelength apart in time. Since the span is equal to the wavelength,
the drop point in the calculation has exactly the same value as the next

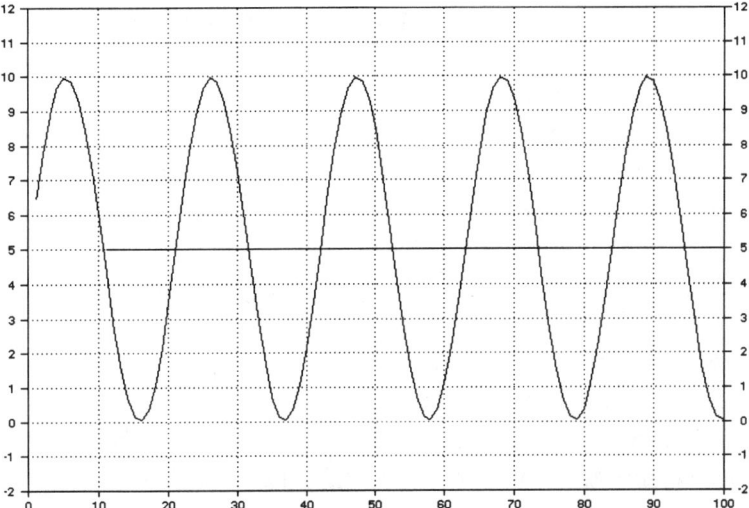

Figure 7.3. *A moving average of span 21 is applied to the cyclic data from Figure 7.2. The average is the horizontal line at the $5 level. Thus the sinusoidal movement has been totally removed. Note that the average starts at week 11 because it is centered and the first 10 data points are lost.*

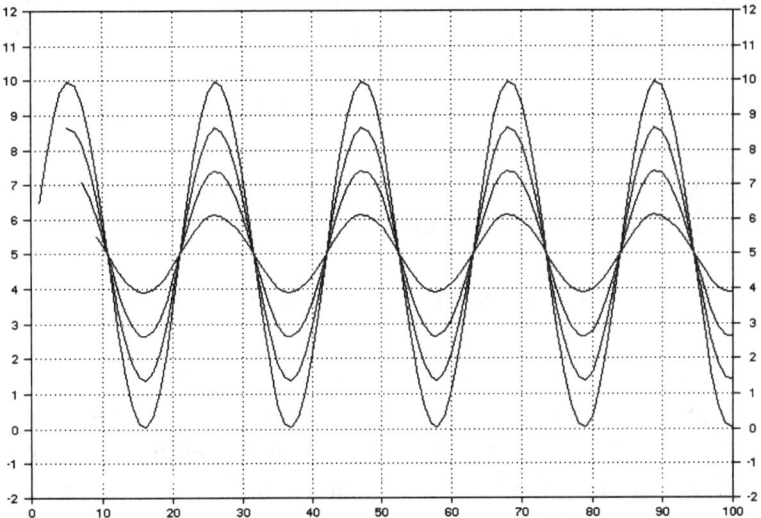

Figure 7.4. *The result of applying moving averages with spans less than that of the wavelength. Averages of spans 9, 13 and 17 weeks have been applied to the sine wave of 21 weeks wavelength. The original sine wave is shown with magnitude $10. As the span increases the magnitude of the smoothed data decreases. The most shallow wave is due to the application of the 17 week average.*

data point to be added. Consequently the running total and so the average, remain constant.

This effect (when the span is equal to the wavelength) is simply a special case of the more general one that removes a cycle completely when the span is an exact multiple of the wavelength: **span = n x wavelength**

Spans less than the cycle wavelength

In the second rule above we pointed out that using a span less than the wavelength of the cycle should lead to a reduction in the magnitude. In order to check this point, averages with spans of 9, 13 and 17 were applied to the cyclic data shown in Figure 7.2. The result is shown in Figure 7.4. The original sine wave is shown, and is the one with the greatest magnitude ($10) in the Figure. The other three waves of decreasing magnitude are the results of applying each of these averages. The wave with the smallest magnitude is the result of applying the 17 week average, and, as predicted, the magnitudes increase as the span decreases through 14 and 9 weeks. So, as long as the span is less than the cycle wavelength, the smaller the span used, the less is the attenuation of the data. The smoothed data sets are also aligned perfectly in time with the original data. The first plotted points of the 9, 13 and 17 weeks averages are at weeks 5, 7 and 9 respectively because they have been plotted as centered averages.

Spans greater than the cycle wavelength

In the third rule we pointed out that using a span greater than the wavelength of the cycle should lead to a reduction in the magnitude, but could also lead to an offset of the result so the original alignment was lost. In order to check this point, averages with spans of 35 and 45 were applied to the cyclic data shown in Figure 7.2. The result is shown in Figure 7.5.

The 35-week average starts at week 18 and the 45 week average at week 23 due to the fact they are plotted as centered averages. The interesting point is that while the 45 week average is aligned with the original data as

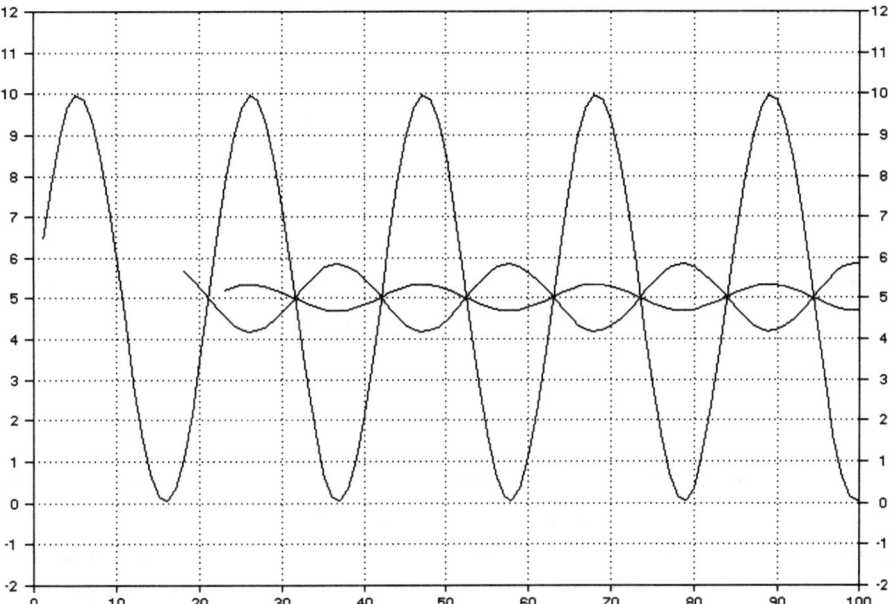

Figure 7.5. *Averages of spans 35 and 45 weeks have been applied to the cyclic data from Figure 7.2. The 45 week average is the cycle whose peaks and troughs are still aligned with the original data. On the other hand, the 35 week average is shifted by half of a wavelength to the right.*

far as peaks and troughs are concerned, the 35 week average is shifted one half of a wavelength to the right.

The effect of averages (with spans greater than the wavelength of the original data) suffers from the effect of the shifting of some averages. It also suffers from the fact that the magnitudes do not change in a straight-forward manner, as was the case with averages, that have spans less than the wavelength of the data.

The shifting of some averages while others remain aligned with the original data is not a random effect, but does have a mathematical basis.

In the equation:　　　**span = n x wavelength**

the averaged data remains shifted by one wavelength from the original data for spans which lie between an odd value of **n** and the next even value of **n** in the above equation. The first range of these spans would be from 22 to 41.

The averaged data remains aligned with the original data for spans that lie between an even value of **n** and the next odd value of **n** in the above equation. Thus the first range of these spans that are greater than the wavelength would be from 43 to 62.

In both of these cases, the magnitudes of the averaged data rise to a maximum and then falls back again. Therefore the least attenuation of the data occurs with a span of around 31 (shifted from original data) and 51 (aligned with original data.)

This shifting of the averaged data is something that the investor must guard against when it comes to the application of moving averages to real market data. We will see that averages will be used to highlight particular cycles, but that one has to be careful that a cycle is actually rising or falling, and not giving the impression simply because it has been shifted by half a wavelength because of the relationship between the span of the average and a cycle in the data. In such cases, the cycle will be moving in the opposite direction of that indicated on the plot. As long as the investor is aware of the possibility, it will be easy to check the exact status of the cycle by applying an average with a different (and very carefully chosen) span and viewing the result for consistency.

From these examples of the effect of different spans of average, the conclusion is we should use a moving average span less than the wavelength of the cycles we wish to observe. We will see later that we also have to take into account the presence of other cycles when deciding on the span most suited to our needs. Sometimes we may wish to remove a particular cycle totally, in which case we can choose a span equal to the wavelength of this cycle.

NUMERICAL ANALYSIS—THE BASICS

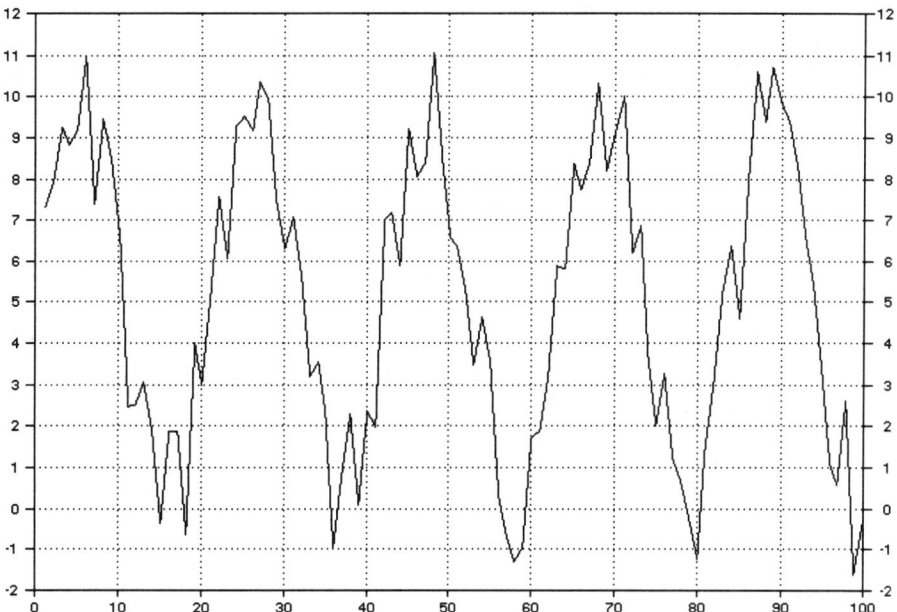

Figure 7.6. *The sine wave from Figure 7.2 with random movement added.*

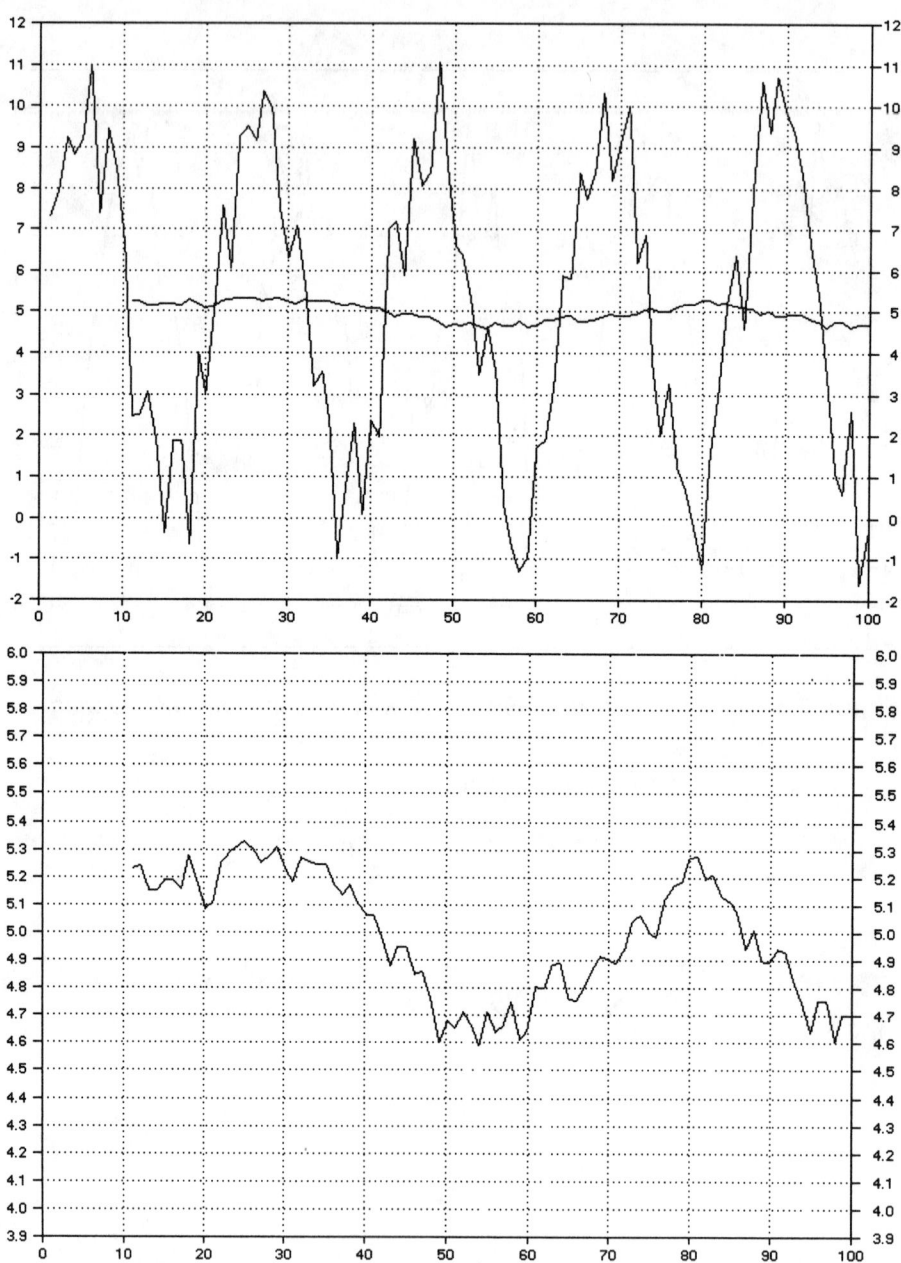

Figure 7.7. *Upper panel: the result of applying a 21-week average to the data from Figure 7.6. Lower panel: the vertical axis has been expanded to show the random movement more clearly. There is no trace of the 21-week cycle.*

ONE CYCLE PLUS RANDOM MOVEMENT

In chapter 5 we showed how, if we took a mixture of cyclic and random movement, we could, by a graphical method, separate each of these components. Now it is necessary to look at the effect of moving averages on data also contains some random movement in order to see if we can achieve the same thing by purely numerical methods. The data for this exercise lies in Figure 7.6, where we have taken the cycle used in Figure 7.2 and added random movement swings from +$2 to -$2.

Isolating the random movement

Since we know that the application of a 21-week average should eliminate the cyclic movement altogether, we are not surprised by the result that is shown in Figure 7.7. The cycle of wavelength 21 weeks has totally disappeared, and what is left is essentially the random movement that was incorporated into the combined complex movement. This can be seen in enlarged form in Figure 7.8.

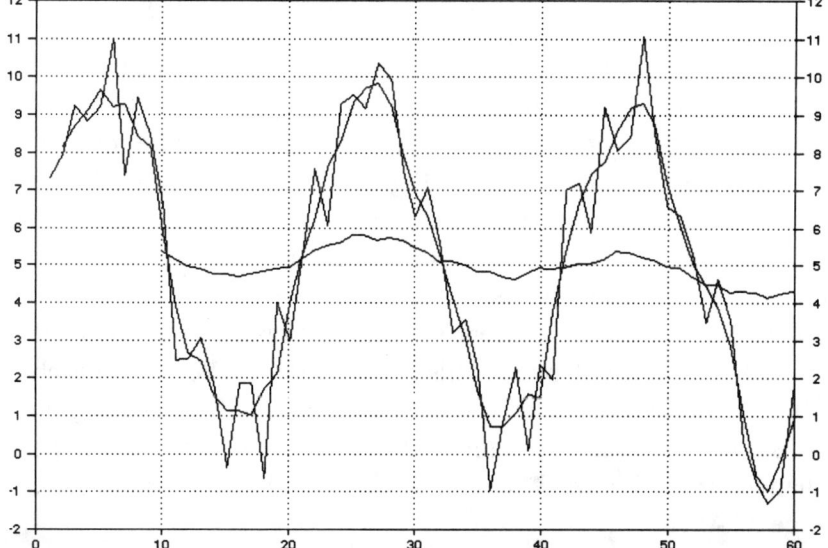

Figure 7.8. *The application of 3-week and 19-week moving averages to the data from Figure 7.6. The 3-week average is the line closest in magnitude to the original data. The magnitude of the 19-week average is sharply reduced.*

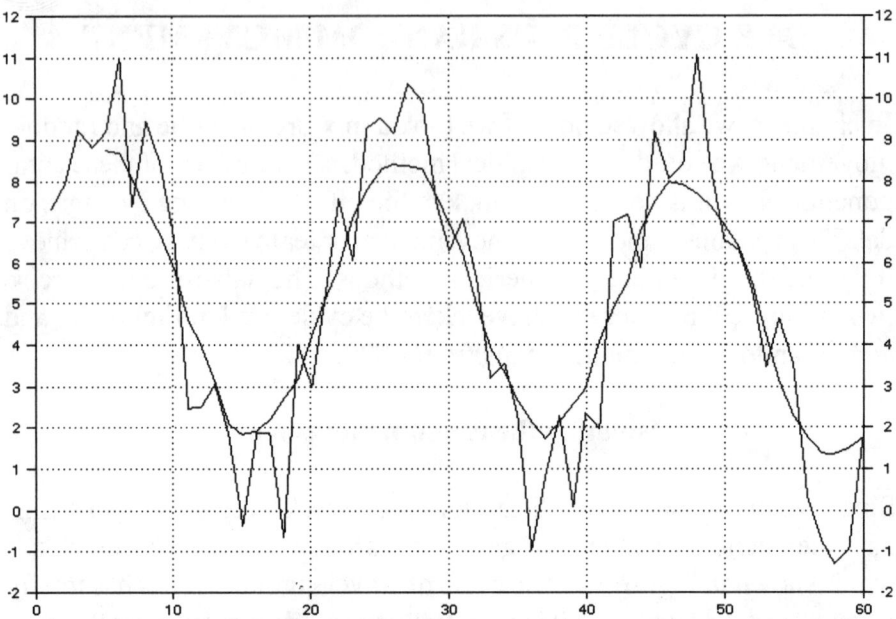

Figure 7.9. *The application of a moving average of span about half of the wavelength of the cycle gives the cleanest result, as shown for this 9-week average of the noisy 21-week cycle. The penalty is that the magnitude of the result is reduced to around $7.5 compared with $10 in the original.*

The phrase 'essentially the random movement' is used because there will be some obvious differences. First the averaging process will result in the magnitude of the averaged data being less than that of the original random movement, as can be seen in Figure 7.7. Second, if we think more carefully about the averaging process, especially the relationship beween the drop point and the next data point added in to the running total, we realize there will be few occasions when these two could be the same. As an example, suppose the current value of the random data is $1.25 and next week the value will be $2. This means there will be a positive change of $0.75. If, however, the drop point 21 weeks ago happened by chance to be $2, then the running total, and hence the average, will appear as unchanged from this week to next week, even though it should reflect a change of $0.75.

Quite clearly, because of these considerations, we will never be able to isolate the random movement by the application of a simple moving average as other than a very good approximation to the original. However, we will soon see that we will be able to do this by another means.

Isolating the cycle

Our prime aim in using a moving average on this data is to try to isolate the original cyclic movement as far as possible, unencumbered by random movement. The result therefore needs to be close to the original cycle in terms of magnitude and position. As far as retaining the original position is concerned, this can be achieved if we use a span that is less than the wavelength of the cycle and avoid using a span that is greater. We also noted that with such spans the magnitude of the resulting averaged data was reduced as we increased the span.

In order to gain some understanding of the effect of the two possible extremes of averages, we show in Figure 7.8 the application of a 3-week average and a 19 week average. Both of these averages remove most of the random movement, leaving a cycle that retains the correct wavelength and position. However, as expected, the 3-week average produces a result that is closest in magnitude to the original sine wave, giving a magnitude of around $8 compared with the $10 of the original. On the other hand, as expected, the 19-week average reduces the magnitude sharply, down to only around $1. Both of these averages suffer from the drawback that there is still a trace of random movement coming through.

Of all the possible odd values of span between 3 and 19, the most successful in removing the random movement is the 9-week average (Figure 7.9). There would be no doubt in the mind of the observer that there is a cycle of wavelength 21 weeks present in the data, but this clarity is obtained at the expense of a good estimate of its magnitude, which is now reduced to about $7.5.

Quite clearly, in using a moving average to isolate a cycle from a mixture of random and cyclic data, we have to balance the requirement to achieve a clean result in terms of the shape and position of the cycle that comes through in the smoothed data against the requirement to arrive at a meaningful measurement of the magnitude of this cycle.

We will find that in general, the optimum result in balancing these two requirements is obtained when the span of the average is close to half of the wavelength of the cycle. In the present case of a wavelength of 21 weeks, and bearing in mind the necessity to use an odd value, the optimum span should be either 9 or 11 weeks. As we have seen, the 9 week average is the best in this particular case.

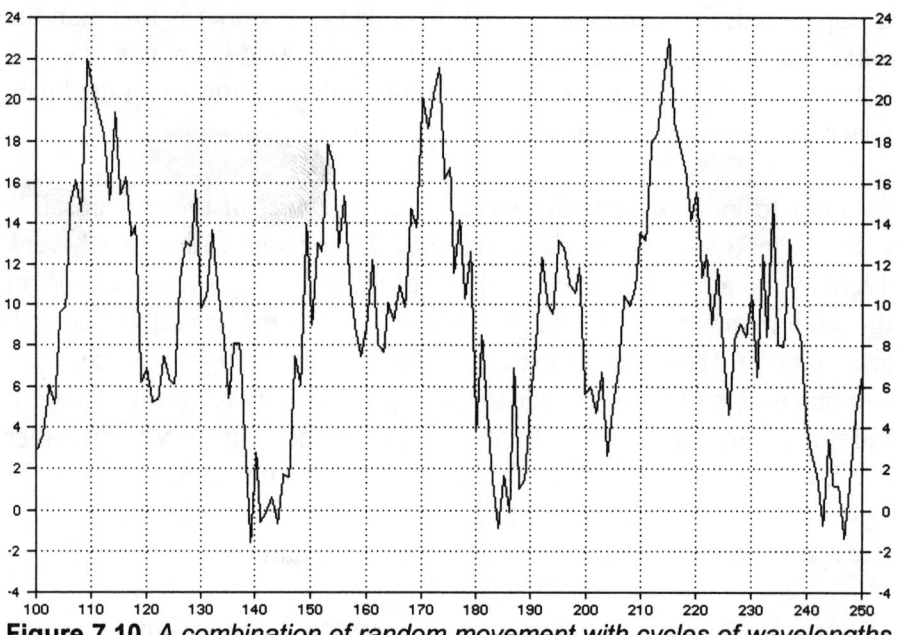

Figure 7.10. *A combination of random movement with cycles of wavelengths 21 and 52 weeks and magnitudes $10.*

Two cycles plus random movement

It is now of interest to apply the knowledge we have acquired so far of the properties of moving averages to the complex wave form used in chapter 5 (Figure 5.7), where we combined two cycles, of wavelength 21 weeks and 52 weeks with an amount of random data. Figure 5.7. is repeated here as Figure 7.10.

Since we know that a span equal to or very close to the wavelength of a cycle will essentially remove that cycle, we should try an average of span 21 weeks, and another of 52 weeks. Since, for reasons discussed earlier, we should use an odd span, in the latter case, the most appropriate span would be 51 or 53 weeks.

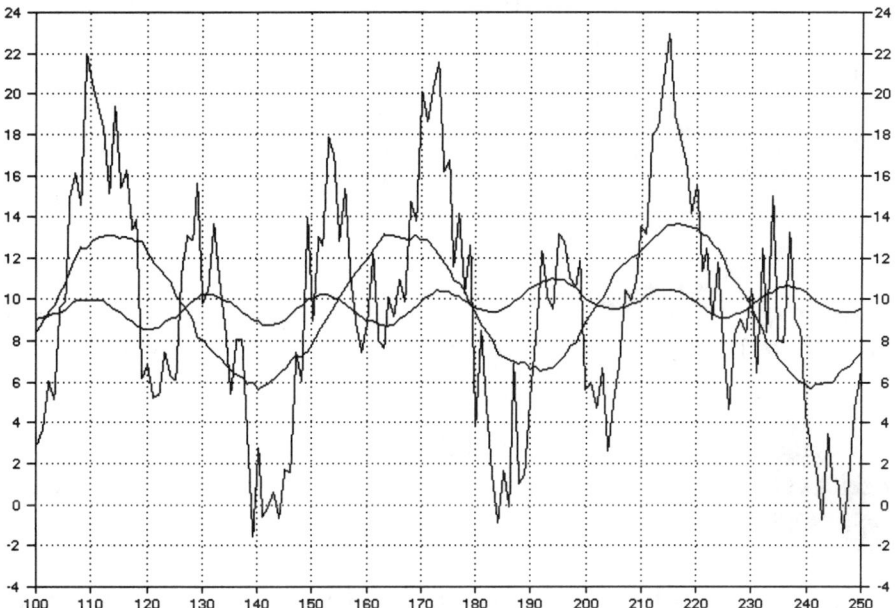

Figure 7.11. *Two averages, of spans 21 and 53 weeks are applied to the data from Figure 7.10. The 21-week average has allowed the 52-week cycle to come through, while the 53-week average allows through the 21 week cycle. Each of these still contains traces of the random movement.*

In Figure 7.11 we see the result of applying a 21-week average and a 53-week average. As expected, each of these eliminates the cycle of similar wavelength, but allows the other cycle through. In each case a trace of the original random movement remains. From our understanding of the effects of various averages, we expect the 21-week average to leave the position of the 52-week cycle exactly as it was in the original data, since this is an example where the span of the average is less than the 52 week

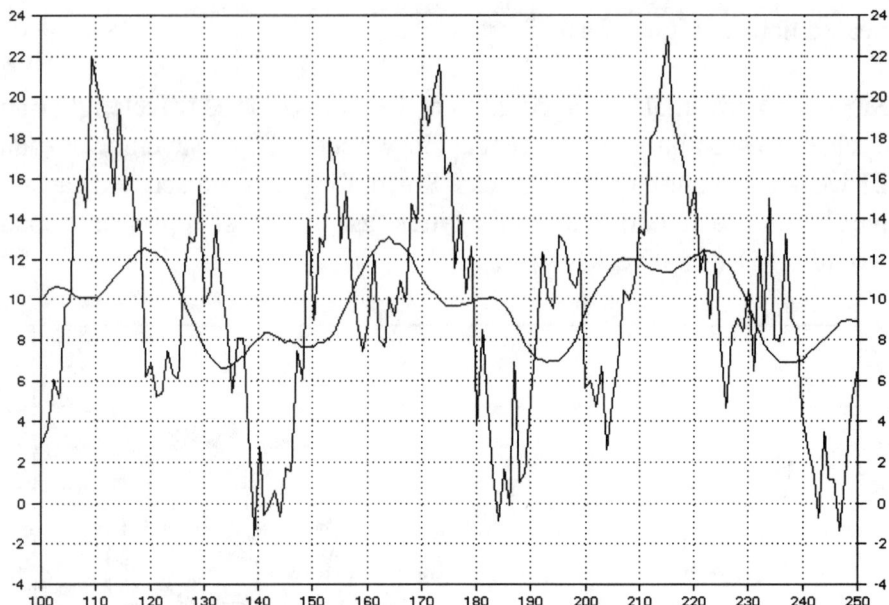

Figure 7.12. *The effect of applying a 31-week moving average to the data in Figure 7.10. There is a shift in time of either one or both of the cycles.*

wavelength. In the other case of the 53-week average as affects the 21 week cycle, we note that the value of 53 lies between 2 x 21 and 3 x 21, *i.e.* it is a case that will not shift the alignment of the cycle.

The magnitude of the 52 week cycle comes through as about $7 compared with the original value of $10, while the magnitude of the 21 week cycle is drastically reduced to about $1. The main message that comes from applying these two averages to the data in this example is that we can isolate two cycles, of wavelengths 21 weeks and 52 weeks, and an amount of random behavior.

It is useful to see the effect of applying an average that is intermediate in span between the two values of 21 and 53. For this purpose, in Figure 7.12, we show the effect of applying a 31-week moving average to the data. Quite clearly, two cycles are present, and very little trace of random movement exists.

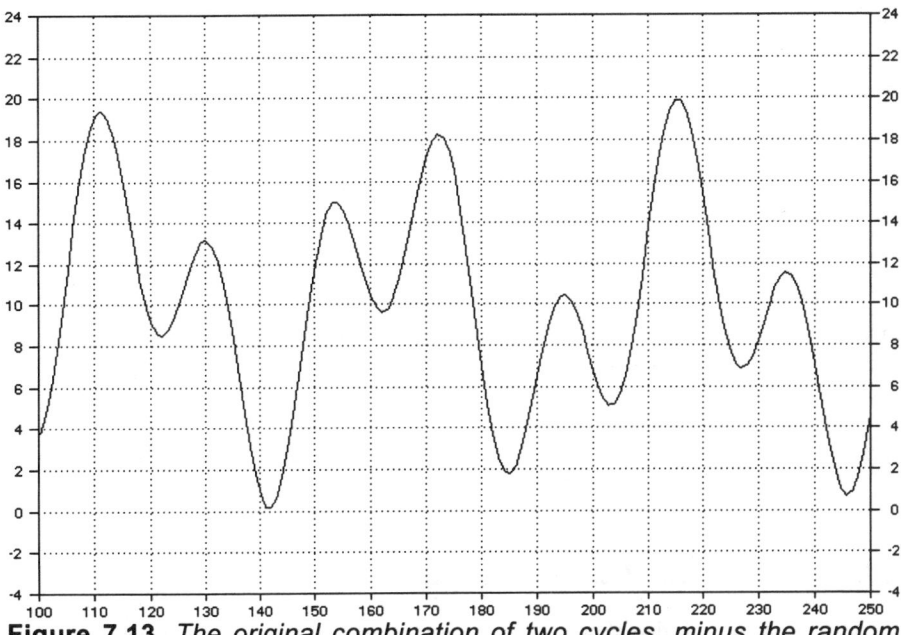

Figure 7.13. *The original combination of two cycles, minus the random movement is shown here for comparison with the plot of the 31-week average as shown in Figure 7.12.*

Since the original combination of two cycles without the addition of random movement is available (Figure 7.13), we can see how efficient a 31-week average is in removing the random movement while leaving the combined cycles to come through the averaging process. There is a considerable loss in the magnitude compared with the original. What is extremely confusing is the total lack of correlation in the position of the cycles in the averaged data in Figure 7.12 compared with their position in the original in Figure 7.13.

The reason for this difficulty is that the 31-week span of the average when compared with the wavelength of the shorter wavelength cycle, 21 weeks, is in the range 1 x wavelength to 2 x wavelength, that is one of the ranges where we get a shift in the position of the cycle. This is the reason we stressed earlier that it is imperative to think carefully about the span of average required for a specific purpose.

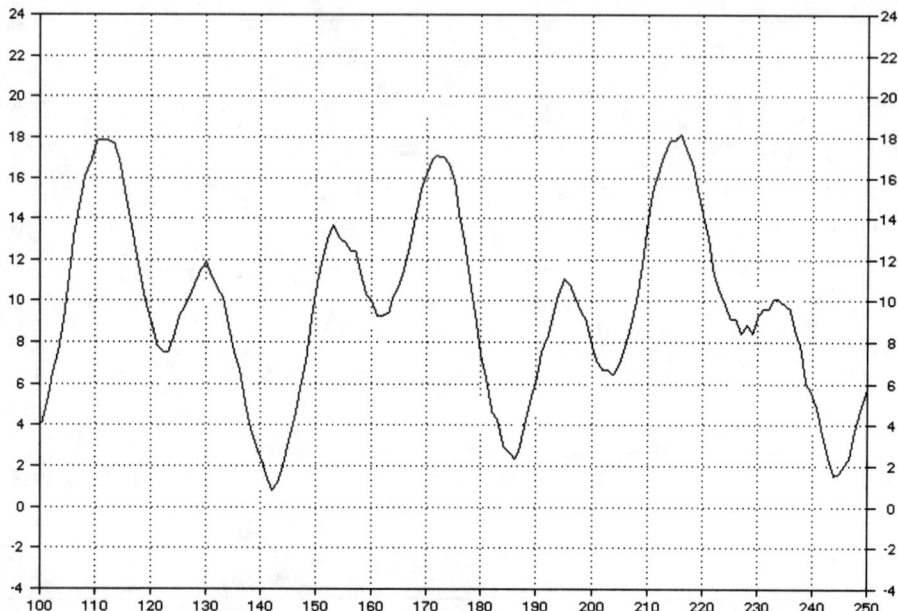

Figure 7:14. *The application of a 9-week average to the data from Figure 7.10. The majority of the random movement has now been removed, and the trace is similar to the original two cycles as shown in Figure 7.13. The magnitude is only slightly decreased compared with the original.*

Since a 9-week average was the most efficient span for studying the 21-week cycle in a combination of that cycle and random movement, it should be obvious that this would also be a good average to apply to the combined data from Figure 7.10. This is for two reasons—1)first we saw the 9-week average removed the vast majority of the random movement, and 2) second since this span is less than the wavelength of either cycle, we would not run into difficulty with a shift in the position of either cycle in the final output.

The result of applying a 9-week average to the data from Figure 7.10 is in Figure 7.14. Quite obviously, this average has been extremely good in removing the random movement, and has had a minimal effect on the magnitudes of the cycles in the data. The vertical positions of the peaks and troughs are not very different from those in the original in Figure 7.13.

SMOOTHED AVERAGES

One of the problems we ran into with simple moving averages was a certain amount of the noise came through when these averages were applied to noisy data, *i.e.* the data that had random movement built in. A way of overcoming this is to smooth the average itself by the application of a second average. In other words, the data is smoothed by the first average, and this average is then smoothed by the second average. It is usual to use a smaller span for the second average than for the first.

Of course, there is a bewildering array of combinations available once the span of the first average gets into double figures. Even if we stick to odd values, using a span of 11 for the first average, then we have available spans of 3, 5, 7 and 9 for the second average. The number of second averages available if we stick to odd spans will be $(n-1)/2 - 1$, where **n** is the span of the first average. In the case of a 201-day average, we can combine this with 99 different second averages. Quite obviously, we have to bring some logic to bear on the situation in order to simplify our selection of the second average. By experimentation, we find the best second average to use is one that is around half of the span of the first average, while still using an odd span. Thus, with a 21-point first average, we could use a 9- or 11-point average as the second one. Either of these will have similar properties.

The way of calculating such a smoothed average is identical to the way the 5-point average was calculated in Table 7.1. Once we have a column of running totals up to the latest point, we use those totals as the input into the second average calculation. There is no point in computing the first average by division of the first column of running totals, since this first average will not be needed. As before, we can use another column as a reminder of which value of the first running total we drop when adding in the next. This process is shown in Table 7.2 for a 11-week average of a 21-week average of the data used to produce Figure 7.10.

Date	Index	Subtract	21-wk total	21-wk average	Subtract	11-wk total	11-wk average
071197	7921.82	X					
071897	7890.46	X					
072597	8113.44	X					
080197	8194.04	X					
080897	8194.04	X					
081597	7871.88	X					
082297	7776.19	X					
082997	7680.26	X					
090597	7680.26	X					
091297	7615.45	X					
091997	7879.56	X					
092697	7913.83	X					
100397	8105.38	X					
101097	8030.23	X					
101797	7876.99	X					
102497	7799.15	X					
103197	7377.74	X					
110797	7577.88	X					
111497	7481.37	X					
112197	7860.18						
112897	7842.03		164682.2	7842.009	X		
120597	8103.87		164864.2	7850.678	X		
121297	7848.99		164822.8	7848.703	X		
121997	7846.50		164555.8	7835.991	X		
122697	7696.75		164058.5	7812.311	X		
010298	7923.94		163788.4	7799.449	X		
010998	7722.16		163638.7	7792.320	X		
011698	7761.02		163623.5	7791.597	X		
012398	7665.36		163608.6	7790.888	X		
013098	7954.83		163883.2	7803.962			
020698	8194.72		164462.5	7831.547		85999.45	7818.132
021398	8340.20		164923.1	7853.482		86010. 93	7819.175
022098	8335.72		165345.0	7873.572		86033.82	7821.256
022798	8545.72		165785.4	7894.540		86079.66	7825.424
030698	8569.38		166324.5	7920.214		86163.88	7833.080
031398	8602.52		167050.0	7954.763		86306.33	7846.030
032098	8906.43		168157.3	8007.491		86514.38	7864.943
032798	8826.47		169606.0	8076.478		86798.53	7890.776
040398	8971.20		170999.4	8142.827		87149.76	7922.706
041098	8994.86		172512.9	8214.898		87573.77	7961.252

Table 7.2. *The calculation of a 11-week average of a 21-week average for the Dow-Jones Index*

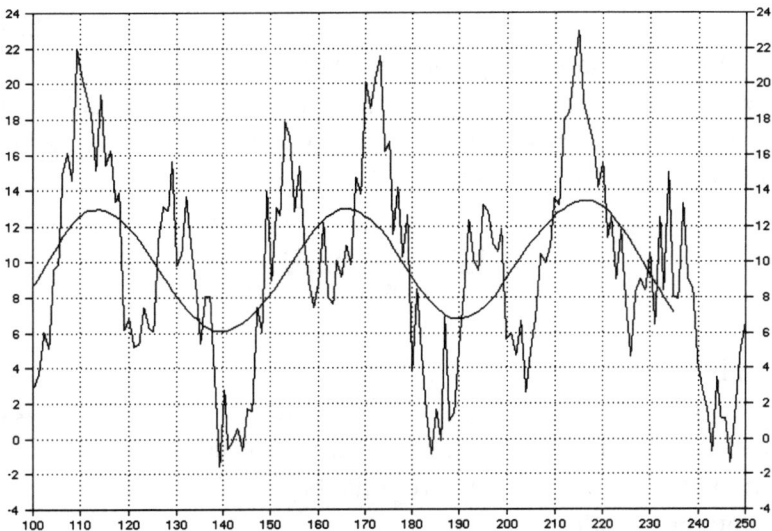

Figure 7.15. *A smoothed 21-week average has been applied to the data from Figure 7.10. There is now no trace of the random movement coming through. The averaged data has a wavelength of 52 weeks, but its magnitude of about $7 is much less than that of the $10 in the original data. Note that the last plotted averaged point is at week 235, i.e. there is a loss of 15 points at the end of the plot.*

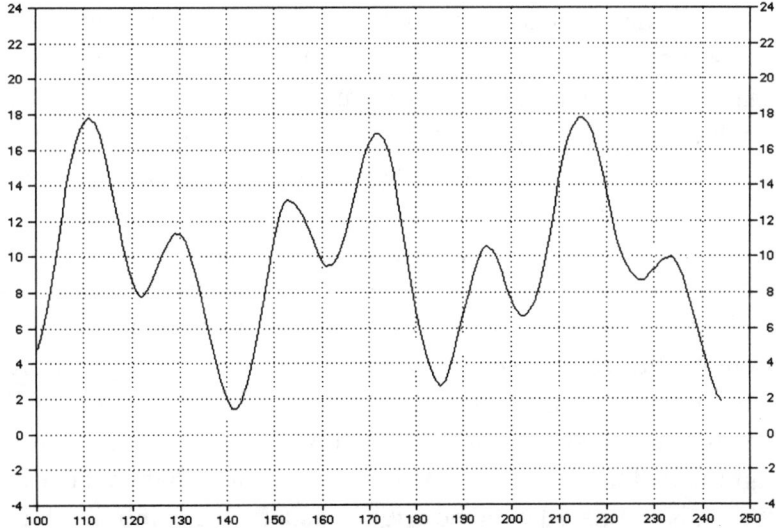

Figure 7.16. *The result of applying a smoothed 9-week average to the data in Figure 7.10. Compare this trace with that from obtained from a simple 9-week average as shown in Figure 7.14.*

As calculated, the value of the final average points are written at the same point in time as the last data point used in the calculation. In order to plot the correct relationship with the data from which the smoothed average is derived, we have to offset the smoothed average point by two amounts. Each of these follows the formula given previously:

$$\underline{\textbf{shift} = \textbf{(span - 1)}}$$
$$\textbf{2}$$

We simply add the two shifts together. For the first 21-week average the shift is 10 weeks back in time, while for the second 11-week average it is 5 weeks back in time. The smoothed average would be plotted 15 weeks back in time. Correspondingly, from the beginning of the data, the first point would be plotted at week 15.

Figure 7.5 presents a plot of this smoothed average. There is a great improvement, in terms of smoothness of the trace compared with the corresponding plot of the simple moving average, as was shown in Figure 7.11. There is no trace now of any random movement coming through. The only difficulty is that the magnitude of the 52-week cycle allowed through is about $7, compared with the $10 in the original sine wave. Note that while the data terminates at week 250, the last plotted point of the smoothed average is at week 235, *i.e.* 15 weeks back in time as expected for a 11-week centered average of a 21-week centered average.

The most effective span to use for a simple average in order to remove the random movement was seen to be 9 weeks, as was shown in Figure 7.14. This still suffered from a small amount of random movement coming through. We would expect a 9-week smoothed average would improve the situation considerably. This is indeed the case Figure 7.16 reveals. Now there is no trace of random movement in the result, although the magnitude of the averaged data is somewhat less than in the original. If this result is compared with the original data for the combined cycles in Figure 7.13, the closeness of the smoothed data to the original is very gratifying. However, as will be discussed later, we have the penalty of a loss of the last 15 points of the averaged data, that will have an implication when we come to the use of smoothed averages as templates for channels.

Weighted Averages

There is another type of average available to us commonly used in computer programs, the weighted average. Unfortunately, it is extremely tedious to calculate, and so only appropriate for those with a computer. It differs from the calculation of a simple average as shown in Table 7.1 by the fact that rather than just adding together each of the **n** data points to give a running total, each point has to be multiplied by a fixed value (a 'weight') before the addition. The maximum weight is applied to the central point. A simple average can be viewed as a weighted average whose weights are all 1. Without going into the mathematics, you can see that a smoothed average is a form of weighted average, where the weights depend upon both of the spans being used.

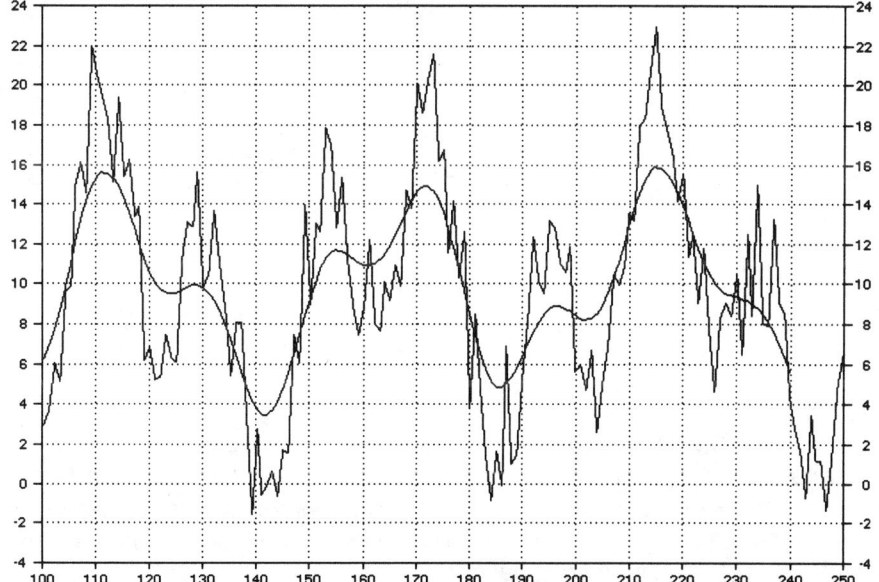

Figure 7.17. *The effect of applying a weighted 21-week average. Unlike the case of a simple average, the cycle of wavelength 21 weeks is not removed, although there is no trace of the random movement. The average terminates 10 weeks before the last data point.*

Because of the weights, the effect of eliminating a cycle of the same wavelength as the span of the average, apparent with simple and smoothed averages, is lost. This can be seen in Figure 7.17, where a 21-week weighted average has been applied. Where the simple average, Figure 7.11, allowed through just the 52-week cycle, with a trace of random movement, the weighted average allows both cycles through, but has eliminated the random movement. As expected, the average cuts off 10 points before the last data point.

The weights used in these examples, require a weighted average of span twice that of the wavelength of a cycle to remove that cycle from the resulting data. A 42-week weighted average would achieve this.

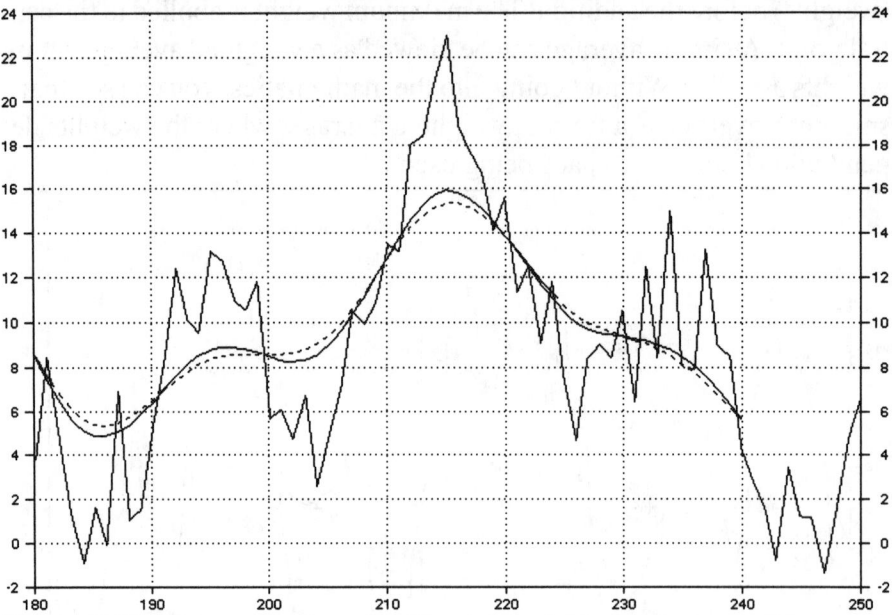

Figure 7.18. *The application of a 21-week weighted average (solid smooth line) and a 15-week smoothed average (dashed line) to the data from Figure 7.10. Both averages lose the last 10 points. The weighted average is marginally superior because the magnitude of the result is slightly larger and therefore slightly closer to that in the original data.*

Since smoothed averages are a form of weighted average, and we lose points at the end of the plot in both smoothed and weighted averages, it is of interest to compare whichever span of smoothed average would cause the same number of points to be lost with the 21-week weighted average. A 15-week smoothed average would also cause the loss of 10 points at the end of the plot. In Figure 7.18 we show the result of applying both a 21-week weighted average and a 15-week smoothed average to the data. Because the two results are so similar, the smoothed average is plotted as a dashed line for clarity. The only apparent difference is that the magnitude of the cycles that come through in the smoothed average are slightly less than those in the weighted average. The weighted average is preferred. What this means, of course, is that the investor without a computer, who calculates a smoothed average is only marginally disadvantaged compared with an investor with a computer who computes and plots weighted averages.

AVERAGES AS TEMPLATES FOR CHANNELS

We mentioned at the start of this chapter that a trend could be represented by a centered average. We also came to the conclusion in chapter 5 that channels had the same shape as the trends we drew through the center of the data, so it follows that we should be able to draw a channel by using the exact shape of a centered average as a template. The reason we have spent quite a bit of time in this chapter discussing the properties of simple, smoothed and weighted averages is to make sure that when we analyze stock real data we apply logic to the selection of the averages from which channels can be produced. Since we also came to the conclusion that a smoothed average was superior in eliminating random fluctuations and cycles of shorter wavelength than the span of the average, we will use smoothed averages as the templates for drawing channels.

We will start with a consideration of what we called the inner channel in previous chapters. We will choose the lowest span of smoothed average that removes the fluctuations (whether random movement or cycles of shorter wavelength than this span). We will see that when we draw the channel and plot the original data, these fluctuations will be contained in the channel. In the case of our test data from Figure 7.10, our inner chan-

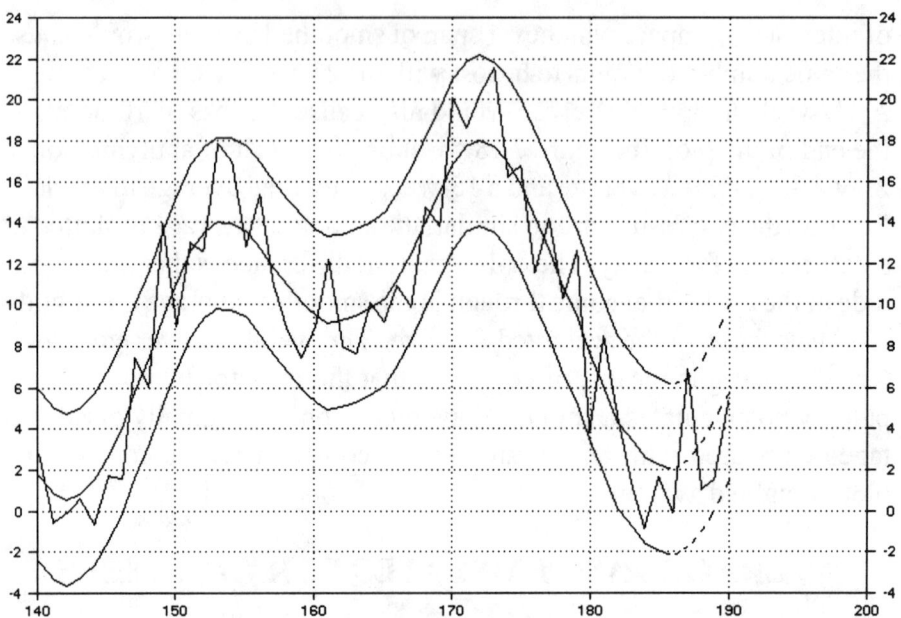

Figure 7.19. *A 7-week smoothed average is plotted on the data. The two channel boundaries are exact copies of this average, placed at equal distances above and below the original position. The dashed lines are estimates of the position of the average between the last calculated point and the last data point.*

nel is the channel that will contain the random movements. We drew such a channel graphically in chapter 5 (see Figure 5.10). The aim is to reproduce this channel by this numerical method as closely as possible. When we come to real data, this selection of the correct span of average for channel production will tend to be by trial and error.

In Figure 7.19, we show a plot of the 7-week smoothed average superimposed on the data. Note of course the average terminates before the last data point. It can also be viewed as a center line, since it runs through the center of the data. The channel is now constructed by duplicating the exact shape of this average twice, plotting one above the original and one below it. These duplicates must always be kept equidistant from the original average in order to preserve the rules of channel analysis. Since they are exact copies, this act of placing them above and below the original will preserve the essential feature of a constant depth. It is now only necessary to move the two duplicates closer to or further from the center line until the acceptable minimum of small violations of these boundaries is reached.

This process is done automatically in a computer program such as **Microvest 5.0™** by storing the distances between each data point and the position of the central average at that point. This gives a distribution of points that will get closer to the theoretical shown in chapter 6 (Figure 6.21) as the number of data points increases. From this distribution it then selects the position of the boundaries to enable a pre-determined number of points to lie outside of the boundaries. Although this number may need to be different in different sets of data, a good starting point is to allow about 3 to 4% of the points to lie outside of the boundaries.

Once the channel has been drawn in this way, it allows us to estimate the magnitude of the random movement. This is of course, the channel depth. The channel contains all of those fluctuations that are of wavelength less than the span used to calculate the average and so construct the channel. As you can see from Figure 7.19, the channel depth is just over $8, which is in line with the actual magnitude of the random movement as running from +$2 to -$2.

Figure 7.19 demonstrates the problem in using the centered average as a template for the channel. We have a gap at the end due to the missing point, and the average and channel terminates 4 points back in time in this case. As we move into the future from the last data point, each new week will bring in a further calculated point for the average, and so the gap will be filled. At a point 4 weeks into the future we will know exactly how the average traversed the gap. At the point we are in Figure 7.19, at week 190, we have to estimate the position of the average over these last four weeks. We are into the same problem addressed in chapter 6, where in the case of real data we will have to examine peaks and troughs in this gap closely in order to provide evidence of what has happened to the channel. In the current example we take into account the large peak at week

187.This forces us to put an upward bend into the channel at the point shown. The estimated positions of the last four points of the average and hence of the channel boundaries are shown as dashed lines.

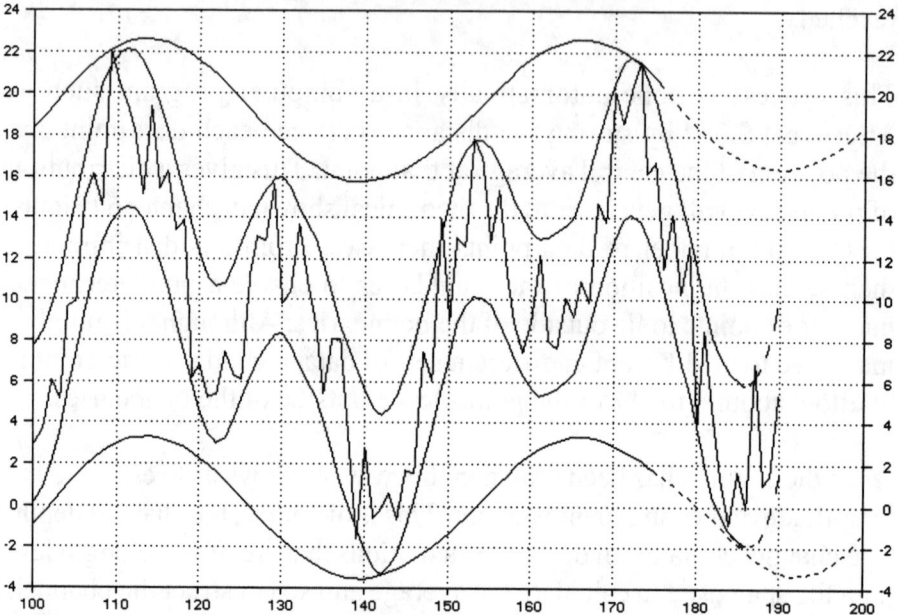

Figure 7.20. *An outer channel has been constructed by plotting a smoothed 21-week average on the top of the previous chart and making duplicates of this average as before. The positions of these were adjusted so as to allow the two boundaries just tough the main peaks and troughs in the previous channel. The original 21-week average has been left out for the sake of clarity.*

In order to isolate the 52-week cycle we can use a smoothed 21-week average, knowing that this will remove the 21-week cycle and the random data. Now that we know the process we place the channel boundaries as exact duplicates above and below the original position of this average we can leave it out of the plot, Figure 7.20. This channel is superimposed on the channel drawn in Figure 7.19. The boundary positions have been adjusted so that the main peaks and troughs in the inner channel just touch the outer boundaries.

The depth of this second channel is just over $18. Since the channel represents the 52-week cycle, this means that the channel contains all fluctuations of wavelength of less than 52 weeks, i.e. wavelengths of 21-weeks or less, and they have a combined magnitude of $18. Since we have established that the random movement is just over $8 in magnitude, this leaves a difference of $10, which is our estimate of the magnitude of the 21-week cycle. We know the latter in the original data to have been $10, so this estimate is excellent.

Although we could draw a third, outer channel by selecting a smoothed average with a span greater than 52 weeks, it is hardly necessary in this case because the outer channel will be running horizontally. The upper boundary would be drawn to touch the two peaks in the second channel just drawn, while the lower boundary is drawn to touch the troughs in this channel. The depth of such a channel is the vertical distance from peak to a trough in the second channel. This is approximately $26, and is due to all the cycles and random behavior present.

From the way the test data was created in the first place, this total should include $10 for the magnitude of the 52 week cycle, $10 for the magnitude of the 21 week cycle and $8 for the magnitude of the random behavior, *i.e.* a total of $28 in all. Thus our estimate of $26 is quite good. By difference between the two channel depths, we estimate the magnitude of the 52 week cycle as being $26 - $18 = $8.

The reason for the estimate of this magnitude being slightly low is because of the overall effect of the application of averages in reducing the magnitude of the cycles which the average lets through. We saw this effect in Figure 7.15.

The general strategy in applying centered averages as templates to stock market data is to increase the span until it is obvious there are no more cycles left in the data. In the interests of efficiency, it is sensible to carry out this process quickly by using fairly large increments rather than step through a large number of averages that are very close together.

CHAPTER 8

Numerical Analysis—More about Cycles

We saw in the last chapter how moving averages, both simple and smoothed, were able to remove cycles with wavelength equal to the span of the average. We also saw that averages would allow through cycles of wavelength greater than the span of the average, although with reduced magnitude, and would mostly remove cycles of wavelength less than the span of the average. In a mixture of two cycles and random data we were able to isolate the cycle of largest wavelength only by the application of an average span equal to the wavelength of the second cycle. It was not possible to isolate the second cycle simply by applying an average, although channel analysis gave a good indication of the wavelength and magnitude of each cycle, and indeed of the random movement present.

Obviously, if we had three different cycles present in the data, we would not be able to isolate just one of these, because applying an average of the same span as one of the cycles would still leave the combination of the other two cycles coming through. Thus, it is apparent that we cannot use moving averages in the normal way to isolate an individual cycle from a mixture of more than two. With a mixture of two, we are only able to isolate the cycle of largest wavelength.

This chapter shows the use of average differences will overcome some of the problems associated with the isolation of particular cycles. **However, since these calculations will be based on centered averages, they will**

still suffer from the same drawback of loss of data points at the beginning and end of the plotted result. As is the case with averages, we will not be sure what is happening at the present time, and will have to estimate how the calculated data might have unrolled across the gap from the last true calculated point to the present and where desired, into the future.

SIMPLE AVERAGE DIFFERENCES

We showed in chapter 5 (see Figure 5.3) how the random content of a cycle with added random movement could be extracted by taking the differences between the line drawn through the center of the data and each individual data point. This is simply a manifestation of the general principle of average differences. The fluctuations that have been removed by the averaging process, for example, the random movement when, say a 9-week average has been used, can be recovered by taking the difference between the value of the centered average and the value of the data at each point between the beginning and end of the centered average. The

Date	Index	Subtract	5-week total	5-week average	Centered	Avge Diff
02/06/98	8194.72					
02/13/98	8340.20					
02/20/98	8335.72				8397.148	61.428
02/27/98	8545.72				8478.708	-67.012
03/06/98	8569.38	X	41985.74	8397.148	8591.954	22.574
03/13/98	8602.52	X	42393.54	8478.708	8690.104	87.584
03/20/98	8906.43	X	42959.77	8591.954	8775.200	-131.23
03/27/98	8826.47	X	43450.52	8690.104	8860.296	33.826
04/03/98	8971.20	X	43876.00	8775.200	8973.292	2.092
04/10/98	8994.86	X	44301.48	8860.296	9004.930	10.07
04/17/98	9167.50	X	44866.46	8973.292	9069.050	-98.45
04/24/98	9064.62	X	45024.65	9004.930	9085.840	21.22
05/01/98	9147.07	X	45345.25	9069.050	9106.068	-41.002
05/08/98	9055.15	X	45429.20	9085.840	9095.456	40.306
05/15/98	9096.00	X	45530.34	9106.068	9076.572	-19.428
05/22/98	9114.44	X	45477.28	9095.456	9054.700	-59.74
05/29/98	8970.20	X	45382.86	9076.572	9010.658	40.458
06/05/98	9037.71	X	45273.50	9054.700	8934.032	-103.678
06/12/98	8834.94	X	45053.29	9010.658		
06/19/98	8712.87	X	44670.16	8934.032		

Table 8.1. *Calculation of average differences for the Dow-Jones Index*

result is known as the average difference. Once the average has been calculated and centered, the process is quite simple, as shown in Table 8.1.

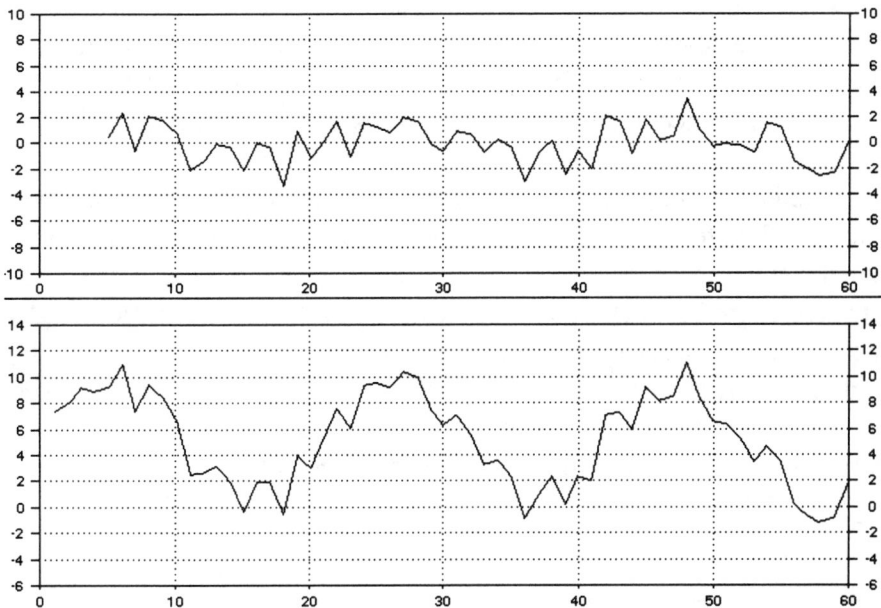

Figure 8.1. *Lower panel: a sine wave of wavelength 21 weeks and magnitude $10 with random movement ranging from -$4 to +$4 added. Upper panel: a 9-week average difference plot which just the random movement. Note the loss of 4 calculated points at the beginning of the upper plot because the calculation involves a centered average. A similar cut-off would be seen at the end of the data, terminating at week 1000.*

In chapter 7 (Figure 7.9) we showed that the cleanest result was obtained using an average with a span of 9 weeks when applying simple moving averages to the 21-week cycle with added random movement. Now we show the result in Figure 8.1 of taking the 9-week average difference of the same data. The original cycle with its random movement is shown in the lower panel, while in the upper panel you can see that the cycle has been eliminated and only the random movement allowed through. Note the cut-off of the first four calculated points in the upper panel because the calculation is derived from a 9-week centered average. There is not an equivalent at the right hand side of the plot since the display is just the first section of a much longer set of data that runs to week 1000.

If we apply this same principle to a combination of two cycles, such as the 21-week and 52-week combination used in earlier chapters, we would expect that a 21-week average would highlight the 52-week cycle, since the 21-week cycle would be eliminated. We now expect that a 21-week average difference to show us this 21-week cycle and eliminate the 52-week cycle. This is indeed true, as shown in Figure 8.2. The 21-week average is superimposed on the combination of two cycles in the lower panel, and quite clearly shows the 52-week cycle in isolation. The upper panel shows the 21-week average difference. This is obviously the cycle of wavelength 21 weeks, as the successive peaks and successive troughs are exactly 21 weeks apart. There is a minor fluctuation in the magnitude, and this is due to a trace of the 52-week cycle still coming through. Even so, you can see that by the use of an average and an average difference we can isolate each of the two cycles present in the data.

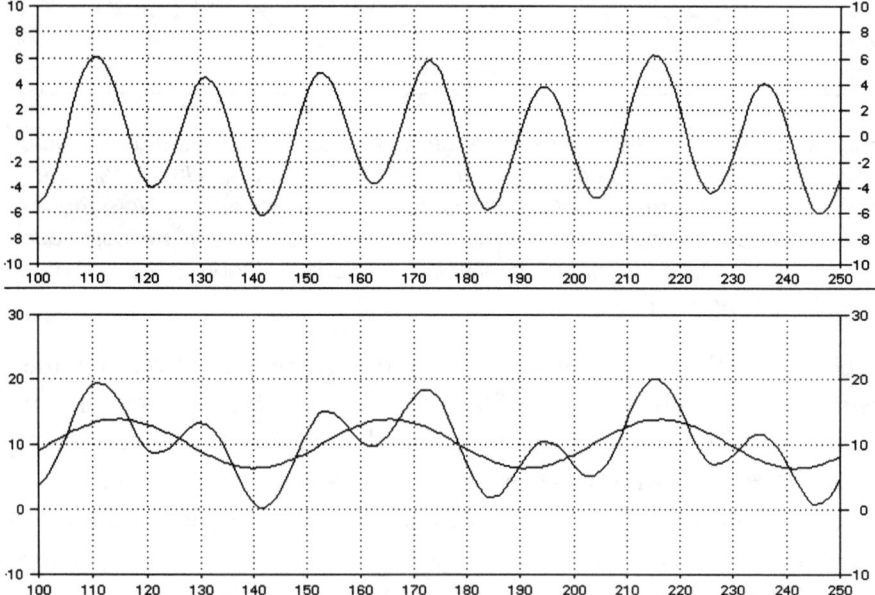

Figure 8.2. *Lower panel: the combined 21-week and 52-week cycles. The superimposed 21-week average highlights the 52-week cycle. Upper panel: the 21-week average difference highlights the 21-week cycle. The lost points at either end are not seen because this is a section of a longer set of data.*

Because the displayed data is just a central section of a much longer data set that runs to 1000 weeks, we do not see the cut-offs. In this case a 21-week average amounts 10 weeks at either end.

If we turn to the combined cycles with added random movement, we show in Figure 8.3 the effect of applying a 21-week average difference. Although this has the effect of isolating the 21-week cycle, it also allows through the random movement. Another way of looking at it is that we have removed the 52-week cycle from the combined data, leaving the rest of the components to come through.

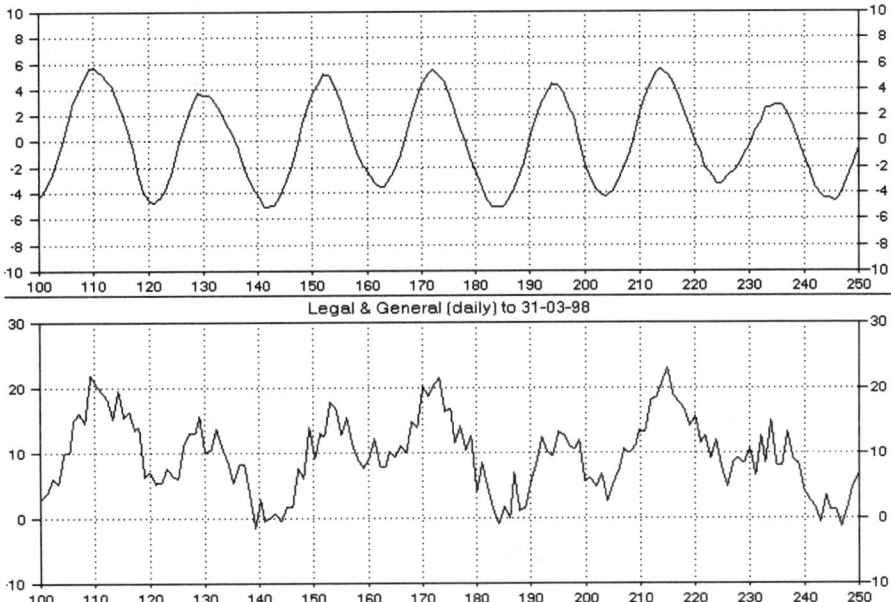

Figure 8.3. *Lower panel: the combined 21-week and 52-week cycles with added random movement. Upper panel: the result of applying a 21-week average difference to the data. Both the 21-week cycle and the random movement can be seen, while the 52-week cycle has been removed.*

We saw in the last chapter how we could remove the random movement from a combination of a 21-week cycle with random movement by using a 9-week average. We can use this same method again, *i.e.* apply a 9-week centered moving average to the calculated data in Figure 8.3 in order to smooth out the random fluctuations and confirm the presence of a clean 21-week cycle. The result of doing this is shown in Figure 8.4, where a 9-week centered average has been applied to the 21-week average difference. By doing this, it is quite clear we have isolated the 21-week cycle free of the random movement.

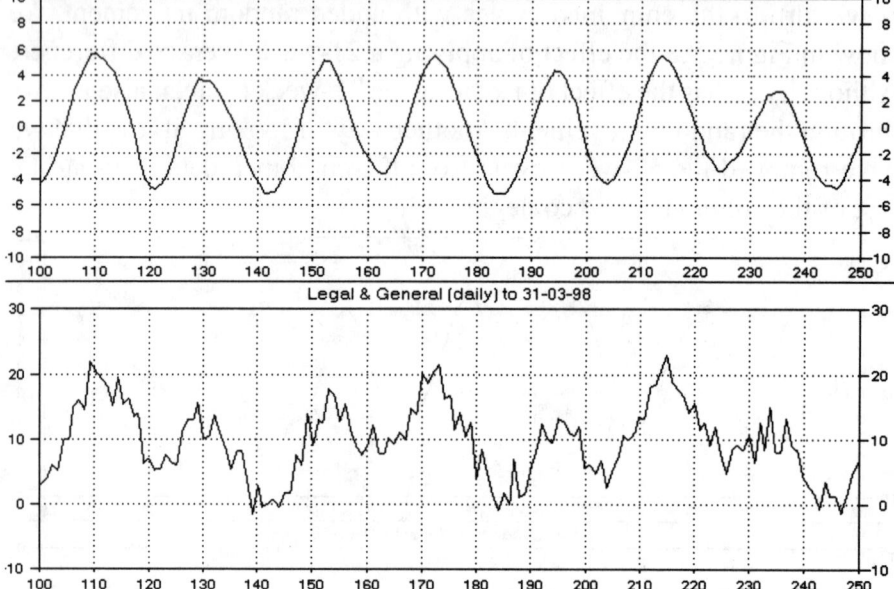

Figure 8.4. *Lower panel: the combined 21-week and 52-week cycles with added random movement. Upper panel: the 21-week average difference has been smoothed by the application of a 9-week moving average.*

What is not obvious, because we are displaying only a central section of the data, is the number of points that are lost at the beginning and end of the final calculation compared with the original data set. We lost ten points at each end by the application of the 21-week average difference, and the use of another 9-week centered average would lose a further four points at each end, giving a loss of fourteen points at each end.

From the next few examples we will be able to see the complementary nature of the two averages. In the case of a complex mixture of many cycles, we will be able to isolate at least two, and possibly more, of the cycles by applying these methods. Of course, as we have seen, the penalty for the sequential application of centered average differences and centered averages will be the increasing loss of data points. While this is of no consequence at the beginning of the data set, it makes it difficult to determine what is happening, because we must estimate the values of the lost points.

The examples are based on a test mixture of three cycles of wavelengths 9, 21 and 52 weeks respectively. Each has a magnitude of $20. The combination is shown in Figure 8.5.

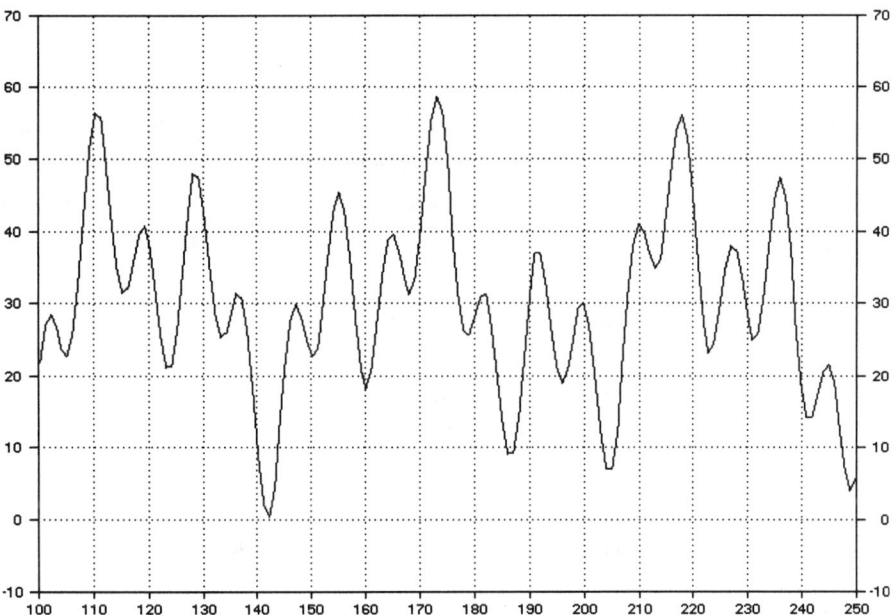

Figure 8.5. *A mixture of three cycles of wavelength 7, 21 and 52 weeks. The magnitude of each cycle is $10.*

Isolating the largest wavelength cycle

Since, by applying a simple moving average, we allow through those cycles with wavelengths greater than the span used for the average, then the strategy is to use an average whose span lies between the wavelengths of the cycles with the two largest wavelengths. This allows us to isolate the largest wavelength cycle.

Isolating the shortest wavelength cycle

Since, by applying a moving average difference we allow through all cycles with wavelengths equal to or less than the span used for the average, then the strategy is to use an average difference whose span is equal to this wavelength.

Other wavelengths

These can be accessed by applying either an average difference and a simple average, or by using two successive averages. A little thought has to go into which of these two combinations should be applied, and which spans should be used. Often there are two routes to isolating an individual cycle from a mixture. The process is analogous to the use of a succession of sieves to separate materials of different diameters.

The problem can be stated as:

> *We have a mixture of cycles of wavelengths **w1** ... **wn**, where the wavelengths are increasing from **1** to **n**. The aim is to isolate an individual cycle, say the one with wavelength **w5**.*

METHOD 1: BY REMOVING SHORTER WAVELENGTHS FIRST

In this method, we first remove all of the cycles whose wavelengths are less than **w5**. This can be done by applying an average with span equal to **w4**. Wavelength **w4** is thus entirely removed. Traces of the shorter wavelengths may come through.

To this combination of fewer cycles we apply an average difference of span equal to the wavelength we wish to isolate, *i.e.* **w5**. This will isolate **w5** by removing all wavelengths greater than **w5**.

In cases where traces of the shorter wavelengths come through, the application of smoothing average of span equal to the shorter wavelength will clean up the cycle.

METHOD 2: BY REMOVING LONGER WAVELENGTHS FIRST

In this method we first of all remove all of the cycles with wavelengths greater than **w5**. This can be done by applying an average difference with span equal to **w5**. Wavelengths **w6** ... **wn** are removed.

To this combination of fewer cycles we apply an average of span intermediate between **w4** and **w5**. This will remove all wavelengths of less than the span, leaving **w5** isolated.

We can see that the isolation of the longest and shortest wavelengths from a mixture is simply a special case of these two methods, where the second stage does not need to be applied because only one cycle is present after the first stage.

By such a method of attrition, we can isolate any chosen cycle. However, the penalty for this will almost certainly be a reduction in magnitude. Because such a reduction will occur at each of the two (or three if additional smoothing is required) stages.

Testing Methods 1 and 2

In the test mixture the three cycles have wavelengths of 9, 21 and 52 weeks. Each has a magnitude of $20. Thus we have **w1 = 9, w2 = 21** and **w3 = 52**.

To isolate the cycle wavelength of 52 weeks, method 1 was applied, using a 21-week average (same as **w2** wavelength). This is a case where there were still traces of the 9-week cycle in the result, so a second average with a span of 9 weeks was used to removed these, giving the clean 52-week cycle shown, superimposed on the original data in Figure 8.6. The magnitude of this cycle is around $10. About half of the true value. As expected, there has been a considerable amount of attenuation of the cycle by the two averaging processes.

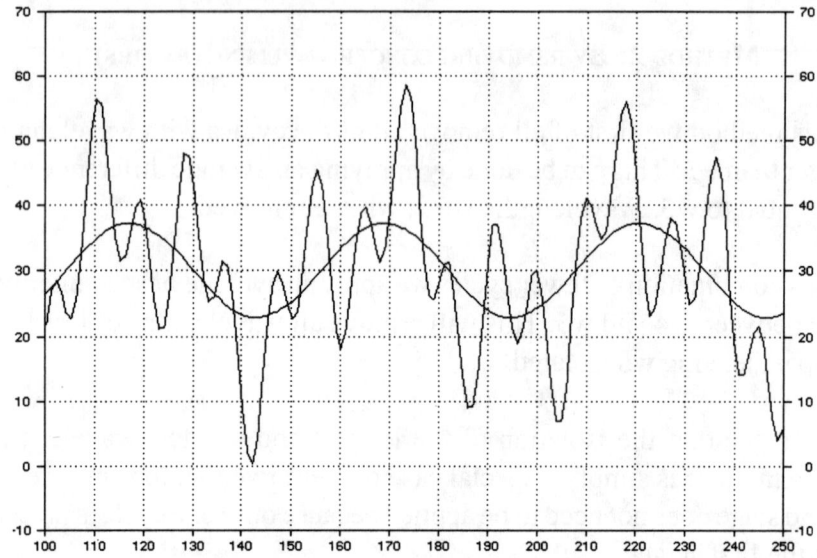

Figure 8.6. *The application of a 21 week average followed by a 9-week average removes the cycles of wavelengths 21 weeks and 9 weeks, leaving a clean 52 week cycle. The 9-week average was required in order to remove traces of the 9-week cycle from 21-week averaged data.*

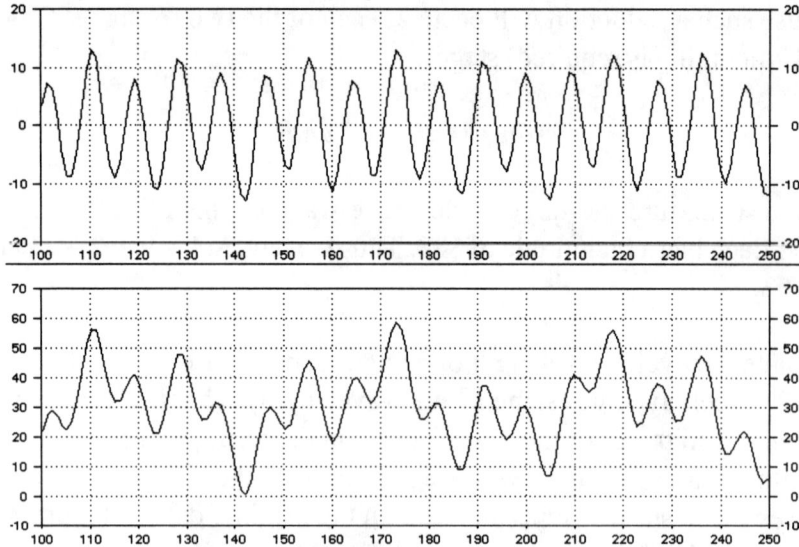

Figure 8.7. *Lower panel: the complex mixture of three cycles. Upper panel: the 9-week average difference isolates the 9-week cycle quite cleanly.*

To isolate the cycle wavelength of 9 weeks, method 2 was applied, using a 9-week average difference (same as **w2** wavelength). The result is shown in the upper panel of Figure 8.7. In this case it was not necessary to apply any further smoothing average, you can see the magnitude of the cycle is around $20. There has been very little attenuation by the application of an average difference.

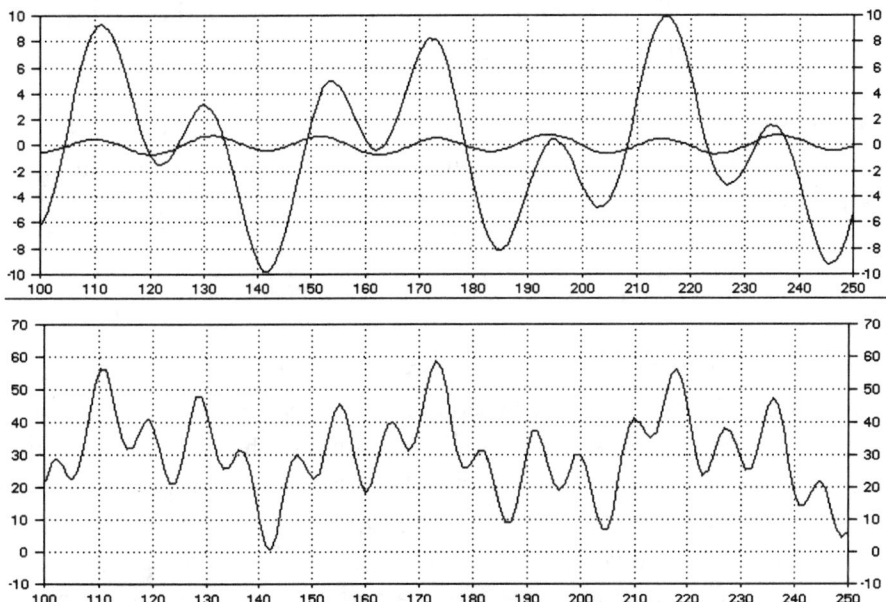

Figure 8.8. *Lower trace: the original three-cycle combination. Upper trace; The trace with the largest magnitude is the result of applying a 9-week average to the original data. A 21-week average difference is then applied to give the clean 21-week cycle. The magnitude of this is severely reduced to about $2 from the original $20.*

To isolate the cycle of wavelength 21 weeks, method 1 was applied, using an average of span 9 weeks. The result of applying this average is shown in the upper panel of Figure 8.8.

At this stage there is little loss of magnitude of the combination of 21-week and 52-week cycles that have come through. At the next stage, however, where a 21-week average difference has been applied to remove the 52-week cycle, there is a drastic reduction in magnitude, down to about $2. Even so, it is quite clear we have proved the existence of a cycle with a wavelength of 21 weeks by this method.

As you can see from this last isolated cycle, the difficulty with this sequential method is that sometimes it is difficult to estimate the magnitude of the various cycles present in the mixture of cycles, although we can deduce their wavelengths quite easily.

The following method of isolating cycles is far superior because it is only necessary to specify one value, the wavelength of the cycle that the user desires to isolate.

AVERAGE MINUS AVERAGE

Although this method is also based on average differences, the difference in this case is the difference between two averages, rather than the difference between an average and the original data. For those investors without a computer, the procedure is to take a moving average with span equal to the wavelength of the cycle to be isolated. The average should be centered as in the previous method. A second moving average is calculated with a span half that of the first average, and this is again centered. The next step is simply to take the difference between these two averages.

For those with a computer, the best result is obtained when the second average is a weighted average. This is the method used in the examples that illustrate this approach. In order to have an even more demanding test, a combination of cycles of wavelengths 9, 21, 53 and 99 weeks was calculated. In order to approach more closely the relative magnitudes of cycles in stock market data, the 9-week cycle was given a magnitude of $20, the 21-week cycle a magnitude of $40, the 53-week cycle a magnitude of $80 and the 99-week cycle a magnitude of $120. There is also a constant amount added to make the lowest point non-zero. The data terminates at week 300, and particular attention will be paid in the examples to an estimation of the isolated cycles between the last calculated point, which will be half a span back from week 300 and a point some weeks into the future.

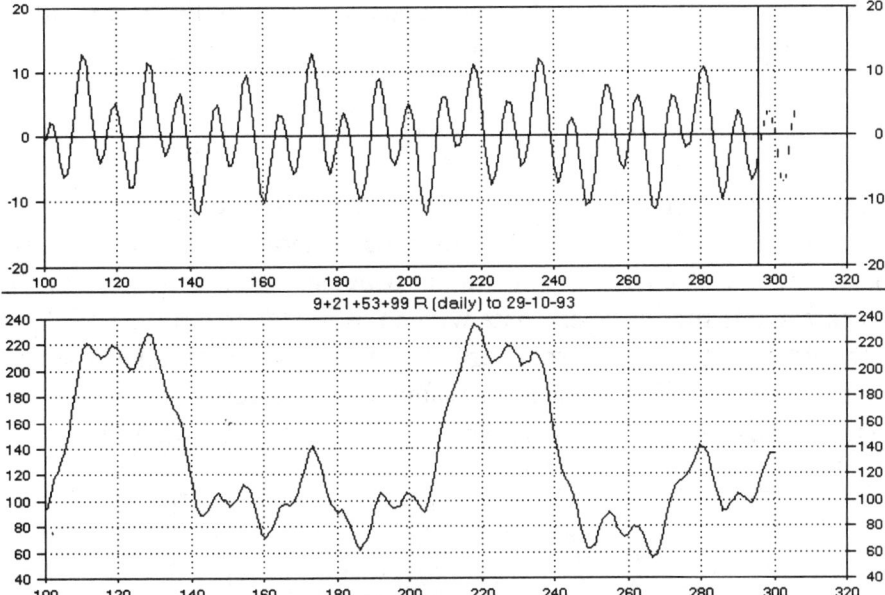

Figure 8.9. *Lower panel, a combination of 4 cycles of wavelengths 9,21,53 and 99 weeks, with magnitudes $20, $40, $80 and $120 respectively. Upper panel: the result of applying a 9/5 week average difference is the presence of a 9-week cycle, and estimated magnitude about $18. The dashed line is the best estimate of the direction the averaged data would have taken from the last true calculated point, which is 4 weeks in the past (at the vertical solid line) and into the future. The present time is week 300.*

For simplicity, the averages used will be described as a 9/5-week average difference. (The difference between a 9-week and 5-week average has been taken). In Figures 8.9 to 8.12 the combination of cycles is shown in the lower panel so the position of the peaks and troughs in the extracted cycles can be compared with the original trace.

As is the case with centered averages, the difference of the two averages will show a loss of points at the beginning and end of the plot. The average with the largest span determines the number of points lost, as with a simple average. The last plotted point is marked by a solid vertical line in the top panels of the following figures, and the dashed line shows the estimated position of the plot up to the latest data point and forwards for some time into the future. The estimated position into the future will be used shortly to try to estimate how the data itself will move in to future.

The 9-week cycle

This combined cycle and the result of applying a 9/5-week average difference are shown in Figure 8.9. The lower panel shows the original combination of four cycles, while the upper panel shows quite clearly the 9-week cycle is present in the data with an estimated magnitude of about $18, close to the original value of $20. Because the calculation is based on a centered average, the last calculated point is 4 weeks in the past. The estimated course of the average from that point into the future is shown by the dashed line.

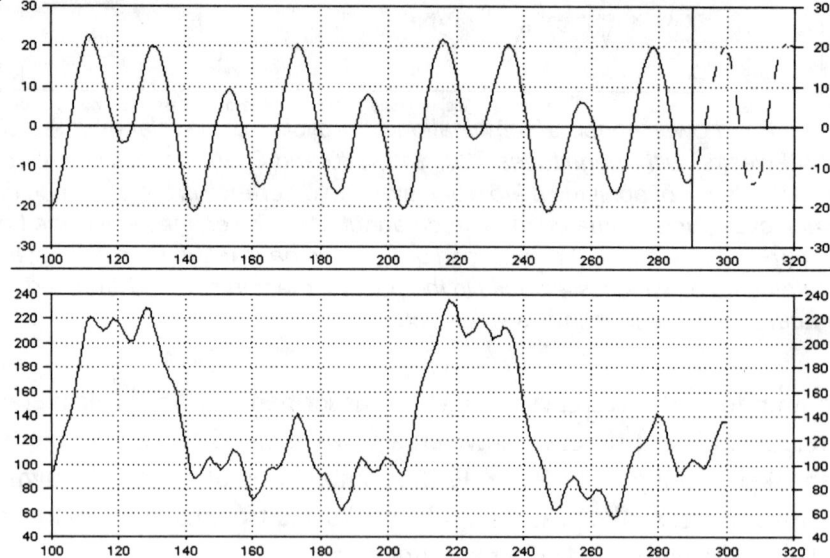

Figure 8.10. *Lower panel, the combination of four cycles of wavelengths 9, 21, 53 and 99 weeks. Upper panel: the result of applying a 21/11 week average difference is to show 21-week cycle, and estimated magnitude about $35. The dashed line is the best estimate of the direction the averaged data would have taken after the last true calculated point, which is 10 weeks in the past (at the vertical solid line). The present time is week 300.*

The 21-week cycle

To isolate the 21-week cycles requires a 21/11-week average difference, as shown in Figure 8.10. The extracted cycle, while not as close in shape to a sine wave as one would like, nevertheless has a wavelength of 21 weeks and an estimated magnitude of about $35, compared with the original value of $40. The estimated course of the average from the last calculated point 10 weeks in the past into the future is shown by the dashed line.

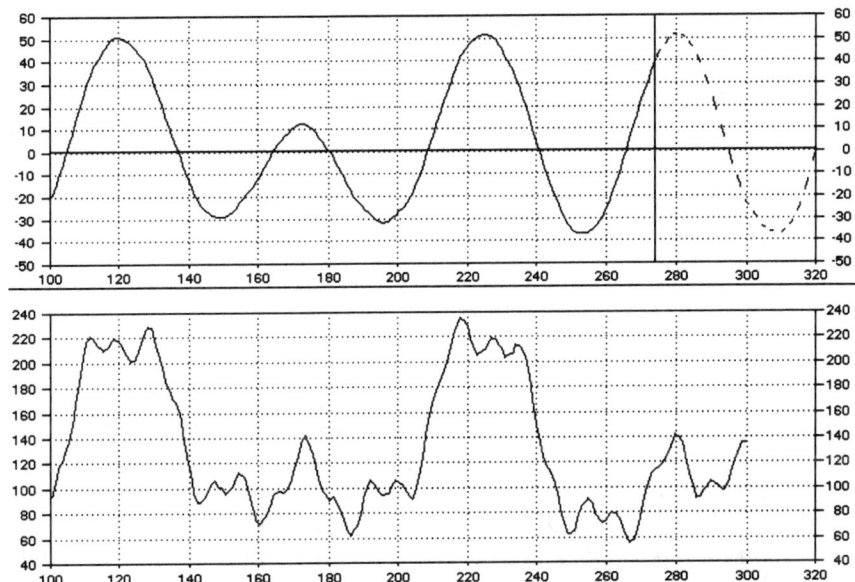

Figure 8.11. *Lower panel, a combination of 4cycles of wavelengths 9,21,53 and 99 weeks, each of magnitude $20. Upper panel: the result of applying a 53/27 week average difference is a 53-week cycle, and estimated magnitude about $18. The dashed line is the best estimate of the direction the averaged data would have taken after the last true calculated point, 26 weeks in the past (at the vertical solid line). The present time is week 300.*

The 53-week cycle

To isolate the 53-week cycles requires a 53/27-week average difference, as shown in Figure 8.11. The extracted cycle shows some variation in the magnitude, but clearly has a wavelength of 53 weeks. The average magnitude is about $85, compared with the original value of $80. The estimated course of the average from last calculated point 26 weeks in the past and into the future is shown by the dashed line.

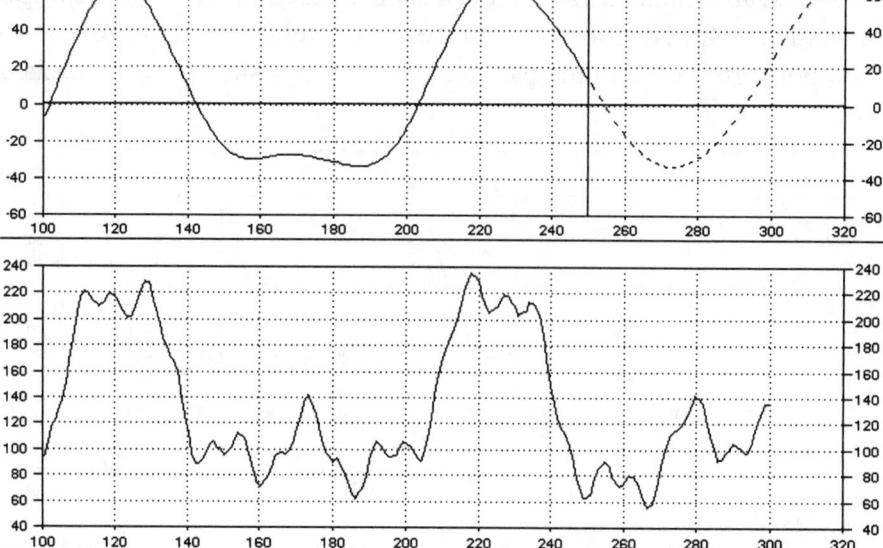

Figure 8.12. *Lower panel, a combination of 4 cycles of wavelengths 9,21,53 and 99 weeks, each of magnitude $20. Upper panel: the result of applying a 111/57 week average difference is to show the presence of a 99-week cycle, and estimated magnitude about $18. The dashed line is the best estimate of the direction the averaged data would have taken after the last true calculated point, or 55 weeks in the past (at the vertical dotted line). The present time is week 300.*

The 99-week cycle

On the basis of the discussion and results so far, we can expect that to isolate the 99-week cycle will require a 99/51-week average difference. However, when this is applied, considerable traces of the 53-week cycle come through, making it difficult to determine the exact wavelength and magnitude. By moving up to a 111/57-week average difference a much better view of this cycle emerge, as shown in the upper panel in Figure

8.12. The estimated course of the average from last calculated point 55 weeks in the past and on into the future is shown by the dashed line.

These examples show that the use of the average-minus-average is an extremely valuable way of investigating a complex mixture for the presence of a particular cycle. It is particularly useful to discover that the magnitude of the extracted cycle is usually only slightly diminished. This will have implications when we apply the method to real stock market data in an endeavor to find out which cycles are present and their influence on the movement of the stock price itself.

The current and future status of the cycles

In these examples, we showed the estimated position of the cycles up to and past the present time, or in these examples week 300. The underlying purpose of these exercises in extracting the cycles is to predict what the combined data will be doing in the near future. Once we have established this is possible, even though there may be limitations, we are in possession of a method that can be applied to market data with obvious benefits.

Since the penalty for isolating a particular cycle is the loss of a number of points equal to one less than half a span of the average, (we are isolating cycles with wavelengths similar to the span of the average being used,) then we lose half of a wavelength at the end of the cycle. Even to bring the position up to date, to estimate the current state of the isolated cycles, requires an extrapolation of over half of a wavelength. Gathering together the results from these examples, we find the status of the various cycles as:

- 9-week, falling, estimated magnitude $18 (actual $20)
- 21-week, just topping out, estimated magnitude $35 (actual $40)
- 53-week, falling, estimated magnitude $85 (actual $80)
- 99-week, rising, estimated magnitude $95 (actual $120)

Since only the longer term cycle is rising and the other three falling for

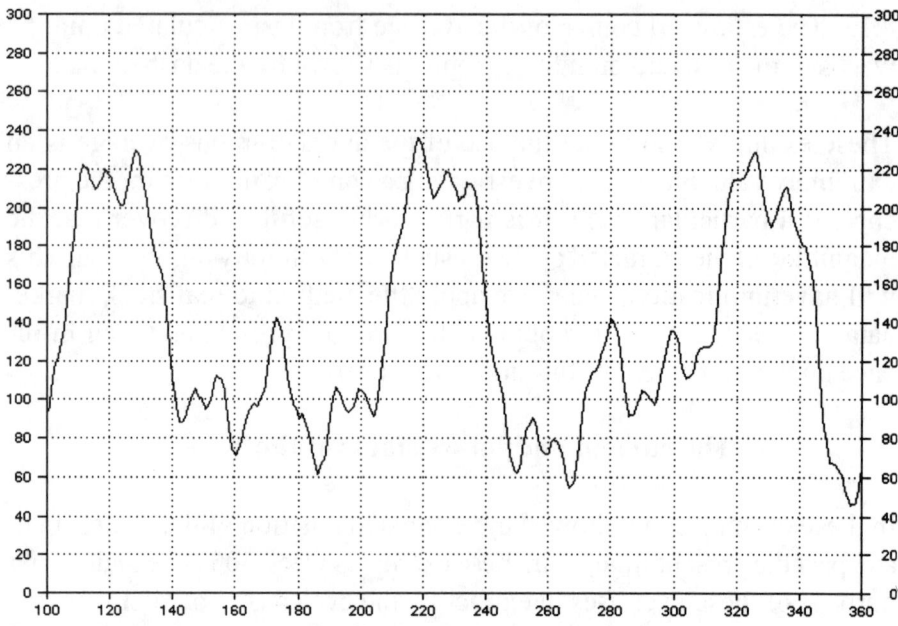

Figure 8.13. *The movement of the complex data up to week 360.*

the next few weeks, we can, without applying any arithmetic, we expect the combination of these cycles to fall over the very near future. Figure 8.13, contains a slightly larger section of data and shows that this happens. The original data fell between weeks 300 and 305 before rising slightly, hesitating, and then making a large advance. This large advance finally topped out around week 325.

We need to see now whether, by applying a little more arithmetic, we can deduce that this large advance will happen over the next twenty weeks or so from week 300. One problem is that this time scale of 20 weeks is greater than the wavelength of the shortest 9-week cycle, meaning that it will pass through two peaks or troughs in the time period. The first step is to measure how far past the last turning point, *i.e.* peak or trough, each cycle is, and the current value:

- 9-week, 2 weeks past peak, current value +$2
- 21-week, just at peak, current value +$20

- 53-week, 20 weeks past peak, current value -$23
- 99-week, 25 weeks past trough, current value +$20

The next step is to deduce how far past a peak or trough the cycle will be in 20 weeks time. Its value can then be estimated by looking at a similar point in the cycle development in the recent past. We will then look at the change this means from the current position and add up all these changes to get an overall change from the current position. This approach is necessary because of the presence of a fixed amount in the complex wave form that was added in order to avoid negative values.

The 9-week cycle

In 20 weeks time, the 9-week cycle will be 22 weeks past the last true peak, and will have passed through 2 more peaks. In 18 weeks time it will be in the same vertical position as now, so by the time 20 weeks have elapsed, it should be about 4 weeks past a peak, *i.e.* nearly at a trough (half of a wavelength past a peak) and have an approximate value of -$10.

This gives us a change of -$12 from its current position. It will rise from this position.

The 21-week cycle

In 20 weeks, the 21-week cycle will be 20 weeks past the last true peak, or week 300. It will therefore be just one week short of the peak, and should have an approximate value of +$20. It will start to fall from this position in two weeks time.

The change from the current position is about zero.

The 53-week cycle

In 20 weeks time this cycle will be 40 weeks past the last true peak. Since there will have been an intermediate trough at around week 306 (half a wavelength, *i.e.* 26 weeks, past the last true peak, week 280), this puts the cycle 14 weeks past this trough, giving it a further 12 weeks or so before it reaches the peak. It is therefore just short of the mid-point of its climb, with a value just below zero, about -$5.

The change from the current position is about +$18. It will continue to climb for 12 weeks.

The 99-week cycle

In 20 weeks time this cycle will be 45 weeks past its trough. It will be 10 weeks short of a peak (half wavelength is 55 weeks). Its estimated value is therefore about $40.

The change from the current position is about +$20. It should top out around week 330 as this 99-week cycle has the greatest magnitude of the three.

From these changes of -$12, zero, +$18 and +$20, we expect a total change of +$26. From Figure 8.13, we can see the change between week 300 and week 320 was approximately $80. Thus, **(very importantly!)**, we have deduced the direction of the change correctly with the estimated amount less than half of the actual change. This is easily explained on the basis of the loss of magnitude when the cycles were extracted using the difference between the two averages.

In summary, we were able to deduce correctly from this study of the individual cycles in the data that the complex data would:

- fall over the following few weeks from week 300
- make a considerable rise by week 320
- probably top out around week 330

Now that we have seen the power of these methods, it is of interest to apply them to some real market data to give us a flavor of what is possible.

CYCLES IN THE MARKET

The discussion in chapter 6 showed there are cycles present in stocks, currencies, etc. These cycles vary from very short term, with wavelengths less than 10 days up to long term cycles with wavelengths of two years or longer. What was not discussed was whether cycles are present in a market index such as the Dow-Jones Index. This index is derived from its 30 constituent companies. If we accept the existence of a four year business cycle, when we consider cycles of shorter wave length, our inclination is to think that each stock is subject to its own individual cyclic movement. Because of this, we expect the cyclic movements of less than 4 years wavelength to have been smoothed out by the averaging effect of the 30 composite stocks. Thus, on the basis of this argument, the only cycle we would expect to see to any great extent in the movements of the Dow-Jones Index would be one with a wavelength of around four years.

In order to view this cycle, a plot of the 207-week (*i.e.* four years) average-minus-average is shown in Figure 8.14. The lower panel shows the Dow-Jones Index from May 1979 to May 1998. The upper panel is the result of the calculation, and is cut off for the last 103 weeks because the calculation is based on a centered average.

The interesting point is that while the four year cycle was fairly regular during the 1980s, it became very distorted around week 700, in 1992. It is now going through a highly unpredictable phase. It could be argued that at the present time (June 1998) the cycle has disappeared. It will return to a regular state some time in the future, but that time is not predictable. During its regular phase it reached a maximum magnitude of around 450 points.

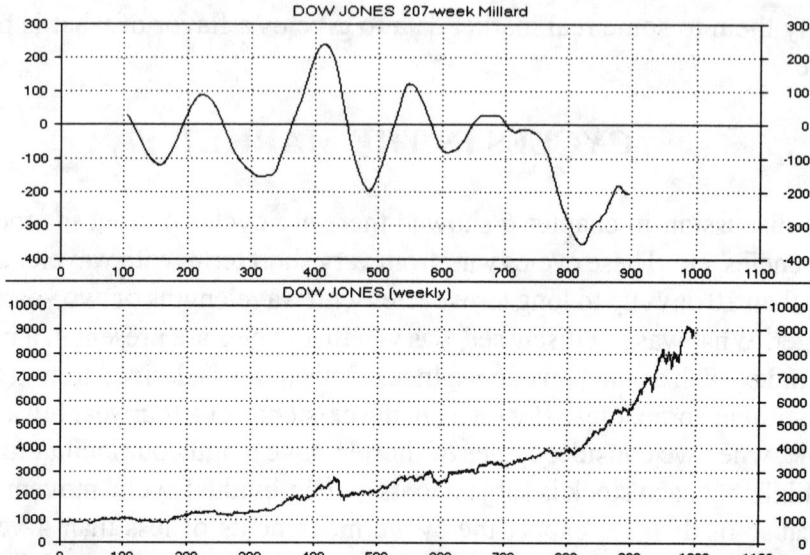

Figure 8.14. *Lower panel: A plot of the weekly closing values of the Dow Jones Index from May 1979 to May 1998. The time axis is marked in weeks to simplify the measurement of wavelengths. Upper panel: the 207-week average-minus-average isolates the four year cycle. The last 103 weeks are lost from the trace.*

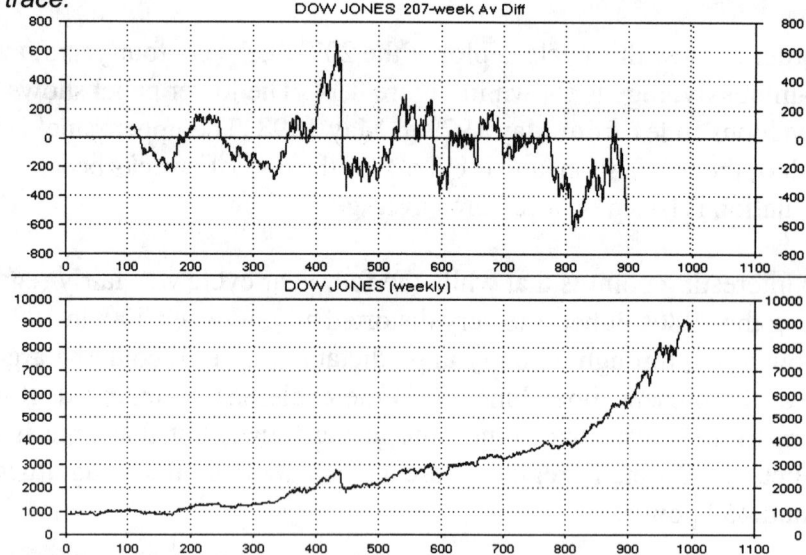

Figure 8.15. *A plot of the 207-week average difference shows the sum of all of the cycles of less than four years wavelength present in the Dow-Jones Index. A number of major peaks about 100 weeks apart can be discerned.*

One laborious way of analyzing for the presence of shorter term cycles would be to use the moving average minus moving average method, running through all the values from say five weeks up to four years. However, we can take a look at the total picture for all cycles of wavelength less than four years by using the four year average difference. If we use weekly data, this means an average difference such as 207 weeks. The result of applying this is shown in the upper panel of Figure 8.15.

A study of this average difference should then tell us if our view that there are no cycles other than four year cycles in the Dow Jones Index is correct. At first sight the plot in Figure 8.15 seems to be meaningless, other than the fact that the sum of all of these movements has made a contribution that has varied from +650 points to -650 points. The time scale has been marked in weeks rather than with dates so the distance between important peaks and troughs can be readily estimated. We note that important peaks occur at approximately 560, 660, 770 and 870 weeks. The differences between these peaks are 100, 100, 110 and 110 weeks. Since this is around two years, we can deduce that there could be a cycle of two year wavelength present in the Dow Jones weekly closes.

This can now be checked by using the average minus average method, using a span of say 103 weeks for the longest span, and 51 weeks for the shortest span (the value of 51 is not critical, similar results will be obtained with 53 or 55). This should isolate cycles of wavelength around 103 weeks if they are present. The result is shown in Figure 8.16. Quite clearly, in the upper panel we see a cycle whose wavelength is a nominal 103 weeks, *i.e.* two years. As expected for real data, we do not have a pure sine wave, but a wave whose wavelength and magnitude are subject to a variation due to the effect of random forces. There is, for example a slight distortion around week 650 due to the presence of a temporary cycle of shorter wavelength. The magnitude has varied from about 250 points to a maximum of about 400 points in 1987. At the most recent calculated point, it is about 350 points. There is a loss of 51 points at the end of the calculation because it is based on a 103-week centered average. Since the cycle is now quite regular, it is possible to estimate how it

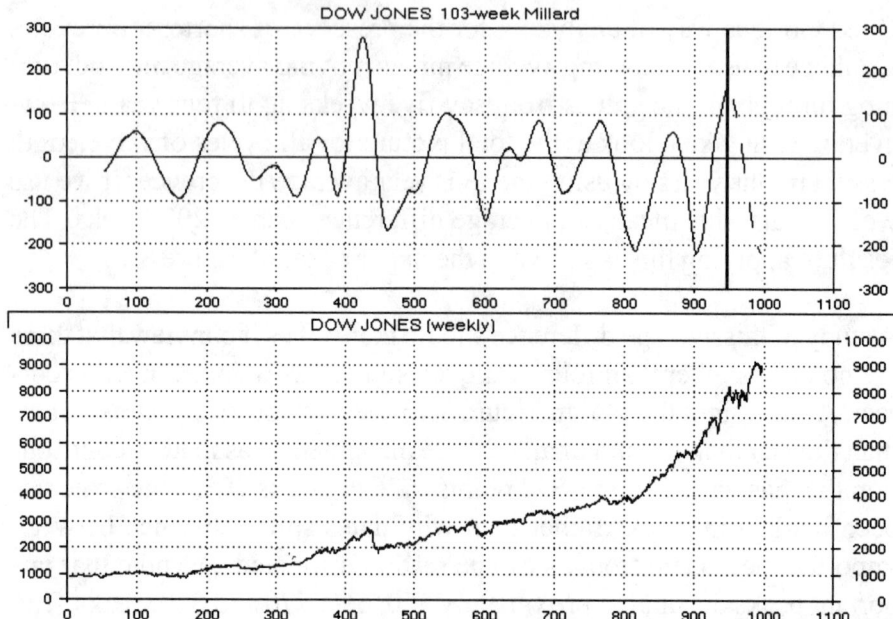

Figure 8.16. *By using a 103-week average-minus-average calculation the presence of a two year cycle in the Dow Jones Index is clearly demonstrated. As expected from real market data, the cycle is subject to a variation in wavelength and magnitude. Since there is a loss of 51 points at the end of the trace from the position of the solid line, the last section (dashed line) of the plot is an estimate. The latest magnitude is about 350 points.*

may have moved over this period, as shown by the dashed line in Figure 8.16.

Many other cycles can be found in the weekly closing of the Dow-Jones Index by this method. In most cases you will find that major peaks and troughs in the cycles in the Dow will be mirrored by peaks and troughs in those stocks containing cycles of similar wavelength. This is the principle of commonality referred to by Hurst.

In the case of individual stocks, we can take **IBM** as an example. The plot of **IBM** weekly closings since February 1994 is shown in Figure 8.17. For anyone skeptical about the presence of cycles in stock market data, this provides an excellent example of the extraction of a clean, 53-

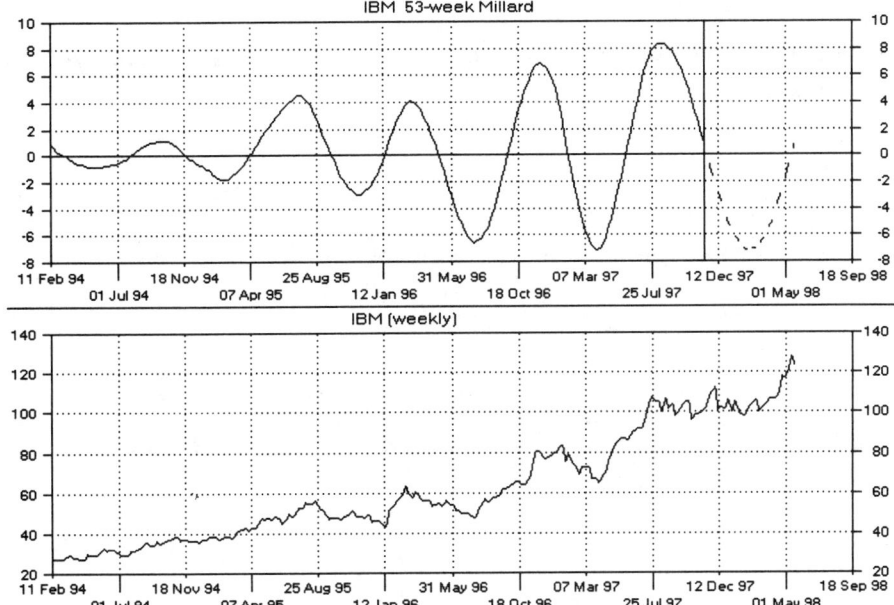

Figure 8.17. *Lower panel: a plot of the weekly closing of IBM since early 1994. Upper panel: the 53-week (one year) cycle extracted by using a 53-week average-minus-average calculation. Since there is a loss of 26 points at the end of the trace from the position of the solid line, the last section (dashed line) of the plot is an estimate. This is an excellent example of the variation in magnitude of cycles in the stock market.*

week (one year) cycle by the use of the average-minus-average method.

The magnitude is steadily increasing over the period. This is an illustration of the principle of variation that operates on cycles in real market data. You can also see a correlation between troughs and peaks in this cycle and the start and end of upward legs in the stock price movement.

The latest magnitude of this cycle can be estimated as $15. Since by the method used there is an attenuation of the magnitude, the real contribution to the most recent upward movement in the stock price will be greater than this. By inspection of the original data, the trough in the stock price occurred on April 4, 1997, with the stock at $64⁵/₈, and by July 25 the price had reached $107. While not all of this rise is attributable to the 53-

week cycle, and shorter wavelength cycles will have made a contribution, this does suggest that the estimated magnitude of the 53-week cycle is much too low.

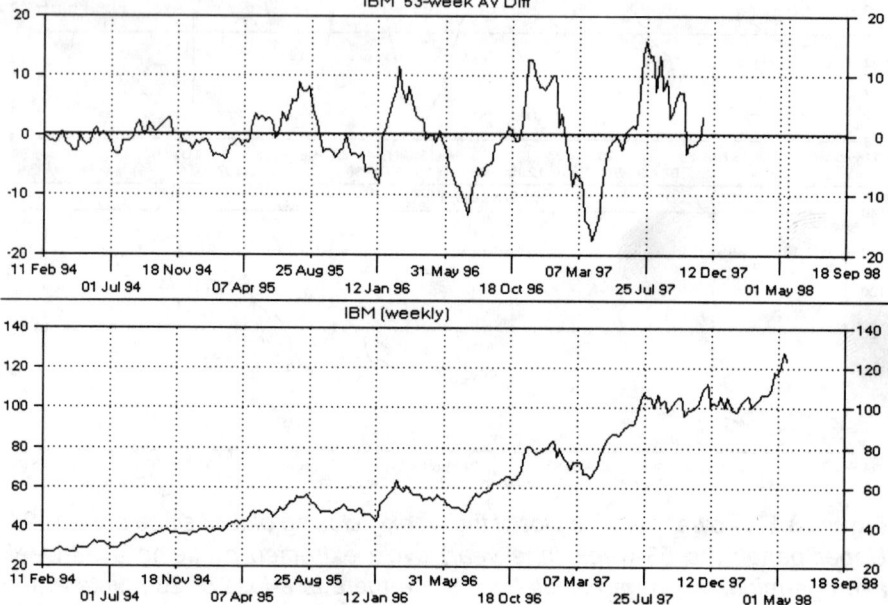

Figure 8.18. *The 53-week average difference of the weekly closing values of* **IBM** *show all those cycles with wavelengths of 53 weeks and less.*

An appreciation of the contribution made by all cycles of 53-week or shorter wavelength can be made by the use of a 53-week average difference. This is shown in Figure 8.18. You can now see that this complex sum of cycles was responsible for a rise of at least $32 from the low point on April 4, 1997.

Cycles can only be used in a predictive sense when they are going through a regular phase. Thus, the four year cycle in the Dow-Jones Index, Figure 8.14 is useless from this point of view. The 53-week cycle in **IBM** is a different matter. Because it is still sinusoidal in shape, we can, extrapolate it to the present time and on into the near future (Figure 8.17). Since we have seen the magnitude increasing, we expect it to peak out at a value of around $10. The time of this peak should be about 53 weeks from the last peak, on August 15, 1997. This gives us August 21, 1998 as the probable maximum of this 53-week cycle. Since at the last data point, on May 22, 1998 the stock was at $123^5/_8$, and the value of the cycle was around zero, we would anticipate a rise of at least $10 in the stock price by late August unless shorter term cycles are already falling and acting in the opposite direction. Similar methods would have to be applied to isolate shorter term cycles before action could be taken. As shown in the next chapter, this method is used together with channel analysis so that investment decisions are taken when the two methods are consistent with each other.

These few examples serve to show how, by a simple, if tedious, set of calculations, important information about the status of various cycles in market data can be determined. The calculations can readily be carried out with a spreadsheet, or a number of investment software packages. We can either look at the total contribution made by a group of cycles, as was shown in the **IBM** case, or that made by a specific cycle, again illustrated by **IBM**. By this means we can find out if that particular cycle is going through a regular phase when its contribution to the overall movement can be estimated, or through a disordered phase when its contribution cannot be quantified.

CHAPTER 9

Applications of Numerical Analysis

In this chapter we apply the methods discussed in chapters 7 and 8 to real market data. For each of the examples we will display channels that are based on templates derived from a smoothed moving average calculation, showing how the particular spans were chosen. The channels will be constructed at points of interest on the historical chart to see how they would have predicted the movement from that point in time. At the same point in time an analysis of the status of important cycles will also be investigated in order to act as confirmation or otherwise of the message being given by channel analysis. Rather than repeating the term *'average-minus-average'* calculation, giving the span of both centered averages, we will use the term *'cycle highlighter'* to mean the same thing, specifying the span of the largest of the two averages, for example *53-week cycle highlighter.*

As in chapter 6, the stepwise approach of using weekly and then daily data is most efficient. Some of the examples used here were also analyzed in chapter 6 by the graphical method. We will see that the channels produced by calculation will be quite similar. Since centered averages produce channels that terminate half a span back in time from the last data point, a computer program such as **Microvest 5.0™** (see Appendix) uses a quadratic curve fitting routine based on the last few calculated points to extrapolate the channels to the present and into the future. Such a program also adjusts the vertical position of the channels to achieve the permitted number of points to lie outside the channel boundaries. If these extrapolated channels are violated by the price, then they have to be bent in one direction or another to remove the violation. To do this, exactly the same logic has to be applied as in the graphical method. A more detailed look is taken in chapter 10 at such turning points in channels.

DELTA AIRLINES IN DECEMBER 1994

The position for **Delta Airlines** with daily data on December 22, 1994 is shown in Figure 9.1. The stock had fallen each day from December 19 when it closed at $47^1/8$ and close of $45^3/4$ on the 22nd before jumping the next day to $49^5/8$. Channel analysis by the graphical method in chapter 6 indicated the stock was near a rising lower boundary and therefore could be bought. The channel calculated from a centered moving average span 201 days is shown in the lower panel. This span was chosen because a 200-day unlagged average is typically chosen by chartists as a sign that the long term trend is rising. The dotted lines show where the boundaries are estimated to lie between the last calculated point (100 days ago) and the current time. Quite clearly the channel is well past its turning point and has been rising for some time. The daily falls in price from December 19 took the stock down to the estimated position of the lower boundary on December 22. The investor could not buy at this point because the price was still falling, and a trough has to be formed to confirm the position of the lower boundary. Thus, as discussed in chapter 6, the investor would be forced to wait until the 23rd. A rise during the early part of the 23rd would have given the investor some indication the stock would close higher, thereby forming the required trough. It is of interest to see if the use of cycle analysis could have anticipated the jump in price by the close on December 23, so the investor could have gotten into the stock a day earlier.

We can see in the lower panel of Figure 9.1 a previous occasion when there was a trough in the data that bounced up from the boundary since the boundary changed direction. This point is October 6, 1994, and is 54 days back from December 22. Since on December 22 we are expecting a bounce up from the boundary within a day or so. This means we would have two troughs about 54 days apart, signifying a cycle with a wavelength of 54 days. We can use a 53-day cycle highlighter to check the status of this cycle. This is shown in the upper panel of Figure 9.1, with the estimated movement of the cycle since the last calculated point 26 days ago shown as a dashed line. We see that the cycle is about to bottom out, and its magnitude is just over $4. Allowing for the loss in magnitude by the process of isolating the cycle, we might expect the true magnitude to be around $6.

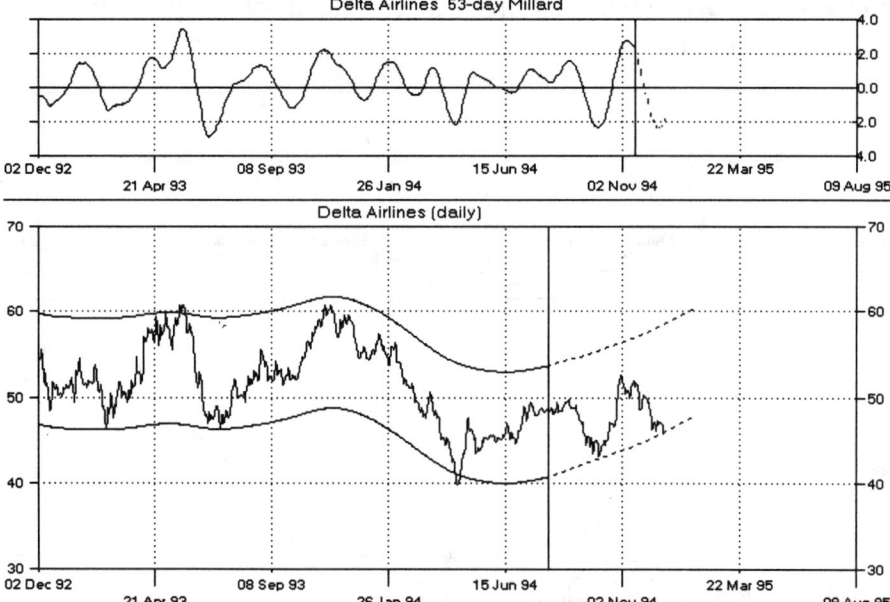

Figure 9.1. *Lower panel: plot of daily closing prices of Delta Airlines December 22, 1994. The channel is derived from a calculation of a centered 201-day average. The estimated portion of the channel is shown by the dashed boundaries. Upper panel: cycle analysis using 53-day cycle highlighter. The last calculated point is indicated by the vertical solid line. The dashed line is the estimation of the cycle from that point in time.*

From this evidence we come to the conclusion that a short term up trend will soon begin, or has perhaps just started, this should take the price up by at least $6 over the next half cycle, 26 days. Since the channel is also rising, and rose nearly $2 during 26 days, this rise will be added in. The expectation is for a rise of nearly $8 from the current level of $45³/₄ over the next 26 days when the 53-day cycle will reach its peak. This gives us a short term target level of around $54. We are comfortable that, on the morning of December 23, with the price rising from the opening of the market, it is correct to buy **Delta**

Airlines, at a price of around $50 to $50¹/₈.

The price rose quite steadily from this point, and it is interesting to see if there was any indication of the topping out of the 53-day trend around 26 days on from December 22. There was such an indication, because the price reached $56 some 20 days on from December 22, compared with the prediction for a rise to $54 in this time.

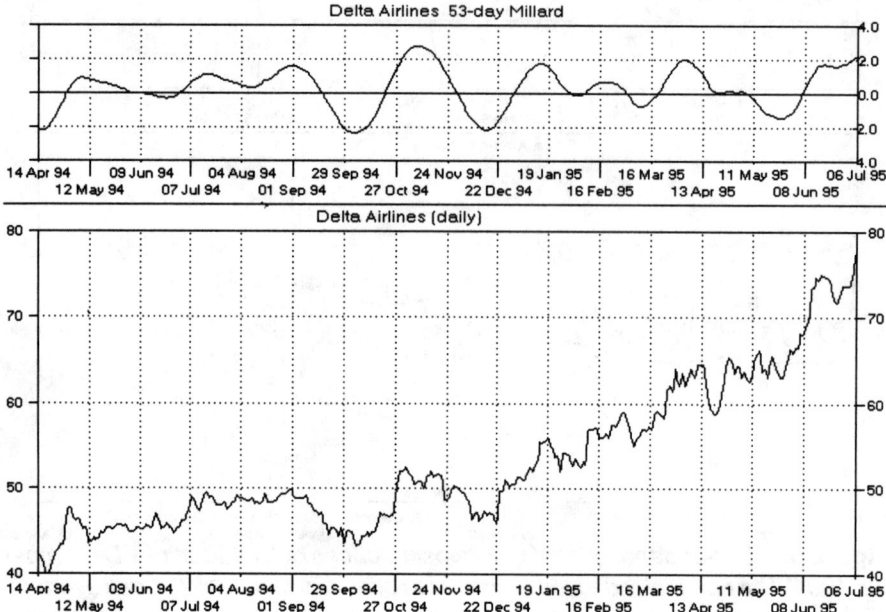

Figure 9.2. *Lower panel: daily closing prices of **Delta Airlines**. Upper panel: the cycle analysis using 53-day cycle highlighter. The 53-day cycle becomes distorted from January 1995.*

Figure 9.2 shows that after a small dip, the price rose quite steadily over the next few months. The upper panel shows the 53-day cycle over the next few months. While it still existed over the months following the decision to buy in late December, you can see it became distorted by interference from cycles of shorter wavelength. We were only able to use this cycle in December as an aid to our decision to buy because it became symmetrical and therefore predictable. It is vital that decisions are not taken when a cycle is distorted, because any extrapolation to the current time from the cut-off point will be subject to considerable error.

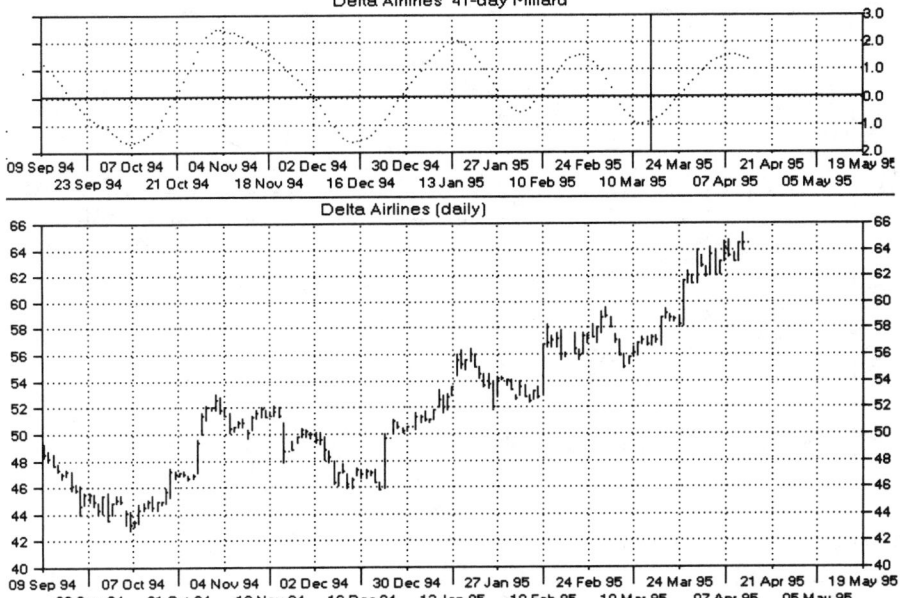

Figure 9.3. *Lower panel: daily ranges in **Delta Airlines** up to April 1995. Upper panel: the 41-day cycle highlighter shows a regular 41-day cycle that is just topping out in April. The cycle is estimated from the last calculated point, the position of the vertical solid line.*

Figure 9.3, shows the daily ranges in **Delta Airlines** up to April 1995. The upper panel shows the result of applying the 41-day cycle highlighter. In this case this short term cycle was quite regular during the period following the buying decision in December.

Japanese Yen in 1995

A channel drawn for the Yen/US$ ratio in August 1995 is shown in the lower panel of Figure 9.4. Only one channel is drawn, because the main point to be made from this chart is the similarity in shape between the 201-day cycle extracted by the highlighter and this channel. The cycle had an estimated magnitude of around 5.1 during 1994/95, but the true value would have been higher.

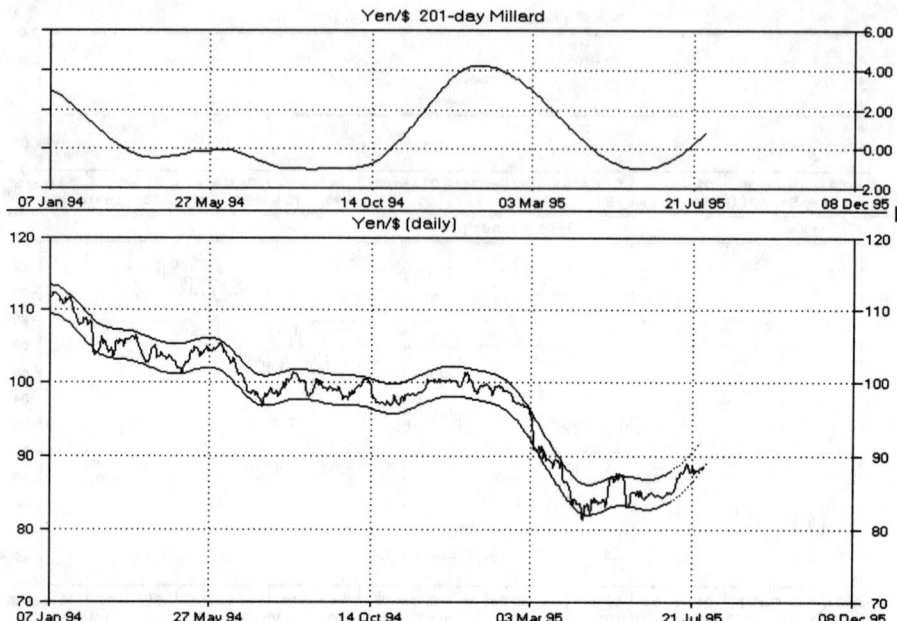

Figure 9.4. *Lower panel: A single channel drawn for the Yen/US$ ratio. Upper panel: the 201-day cycle highlighter shows the 201 day cycle is very similar in shape. This leads us to expect a considerable rise in the channel, therefore carrying the price higher.*

Because of similarity in shape, the investor, when viewing the situation at this point in time, would feel the channel is due for a rise. On the basis of symmetry, you could expect the channel to rise back to the 100 level. Since the cycle would be expected to reach its next peak around September/October 1995, it can be anticipated that the channel would top out at the same time at a ratio of about 100. The ratio of 88.305 on the August 2, as discussed in chapter 6, has placed the ratio at a point close to the rising boundary, so that the investor could now take a decision.

In this instance, the medium term cycle has performed the same function as a second, outer channel in giving a target where the ratio should move. The ratio rose more rapidly than anticipated, reaching 104 within six weeks of the decision point on August 2.

GOLD IN 1993

The chart of the gold price to April 21, 1993 is shown in Figure 9.5. A channel has been calculated and drawn by using a 35-day centered average as a template. The gap of 26 days has been estimated and is shown as a dashed line. The two peaks in July and September 1992 in the channel,

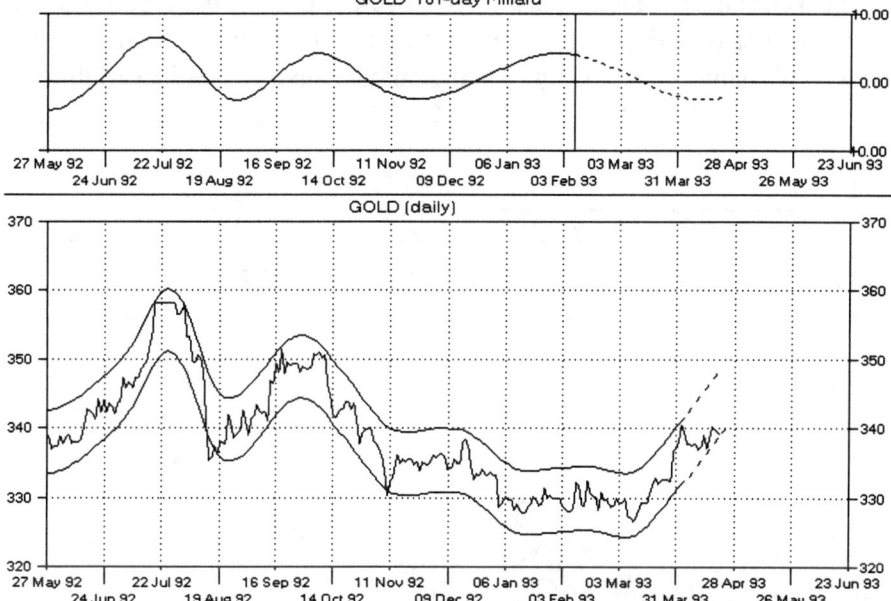

Figure 9.5. *Lower panel: a chart of the gold price to April 21, 1993. The channel drawn is similar to the inner channel in Figure 6.15 (chapter 6). Upper panel: the 101-day cycle has probably just bottomed out and will give an impetus to the upward movement of the channel.*

and the trough in August 1992 were obviously due to a cycle with large magnitude. The separating two peaks is about 52 days, with the trough at midway. This means that a cycle of wavelength 52 days was present at that section of the chart, but unfortunately, this cycle subsequently diminished to a very low magnitude, so it cannot be used for predicting future movement. When a 101-day cycle was tested by the highlighter, the trace given in the upper panel was obtained. This shows that this medium term cycle had just passed its bottom and therefore will be available to give additional impetus to the gold price (already in a channel that has been rising for some 25 days.)

GEC

A **GEC** channel was given in chapter 6 as an example of gradually increasing wavelength and magnitude, and is shown again in the lower panel of Figure 9.6 with just a single channel drawn. When a 207-week highlighter was used to extract the four year cycle, the trace shown in the upper panel was obtained. You can see the nominal four year cycle appears to be responsible for the major peaks and troughs in the channel, but this cycle is subject to a substantial change in wavelength and magnitude. Since the vertical gridlines

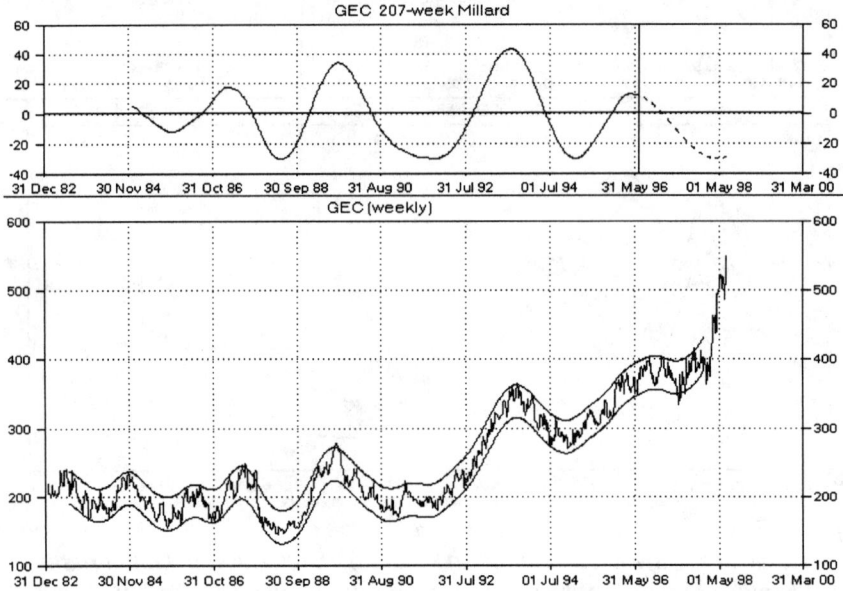

Figure 9.6. *Lower panel: a channel calculated for **GEC**, a good example of the principle of variation in wavelength and magnitude. Upper panel: the 207-week (four year) cycle produced by the cycle highlighter shows that this nominal cycle was mainly responsible for the peaks and troughs in the channel.*

are 100 weeks apart, it is possible to get an appreciation of the wavelength changes by the horizontal distance between successive peaks and troughs. These are 65, 69, 94 and 67 weeks, so the wavelength, being double, passes through the values 130, 138, 188 and 134 weeks. This means the average wavelength of the cycle was closer to three years than four. Since a three year cycle is quite unusual in the UK stocks, the apparent wavelength of three

years is due to a mixture of a four year and a two year cycle which can appear
as a three year cycle.

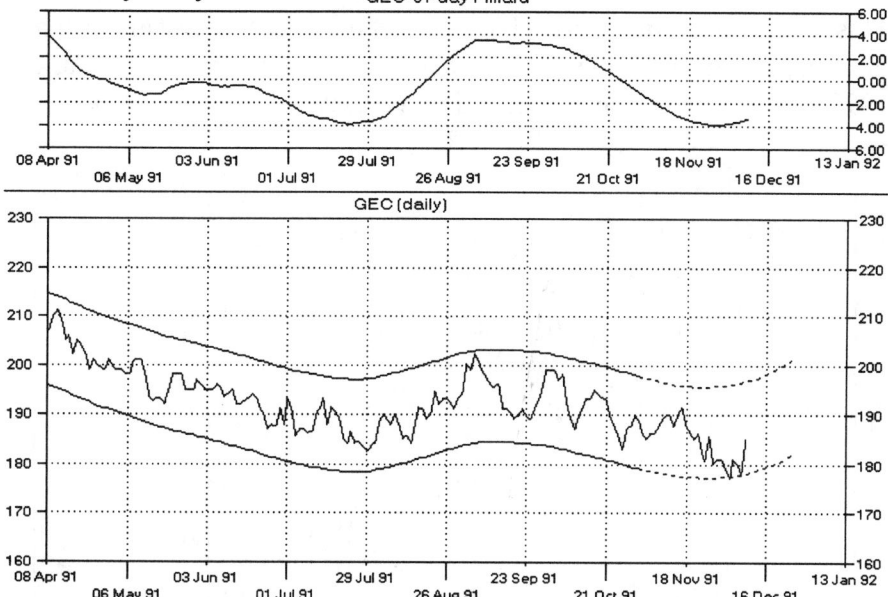

Figure 9.7. *Lower panel: the position in* **GEC** *on December 9, 1991. This point is prior to a very large rise in the stock that almost tripled its price in less than two years. The single channel drawn is now headed up the price having bounced up from the lower boundary. Upper panel: The two major troughs in the channel are about 90 weeks apart. This suggest a 91-week cycle highlighter should be applied as shown. The major cycle is just past the bottom. Its effect should be to boost the rise in the channel.*

Figure 9.7 shows the position in **GEC** on December 9, 1991, a point chosen because the price made a very large advance from that point. The channel has been rising for a few weeks after turning up in early November, and the price has bounced up from the lower boundary that ran through the two closely spaced troughs in the price movement. The two major troughs in the channel itself are some 90 days apart, and therefore suggests that a cycle of this wavelength is becoming important. Because of this the cycle highlighter was used with a span of 91 days, with the result shown in the upper panel. This cycle has just past its low point, and therefore could be expected to make a further contribution to the upward direction of the channel. This confirms that the investor could have bought the stock at that time.

IBM IN DECEMBER 1993

This stock and this time period have been chosen because just after a major turning point in **IBM,** the stock rose from a low of around $20 in August 1993 to over $100 in a few years. It is important to demonstrate that

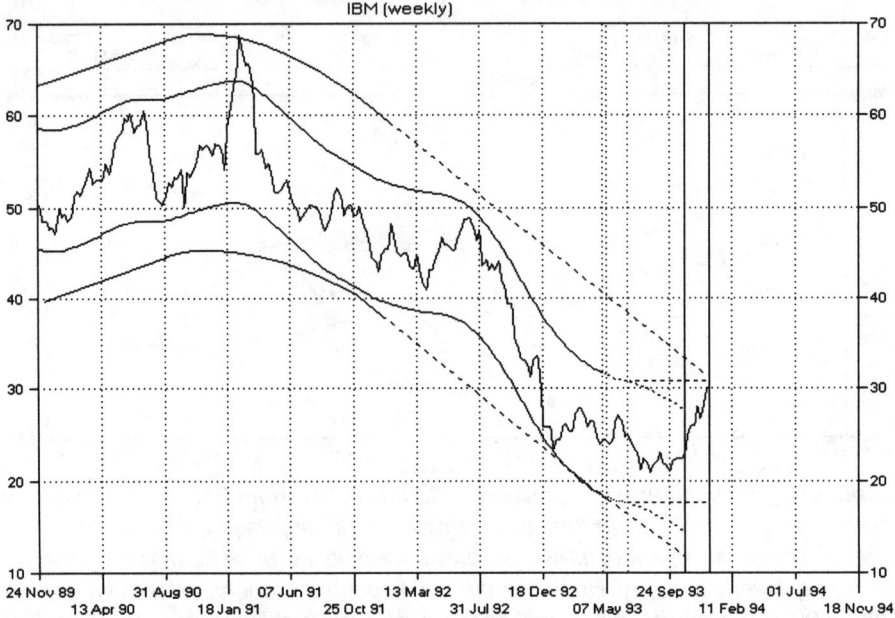

Figure 9.8. *The weekly closing prices of **IBM**. The inner channel is based on a 53-week centered average, and the outer on a longer span. The solid vertical lines show the position at two points in time, October 29, 1993 and December 23, 1993. In October, the extrapolation of the inner channel shows it still falling, by December, the rise in price to just under $30 forces the channel to run horizontally. The investor would now be interested in the stock.*

channel analysis can deal with such turning points, getting the investor into a stock in as short a time as possible after the turn while capturing a large percentage of the rise.

A chart of the weekly closing prices is shown in Figure 9.8. There are two vertical lines on the chart, one at the last data point, on December 24, 1993 and the other two months before on October 29, 1993. The reason for showing these is to emphasize the change that will have occurred in a calculation of the channel at these two points. The inner channel is produced from a centered 53-week average, and the outer channel by a similar calculation using a longer term average.

On October 29, the stock closed at $23. This was a rise of almost $3 from its lowest point on August 13. The inner channel boundaries produced by the channel extrapolation on October 29, are the falling dashed lines. The extrapolation of the outer channel also shows the boundaries as the more or less straight, dashed, lines. This outer channel is also falling on October 29 and is expected to continue at least a few weeks. At this point the investor comes to the conclusion that because the extrapolated outer and inner channels are both falling, there is no opportunity to invest at this point. The investor can also see the stock price is nearing the falling upper boundary of the inner channel, Thus, at this time all the signs are negative.

By December 24, the inner channel can be extrapolated as running more or less horizontally. The main reason for this is the price had risen consistently from its value of $23 in late October to $29 $7/8$ by the close on the 24th. If the boundary was still drawn as continuing in the same direction as it was in late October, then this price level would be considerably above the upper boundary. The only way to avoid this violation of the upper boundary of the inner channel by the price is to force the channel to run horizontally. If the following week's closing price rises even higher, then this would force the channel to an even higher position, so it would then be rising, rather than progressing horizontally. This would be a very positive signal to consider buying the stock.

Since the investor would have been aware in early December that the rate of descent of the 53-week channel had slowed down rapidly, and it would be expected to reverse direction in the near future. It would have been prudent to look at daily data from the beginning of December onward so that changes in the daily channels could be analyzed for early indication of a change in climate for **IBM**.

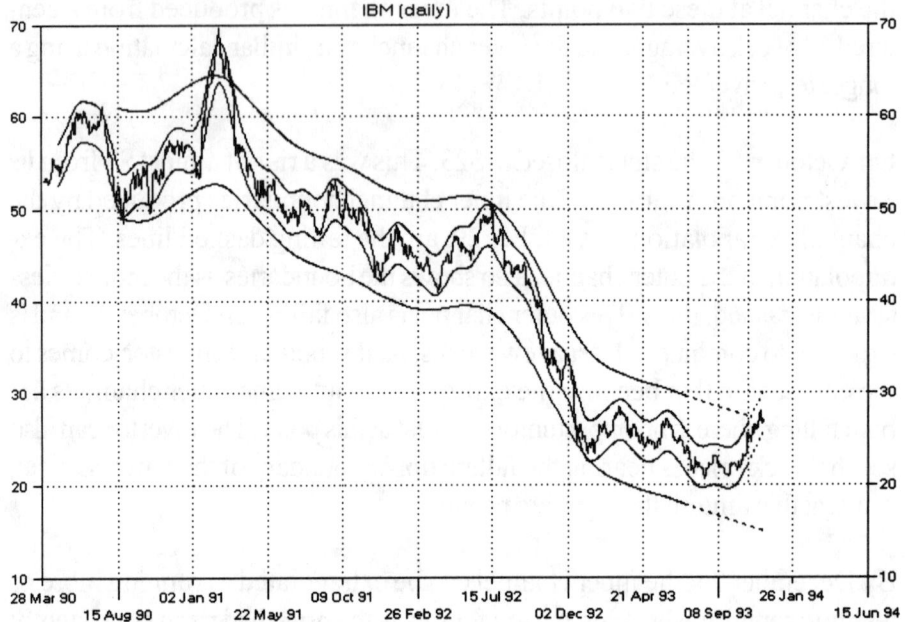

Figure 9.9. *IBM daily closing prices on December 3, 1993. The outer channel is a 210-day channel and the inner a 41-day channel. Each channel has been extrapolated by curve fitting, these sections being shown as dashed lines.*

The position on December 3, 1993 is shown in Figure 9.9. The two channels that have been drawn are based on a 210-day average and a 41-day average. The reason for using a 201-day average has been commented on previously, and is that this, or rather the 200-day version of it, is widely used by technical analysts. The 41-day average is used to show up short term trends because it represents two months of trading days. The averages are extended by curve fitting technique. You can see that this type of extrapolation causes two problems. First, the outer boundary will pass below the level of the most recent prices and second, the rising upper boundary of the inner channel will clash with the falling upper boundary of the outer channel. Obviously the position of the boundaries must be changed.

In our rules for extrapolating channels, it was stated we should work from the outer channels inwards. The first step is to recognize that we must bend the

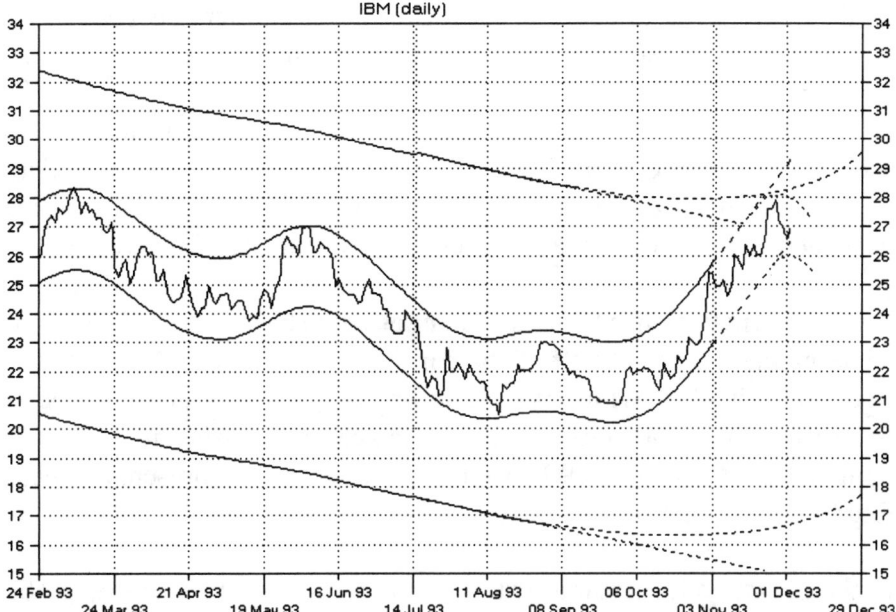

Figure 9.10. *An enlarged section of the plot from Figure 9.9. The original extrapolation of the channels are the straight dashed lines. The curved lines for the outer channel are the result of bending the channel to avoid the peak in November 1993. The curved lines for the inner channel are because it now has to bounce back from the upper boundary of the outer channel.*

outer channel up to an extent that at the very least will pass through the recent high point of $27.875 on November 26. Then we must make the inner channel bounce back down from this. These changes are shown in the expanded plot in Figure 9.10. The original extrapolations are shown as almost straight dashed lines. The new, minimum position of the outer channel to clear the peak of November 26 can be seen as a curved dashed line, and the inner channel is now made to bounce back down. These new positions crystallize the view that the peak on November 26 is the highest to be expected for the immediate future, and that the price will now fall to the rising lower boundary in a period of days. Applying the principle of symmetry to the inner channel at its bending point in late November 1993, we expect the fall to last for perhaps seven or eight weeks. This is how long the inner channel took to rise from its last trough in late September. Since we would not contemplate an investment until we are sure the price has just rebounded from a lower rising boundary, this would mean a wait of perhaps six weeks from the present.

Note that this new position for the outer channel is the lowest in a vertical sense commensurate with avoiding the November peak. The channel might well have risen at a greater rate than that depicted in Figure 9.10, but we have no evidence from the channels or price data that that might be the case.

It is important to realize the **outer channel**, being based on a 201-day centered average, **is the result of the combination of all cycles that are present in the data whose wavelengths are greater than 201 days.** In order to confirm we are correct in drawing this channel as rising from a turning point around November 1993, we need to establish the present and near future status of the important cycles of longer wavelengths.

Of the known cycles in market data, the most appropriate to isolate would be the one year cycle, since it is closest in wavelength to 201 days. There are other reasons why it is a good choice: first, there will be less cut off data than with longer wavelengths, so we have less of a gap across to extrapolate to the present, and second its effect will be more immediate than cycles of longer wavelength if we establish that this cycle is just coming off its low point.

This cycle is shown in the upper panel of Figure 9.11. The extrapolation of the cycle to the present shows its probable position to be past the bottom and about to rise substantially over the next half cycle, *i.e.* six months. Since the message from this is in total agreement with the estimation of the 201-day channel, we now have a very positive climate for the medium term future movement of **IBM** stock. However, the short term climate is quite different. We should never invest in a stock that is near to our estimation of the position of an upper boundary. This is exactly the position with **IBM** on December 3.

Our expectation is that the inner channel will soon move downwards, taking the price with it, so we now need to wait until the inner channel is close to the lower boundary of the outer channel and ready to bounce upwards.

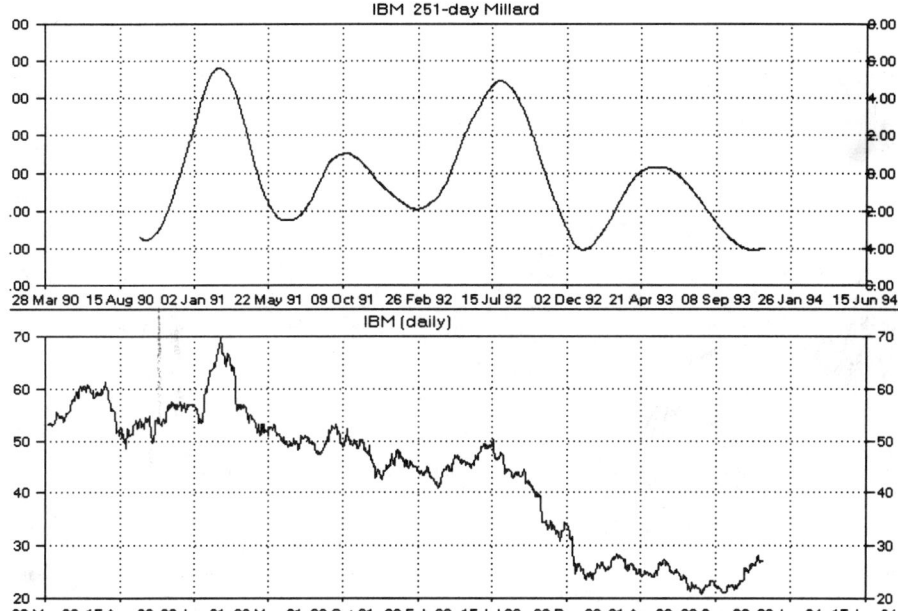

Figure 9.11. *Lower panel: **IBM** daily closing prices on December 3, 1993. Upper panel: the 251-day cycle highlighter shows that the one year cycle has probably just passed its bottom.*

This position is reached in April 1994, as shown in Figure 9.12. The figure shows the channels as calculated in November 1994, so the position of the channels in December 1993 and April 1994 is the real position, these two points in time being well before the last calculated data point in the outer channel. You can see the estimation that the price was near the top of the outer channel was not far off the mark, the price was three-quarters of the way up from the lower boundary. The arrow marks the point in April 1994 it would be considered the time for buying **IBM.** The inner channel had fallen from the top boundary, and the dashed line shows the estimate of the position of the outer channel at that time. Clearly, the inner channel would be estimated as having bounced up from the lower boundary and the time to buy had arrived.

In retrospect, this was an excellent decision. It is interesting to point out the difference between the estimated position of the lower boundary in April, shown by the dashed line, and the real position, showed by the solid channel.

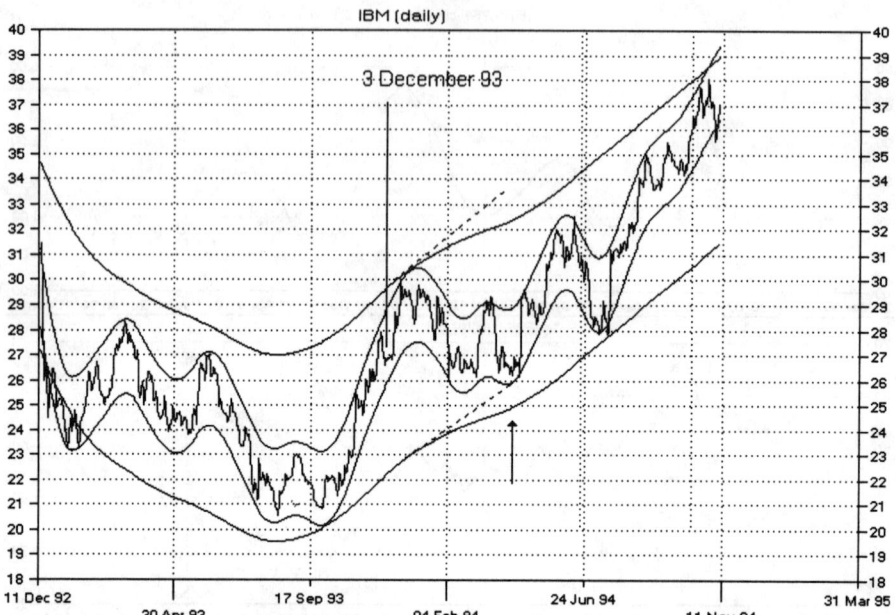

Figure 9.12. *The subsequent movement of **IBM** stock. The channels are now calculated through to November 1994, their actual position on December 3, 1993. Our estimate that the price was near the upper boundary and that it would be premature to buy can now be seen to be correct. The arrow indicates the point (April 1994) where the stock would be bought, since the dashed line shows the estimated position of the outer boundary at that time.*

The estimate of the channel position was high by about $1, but the inner channel never quite reached this low. The inner channel therefore changed direction at the estimated position of the outer channel and not the real position! However, the estimated position still represented a low risk area at the time, and therefore an investment was justified.

If the dashed lines are extended into the future, they give an indication of the target area into which the stock could be expected to move once bought in April 1994. This would be around the $35 to $37 level. As each day went by, the estimate of the channel boundaries would have been updated, and by late May, the estimate of the upper boundary would have been much lower, than the estimate made in April. Thus, when the price reached $32, it would have been quite close to the upper boundary and the investor would be looking for a selling signal.

IBM IN JULY 1994

The chart in Figure 9.12 shows there was another buying opportunity in **IBM** in July 1994 when the inner channel approached the lower boundary of the outer channel. The position on July 19, with the estimated position of both channels is shown in Figure 9.13. The price at the close was \$27³/₄. The investor is now waiting for a rise from this point so as to form a trough in the price at the lower boundary. The price closed on the 20th just below \$28. The trough was formed by this rise, and the investor would be looking for the best opportunity to buy on the July 21.

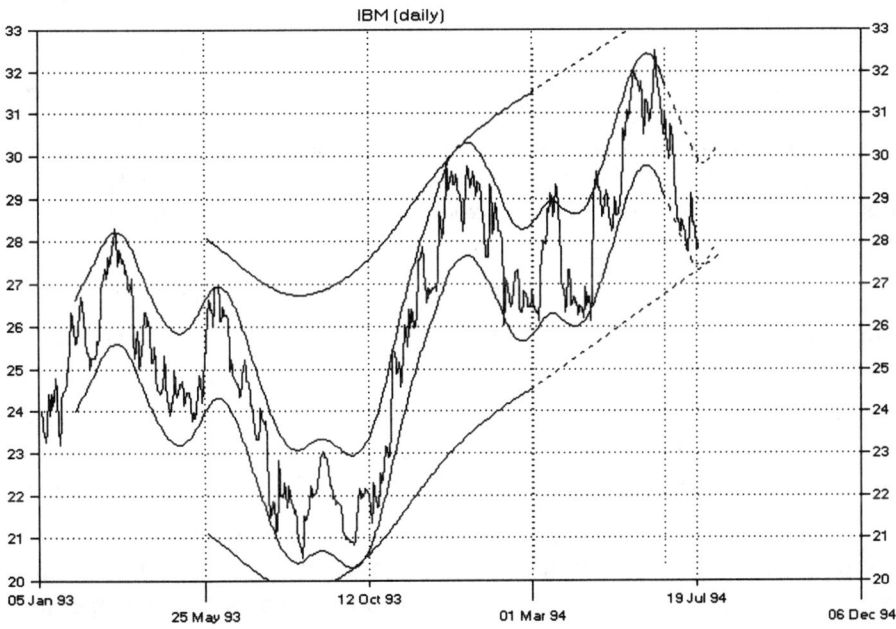

Figure 9.13. *The position in **IBM** on July 19, 1994. The estimated channels are shown as dashed lines. The inner channel is expected to bounce off the lower boundary of the rising outer channel a matter of days. The investor would watch closely for a price rise from the boundary.*

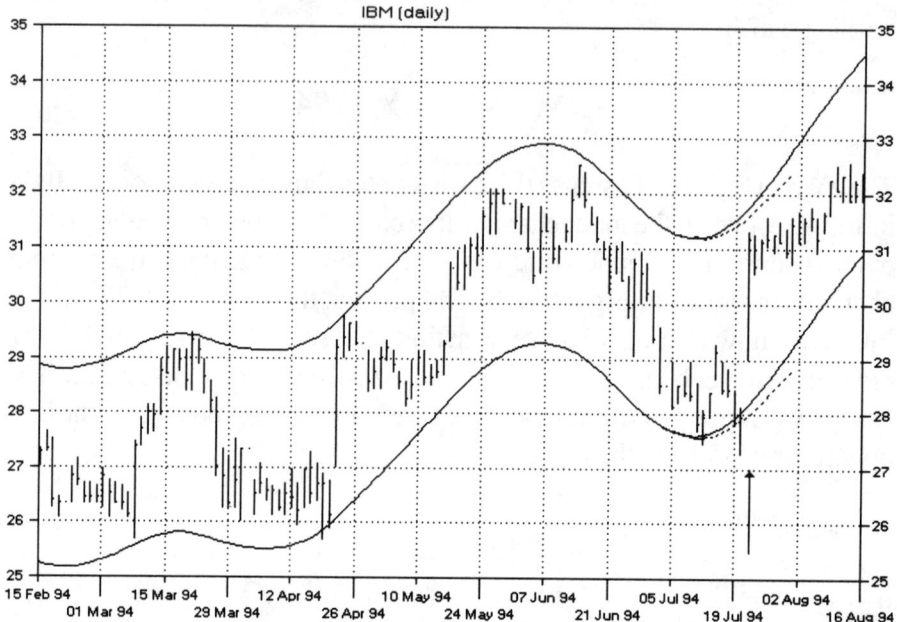

Figure 9.14. *The daily ranges in* **IBM**. *The solid line channel is the actual channel drawn from data that lies in the future. The dashed lines are the estimates of the boundaries made after the close on July 20, 1994 to allow the closing price of just below $28 to lie on the boundary. Note how good the estimate was. The arrow marks July 21.*

A new estimate could be made of the position of the inner channel boundaries after the close on the 20th by making the trough formed by this small rise to lie on the estimated boundary. This is shown in Figure 9.14, that also shows the actual channels as calculated some time in the future. These show how excellent an estimation of the boundary was obtained by this approach. The arrow marks the day of July 21. The price opened at $29³/₄ before falling back to $29. This opening was a long way above the estimated lower boundary, and the investor was now convinced that **IBM** is bouncing upwards at a rapid rate. The careful investor would note that the price fell back from the opening, and, in line with our rule not to buy while the price is falling, would hold off until the price rose from the low point of $29. The investor should have been able to get below $30, and would have been pleased by a close at just over $31. The stock moves sideways for a few days more before resuming a rapid upward rise.

Figure 9.15. *The Sydney All-Ordinary Index showing two major lows during the period. Since they are about two years apart, this suggests that a strong two-year cycle is in being at this time.*

AUSTRALIAN STOCK EXCHANGE

In common with stock exchanges across the world, the Sydney exchange suffered a fall at the onset of the Gulf crisis due to the potential threat to world oil supplies. In retrospect, the fall was not as severe as on other stock markets, you can see from the chart of the Australian All-Ordinary Index in Figure 9.15. You can see that in addition to the sustained 400 point fall during the second half of 1990, a loss of almost similar proportions occurred from mid-1992. These falls created two major troughs at 1204.5 on January 16, 1991 and 1365.1 on November 17, 1992. Since these are just two months short of being two years apart, they could be considered the successive low points of a two year cycle. We will look at both of these interesting points on the chart to see how channel and cycle analysis dealt with the climb back from these falls.

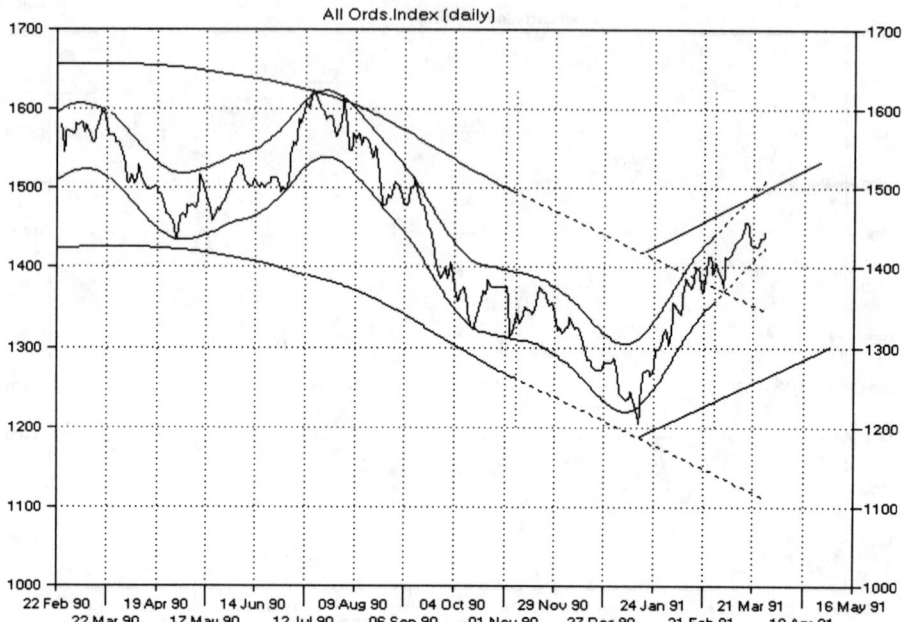

Figure 9.16. *The Australian All-Ordinary Index. The channels as they would be extrapolated in March 1991 would obviously run well below the last month of data. By re-drawing the channels to form a symmetrical turning point as shown, the data is kept within the channel. As now drawn, a rebound of the Index downwards should occur soon.*

Turning point in January 1991

The first major trough in early 1991 is shown on an enlarged scale in Figure 9.16. The extrapolation of the outer 201-day channels by the software curve fit routine (or by eye) results in more or less straight parallel boundaries. The obvious problem is that the level of the Index at the time the channels are drawn is much higher than the upper boundary. As in other examples, the only way to avoid this is to put a bend in the channel to take the upper boundary to at least the level of the highest recent point, which in this example is the latest point.

Since the extrapolated channels are such straight lines, a quick way of gaining an impression of the probable direction of the channels is to invoke the principle of symmetry around the turning point and draw a new channel with boundaries running up at the same slope they were running down to the turning point. The best initial estimate of the position of the turning point in the channel is the major low point on January 16, so this can be made the junction of the two opposing channels. By doing this, the upper boundary then clears quite comfortably the recent peak of 1456.5 on March 19. As drawn, there is no great expectation for a significant rise in the All-Ordinary at this point, since the inner channel, produced by a 41-day centered average, is getting closer to this upper boundary, a bounce down should occur within a few weeks.

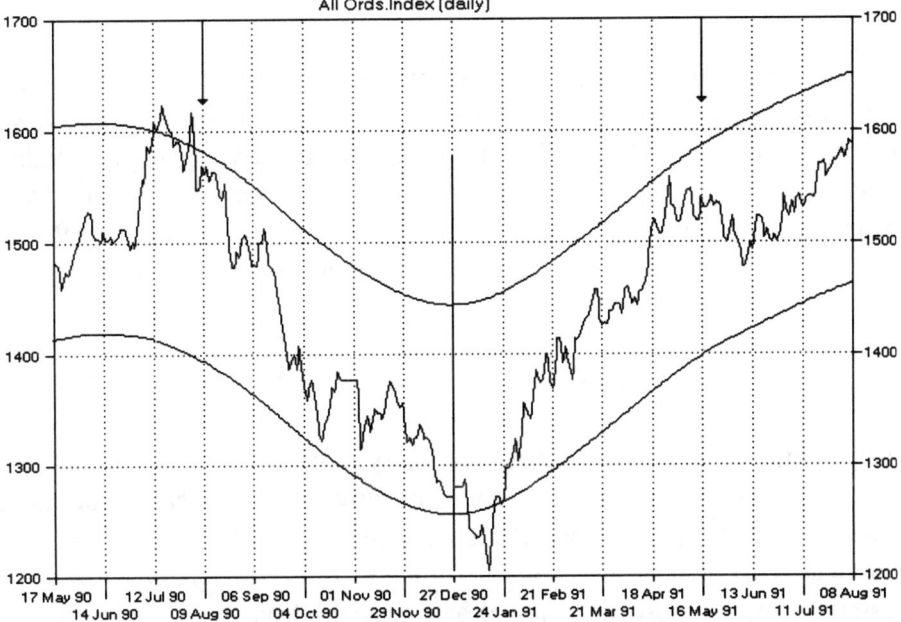

Figure 9.17. *The turning point on January 16, 1991 in the Australian All-Ordinary Index. The 201-day channel is an excellent example of almost perfect symmetry between the two points marked with arrows.*

The interesting point about this exercise in symmetry is that this turning point in the Australian Index is one of the most symmetrical to be found. This is shown in Figure 9.17, where the actual channels are shown. These are real because they were calculated from a point much further into the future. The center point of the turn is shown by the solid vertical line, and the almost perfect symmetry extends out to the arrows on either side. As can be seen, the vertical positions of the boundaries at the positions of these arrows are virtually identical. The position of the boundaries as drawn by the method shown in Figure 9.15 is excellent. The only major difference is that the actual turning point in the channel doesn't exactly coincide with the low point in the Index itself, but this is a frequent feature of channel analysis. It happens because as was stated in an earlier chapter, two components decide the exact turning point—the change between the current data point and the next one, and the change between the first data point in the span, which is due to be dropped from the total and the next one in the data set. This will be discussed in the next chapter.

The reason for this high degree of symmetry is because of the dominance, over this period of time, of the two year cycle which is just reaching its low point on January 16. There is little interference by one year cycles that might have caused distortion. It can also be seen from Figure 9.17 how good an estimate of the upper boundary position were the lines drawn in Figure 9.16. The peak on March 19 is now seen to be comfortably below the upper boundary of the channel.

Turning point in November 1992

The position in the Australian All-Ordinary Index on January 29, 1993 is shown in Figure 9.18. The turning point on November 17, 1992 can be considered to have the same characteristics as the one in 1991, because an extrapolation of outer channel by the end of January 1993 has it falling in almost a straight line. Because of this it is clear that the rise from the major low point takes the Index above the initial estimate of the position of the upper boundary. The first minor peak on December 14, at 1512.4 is just about on the estimated boundary, but the next minor peak on December 21 at 1537 takes the Index slightly above the boundary, while the latest peak of 1464 on January 5 is well above the boundary. This means that quite a major adjustment is called for, and in view of the straight line nature of the extrapolated channel, the same construction can be employed as previously. This is shown in Figure 9.18, where the change of direction is taken to be the low point on November 17, 1992. By doing this, the recent peaks in the data are kept below the new

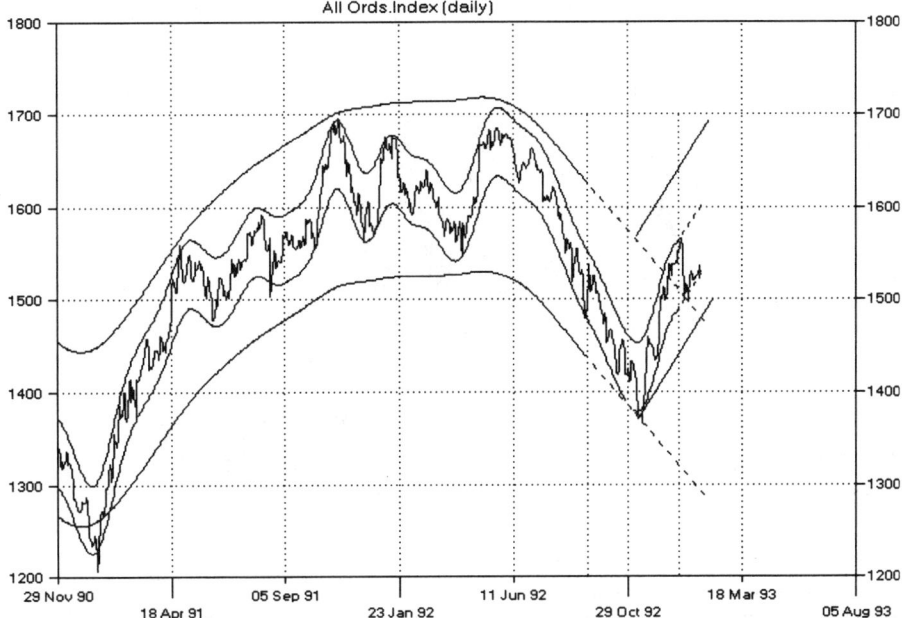

Figure 9.18. *The November 1992 turning point in the Australian All-Ordinary Index. The channels. The outer channel as it would be extrapolated in January 1993 (dashed lines) would obviously run well below the last month of data. The channels have been re-drawn so as to form a symmetrical turning point as shown, keeping the data within the channel.*

estimate of the upper boundary position. The fact that the peaks are now short of the boundary means that a reversal of direction of the inner channel should occur in the not too distant future.

Although not shown, this second turning point in the 201-day channel is also very symmetrical, the symmetry extending out to about 60 days either side of the minimum point in the channel. The channel low point was again slightly offset from the low point in the data, occurring on November 9, some six business days before the Index low on the 17.

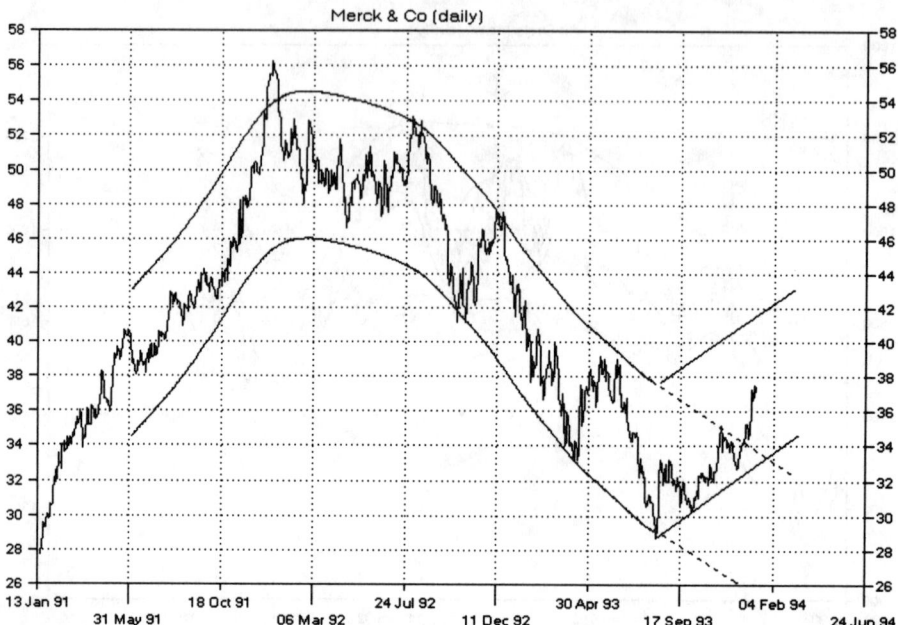

Figure 9.19. *The position in **Merck** on January 11, 1994. The 201-day channel is shown. A few weeks previously the channel would be extrapolated as the dashed lines. The rapid rise over the last few weeks would force a change in direction of the channel, the last section of which would be drawn as shown by the solid lines.*

MERCK & CO

This is an interesting example of a false dawn, where the prediction of a turning point in the stock price, predicted by channel analysis turned out to be rather premature, although not disastrously so.

The position on January 11, 1994 is shown in Figure 9.19, with the stock at \$37¹/₈. A few weeks earlier, the stocks had made a peak at \$35¹/₈ on November 19. The extrapolated 201-day channel at that point in time, appeared to be running downwards in almost a straight line, as shown by the dashed line. The investor would think the channel was more or less in the correct position, because the peak on the 19th just touched this upper boundary. The investor would have nodded happily as the unrolling price moved downwards in line with the expectation of a reversal from the upper boundary. After a few weeks the price had fallen to \$32⁵/₈ by December 14 before a very short term trend reversed direction again and the price was drawn toward the upper boundary of the channel. A very minor peak was formed on December 27 at $35^1/4$. To prevent this minor peak violating the upper boundary would have required an adjustment to the upper boundary. Since this peak is marginally higher than the peak of $35^1/8$ on November 19, the adjustment would mean the upper boundary, and hence the channel, would have to rise at a very shallow angle.

A problem was then caused by the very rapid rise in price of the stock over the next few days at the beginning of January, since the price reached the $37^1/8$ level, as shown by Figure 9.19. This meant a rapid reappraisal of the channel boundary, that would now have to rise at quite a rapid rate to accommodate this new price level. This in turn meant we must have had a major turning point in the channel if it is now apparently rising as fast as it was falling just a few weeks earlier.

If the same procedure is adopted as in the previous example, then the construction of a new channel direction would give a channel similar to the latest section drawn with solid boundaries. This will place the current price level of just over $37 about half way up the channel, so that a further short term rise is to be anticipated. The medium term outlook is also positive since the channel can now be seen to have changed direction only recently.

The careful investor seeks to check this view of the medium term prospects for **Merck** by looking at the position of the 201-day cycle in the stock. By applying a 201-day cycle highlighter, the chart shown in Figure 9.20 was obtained. The best estimate of the status of the 201-day cycle was that it had passed its low point some days ago, and was about halfway up its climb. This means it had about 50 days left before peaking again.

It must be stressed that the investor should not have bought any **Merck** stock at this time because the price was not in the position of having just rebounded off the lower boundary, but was at least half-way up the channel if not higher.

The investor should wait for the next bounce up from the lower boundary to

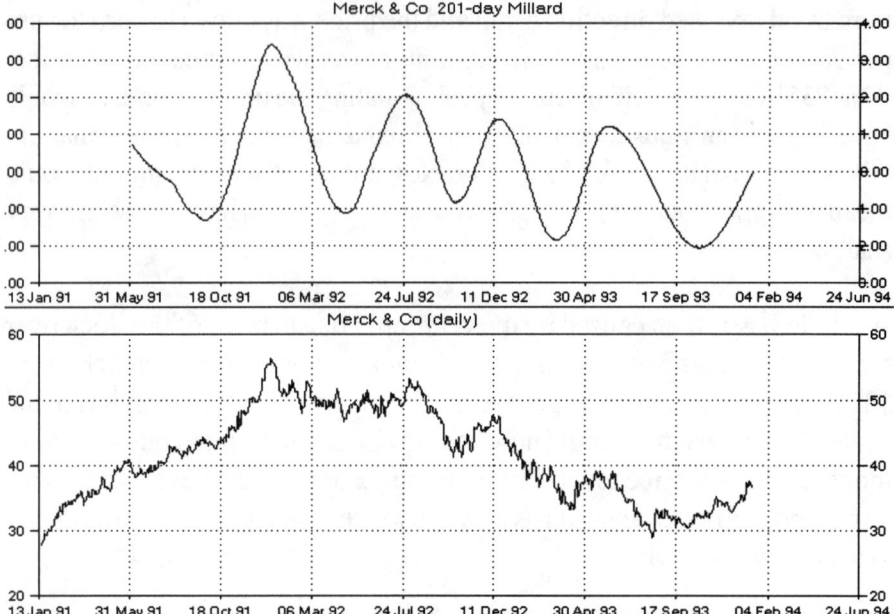

Figure 9.20. *The 201-day cycle highlighter has been applied to the **Merck** price on January 11, 1994.The cycles are fairly regular in wavelength although there is a variation in magnitude. The best estimate of this cycle is that it is halfway up to its peak, some 50 days in the future.*

occur before taking action. The other negative factor to consider is the fact that the 201-day cycle would peak about 50 days on from this point in January, and would then be falling. The investor would hope the price would arrive again at the lower boundary just as the cycle was about to rise again, indicating a wait of perhaps 150 days.

Things did not go quite as anticipated over the next few months, since the price never reached the estimated position of the upper boundary. Instead, it fell back initially to just under $35, rose again slightly to 36^{1/2}$ before falling steadily. A hesitation in early March saw the price rebound from the $31 level on March 4 to just over $32. At that point the investor could have argued that the trough formed at $31 was on the estimated position of the lower boundary. The fact that another trough at a slightly higher level was formed a few days later by a rise to $32 on March 21 would have been a signal to buy the stock, although there would have been some slight unease due to the fact that the 201-day cycle was probably about to fall. The view that the channel had formed a major turning point and therefore should be on course for a sustained rise would have outweighed this uneasiness and the investor would be looking for a good price the next day.

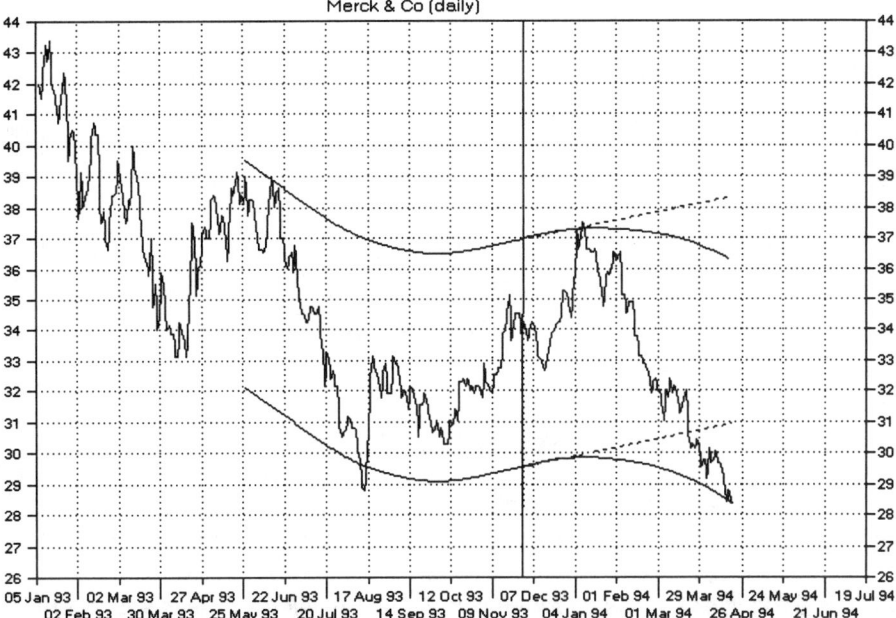

Figure 9.21. *The channel in Merck on April 15, 1994. The vertical line is the last true calculated position. The dashed line is the extrapolation by the curve-fitting process. The curved, solid channel shows how the fall in price has force a bend in the channel.*

Once the stock had been bought, the feeling of optimism would not have persisted for long, since the stock fell back once more. By April 15, the price was down at $28^3/8$ and the position was as shown in Figure 9.21.

The problem at this point was the price had penetrated the rising lower boundary of the channel. This necessitated a change in the estimated position of the channel so that the channel would be forced lower. The only way this could be done while still avoiding a penetration of the upper boundary by the previous high in January would be to put a bend in the channel as shown in Figure 9.21. Thus, the turn up in the channel that was deduced from the data in January has now become a turn down in the channel now that the additional data to April had become available.

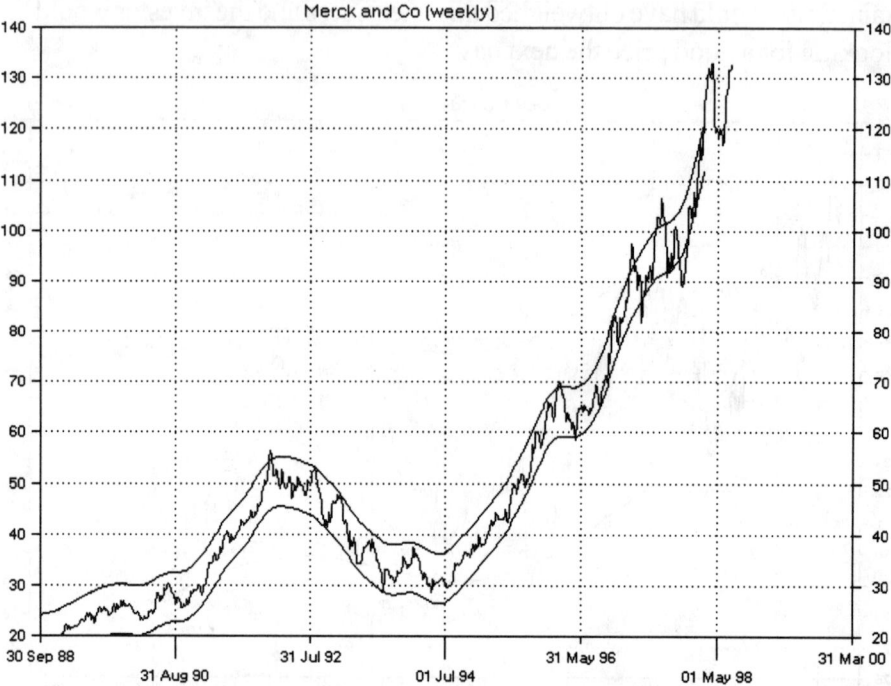

Figure 9.22. *Weekly closing for* **Merck***. The 41-week channel is equivalent to the 201-day channel used in previous charts. You can see the reversal in the channel direction in early 1994 was very temporary, and caused by a double bottom formation.*

The fall in the channel did not last long. It turned out the price on April 15 was the lowest point reached, and a sustained rise was made from that point forwards. In order to cover as large a span of data as possible, the chart in Figure 9.22 shows weekly closings for **Merck**. The 41-week channel is shown as being the equivalent of the 201-day channel in daily data. You can see the reason for the short term change in the channel direction was the fact that a double bottom formation had occurred. At the time this appeared to be quite a strong deformation of the channel, whereas in retrospect, you can see from Figure 9.22, it is hardly more than a blip. The investor who entered the stock in March 1994 and was worried by the fall of a few dollars by April would soon have been feeling very relaxed indeed as the long term trend powered the stock up through $50, $100 and then $130.

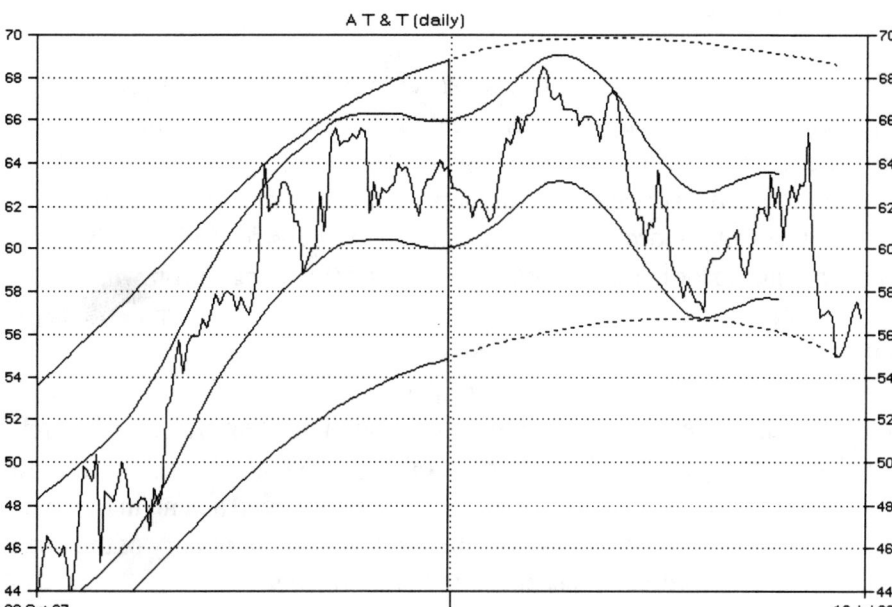

Figure 9.23. *Channels drawn for **AT&T** on July 10, 1998. The outer is a 201-day channel while the inner is a 41-day channel. The last calculated point for the outer channel is shown by the solid vertical line. The outer channel has to be bent as shown in order to avoid penetration of the lower boundary.*

AT&T

So far we have concentrated on positive turning points in channels that have provided buying opportunities. In this example we will look at negative turning points, *i.e.* the topping out of channels, that will interest the short seller. **AT&T** is an excellent example of a stock that made a very large advance over a few years and then, at the time of writing, appears to be topping out and on its way down for the immediate future.

Figure 9.23 is shows the position in **AT&T** on July 10, 1998. Two channels have been drawn on the daily data, the 201-day outer and the 41-day inner. The vertical line shows the position of the last calculated point of the outer channel. The extrapolation of the outer channel to the present time is shown by the dashed lines.

Obviously, as the channel boundaries are extrapolated from the position of the last calculated point, an increasing amount of bend must be applied to the channel in order to allow the trough on May 19 (at just over $57) to be accommodated on or near the boundary. As the extrapolation continues, the even lower trough formed on July 2 by a fall to just under $55 forces an even tighter radius to the bend that by this point is clearly falling. As drawn, you can see the channel has topped out a little later than the peak price in the data, the latter being on March 25, 1998 at 68^1/4$.

As far as the inner channel is concerned, the major feature in the last few weeks was the rapid fall from the peak of over $65 reached on June 23. The price fell in a matter of three days to 56^3/4$. This forced a bend in the inner channel so that it has now fallen rapidly to the lower boundary of the outer channel and has probably just begun to bounce up again.

Since by July 10, the stock had fallen to 56^3/4$ from 68$^1/2$ on March 25, a loss of 17%, the question arises, how soon after the peak price should the invewtor be aware of things going wrong with the stock, so avoiding action could have been taken. The position in **AT&T** on April 21, 1998 is shown by the arrow in Figure 9.24. The calculated 41-day channel terminates at the position given by the vertical line, and the extrapolation to the point given by the arrow is shown by the dashed line.

At this point, the trough formed at a price level of $65 on April 14 fell quite neatly on the estimated position of the lower boundary. The investor now expected a short term rise to the top of this inner channel, giving a target area of at least $70. There appeared to be no cause for alarm when the price, having reached over 67^3/8$ on April 17, fell back to $67 on April 2. The investor would expect the stock to resume its climb to the upper boundary within a few days. However, the stock fell yet again the next day, April 21 to 65^3/8$. It was now exactly at the estimated position of the lower boundary, and the investor would have been waiting anxiously for a bounce upwards to

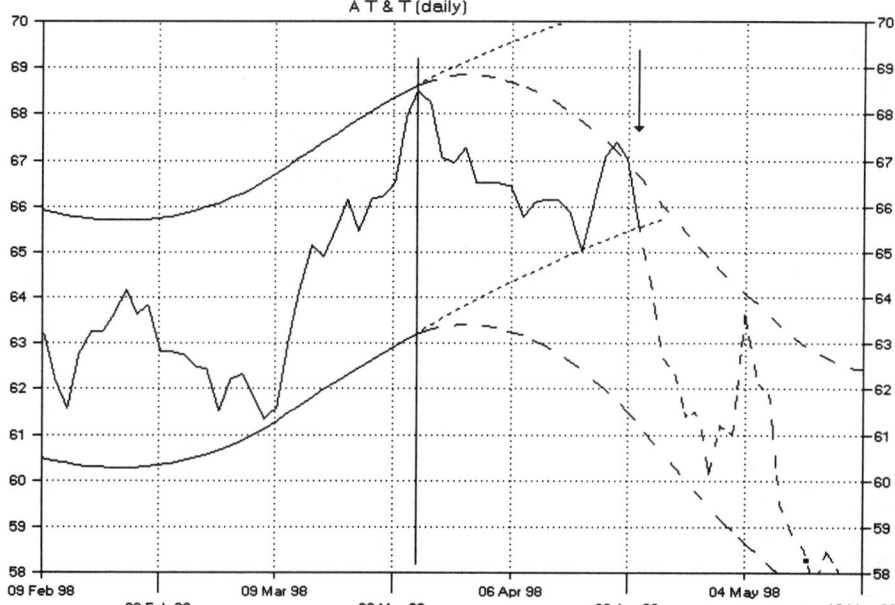

Figure 9.24. *The position in **AT&T** on April 21, 1998 is shown by the arrow. The vertical line is the last calculated point for the 41-day channel. The extrapolation of the channel from the last calculated point to April 21 is shown by the short dashed lines. The price has now fallen below the estimated position of the lower boundary, and is a strong indication of a fall in the near term. Future movement of the stock price and the channel is shown by the long dashed lines, showing that the prediction was correct.*

form a trough that would lie on this boundary. This did not happen, since the stock fell yet again on April 22 to $64^{1}/_{4}$. The stock was then well below the lower boundary, and the conclusion would have been the channel must have changed direction so it was now falling. The investor should have been convinced that **AT&T** was due for a further fall and that it was time to exit the stock, and/or instigate a short sale. A price level of around $64 could have been obtained early the next morning.

The long dashed lines in Figure 9.24 indicates that we took the correct course of action based on the evidence available at the time. The price had fallen to around $57 by July10. Thus the investor had saved some $7 by this careful analysis using a short term channel.

Figure 9.25. *The Dow-Jones Utilities Index weekly closings since January 1978.*

DOW JONES UTILITIES

Figure 9.25 shows a plot of the Dow-Jones Utilities Index since 1978. The data is weekly, and with such a long run it is possible to draw a long term 401-week outer channel, *i.e.* a channel that is the result of cycles of wavelengths longer than eight years. The outer channel itself of course contains the sum total of all cycles with wavelengths eight years or less.

The inner channel is based on a 41-week average. It is interesting that the most prominent of the outer cycles is a three year cycle, with two major peaks in January 1987 and December 1989. The cycle then dies away so that shorter wavelengths take over for a few years, but it then reappears with a major peak in September 1993. The next peak would have appeared in September 1996 but for the intervention of a shorter wavelength cycle that split the peak into two peaks, in February 1996 and January 1997.

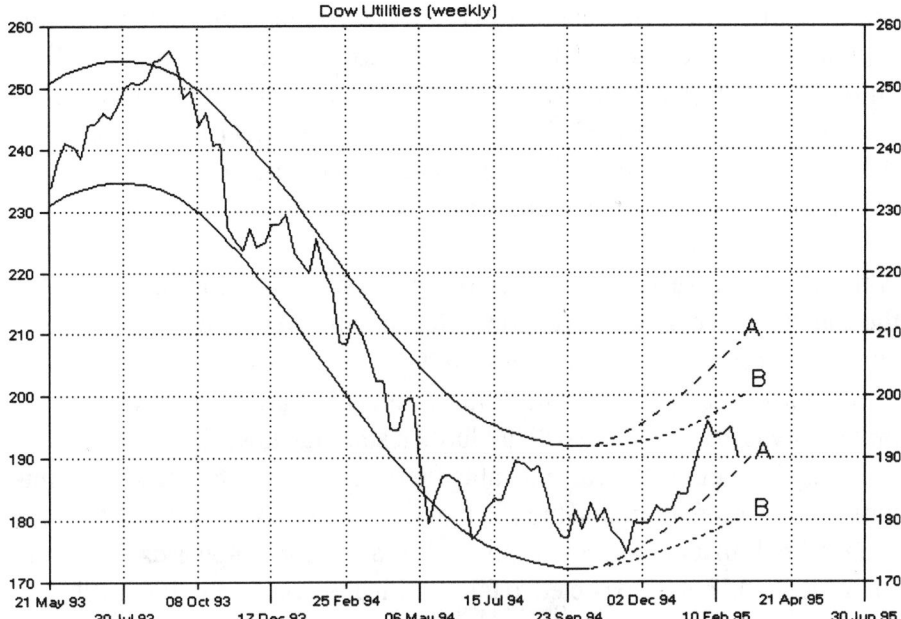

Figure 9.26. *There are two alternative extrapolations, A and B, of the 41-week channel for the Dow-Jones Utilities Index on March 3, 1995. Either the trough on November 18, 1994 or the peak on February 3, 1995 can be at a boundary, but not both.*

Of particular interest is the quite sharp turning point shown in December 1994 in the 41-week channel, the emphasis being on how soon after the turn the investor could be relatively sure the one year downtrend had come to an end. The previous peak in the channel was in September 1993, so that the channel had been falling for over a year before reaching the lower boundary of the long term outer channel. A better idea of the turning point is given by the enlarged section shown in Figure 9.26 for the situation on March 3, 1995. Only the inner 41-week channel is shown, the outer long term channel is omitted since it is not needed in the analysis of the data at this point. The solid boundaries represent the actual calculated channel, while the two sets of dashed lines are estimates of the boundaries.

The reason for the two alternative estimates for the channel boundaries is the relative position of the two recent features, the trough at 174.47 on November 18, 1994 and the peak on February 3, 1995 at 195.62. Obviously, the presence of the peak on February 3, is the crucial factor that determines the channel must have changed direction and is now headed upwards. The difficulty is that unless the channel is distorted badly, a smooth extension of the channel can either have the November trough on the lower boundary (channel A) or the February peak on the upper boundary (channel B) but cannot accommodate both of these features on the boundaries.

Although of course the prime objective of the analysis was to determine that the channel had changed direction, a decision between the two alternative channels would be useful since it would give an indication of the probable movement of the Index in the immediate future. In the case of channel B, the probability is that the Index will fall further, since the lower boundary is considerably lower than the current value for the Index. The target area for this movement would be around the 185 mark. If channel A is accepted, then the probability is that the Index will stop falling and bounce upwards very soon, so that it would not be expected to fall significantly below the 190 level.

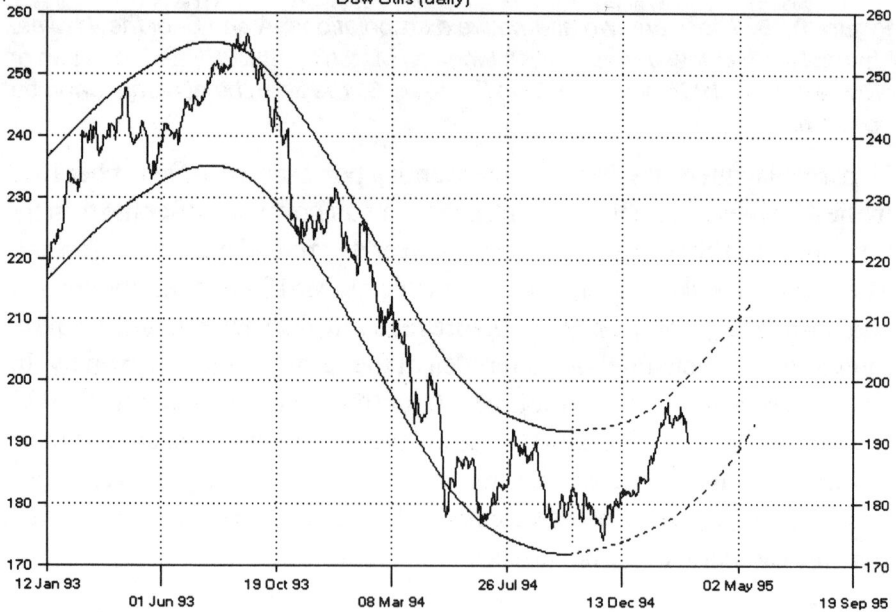

Figure 9.27. *The 201-day channel in the Dow-Jones Utilities Index on March 3, 1995. The estimated boundaries are shown as dashed lines, using the principle of symmetry around the turning point. This shows that a further fall can be expected in the Index over the short term.*

The only criterion that might be used to decide between these two alternatives is the principle of symmetry. It appears to hold on about 80% of occasions where a channel changes direction, and as discussed earlier, a major turning point in the Australian All-Ordinary Index was an excellent example.

In the present case, the channel that is closest to being a mirror image of the actual channel with the turning point as the line of symmetry is channel B. This means we expect the Index to fall somewhat further before hitting the rising lower boundary.

The situation was resolved further by using daily data, as shown in Figure 9.27. In this case, the 201-day channel was used to preserve the close similarity with the 41-week channel used for weekly data. Since it was decided from weekly data that the best channel was the symmetrical one, the same principle was used for the 201-day channel.

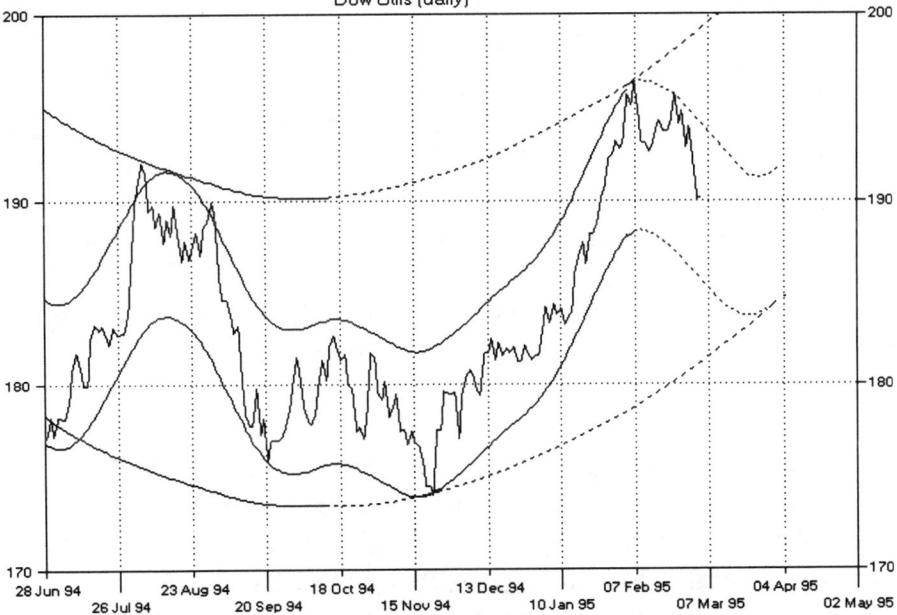

Figure 9.28. *The Dow-Jones Utilities Index on March 3, 1995. An inner 41-day channel has now been added to the 201-day channel. Both have been extrapolated according to the dashed lines. The indication is for a fall in the value of the Index to around 185 from late March onwards and then a rise to over 200 some weeks past the last date on the chart.*

In order to predict more easily the movement of the Index in the immediate short term, it is necessary to view an inner channel so that its relationship with the 201-day channel can be deduced. In Figure 9.28 a 41-day inner channel has been added. The extrapolation of this channel is shown as a dashed line, as is the extrapolation of the 201-day channel. Now that the estimate for the 201-day channel boundaries has been put in place, these boundaries now limit the excursions of the 41-day channel. Thus, it has to be made to bounce downwards in early February, and made to continue its journey down to the rising lower boundary of the 201-day channel. It can be estimated as reaching that point in late March, from where it should rise again. Although off the right hand side of the chart, the inner channel should meet the upper 201-day channel boundary in late May at the soonest, and could be delayed much longer. The longer this arrival at the upper boundary takes, obviously the high will the Index rise. If it reaches the boundary in June, then a target of around 210 is likely.

The Index behaved perfectly, hitting the upper boundary at 196.35 on February 2, and as predicted, fell from its value of 190.09 on March 3 to 185.61 on March 21. This is the point when it bounced up again, and rose steadily until it reached a temporary peak of 209 on June 5, 1995. You can see from the extrapolations in Figure 9.28. the estimation of the channel positions, and hence the value of the Index, in the near future was extremely accurate.

In retrospect, you can see this was another example of where to apply symmetry as an aid in determining the channel position correctly, and predicting future movement.

The examples so far have concentrated on turning points in channels, since a knowledge of when a trend has changed, or is about to change, direction is essential if consistent profits are to be made. If we move on slightly in time in this example of the Dow-Jones Utilities, we can see a situation where the prediction is not for a turn, but for the channel to continue forwards in more or less the same direction. This is shown in Figure 9.29 where the extrapolation of the 201-day channels as calculated in September 1995 is shown. The indication is that the channel will continue to rise, carrying the Index with it. The

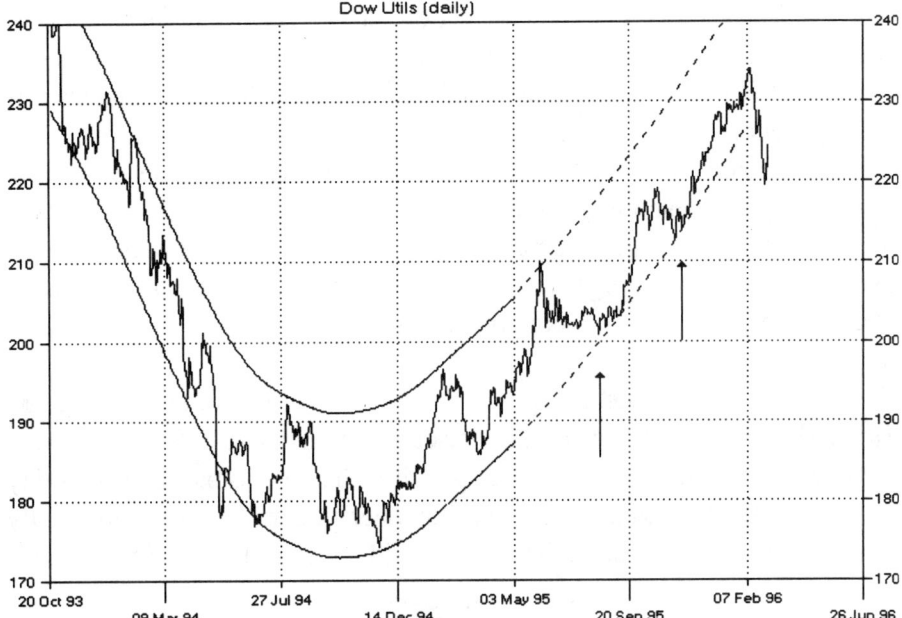

Figure 9.29. *The 201-day channel as estimated on September 8, 1995 (indicated by the left hand arrow). The extrapolation takes the channel into the future. The channel was accurate enough to predict the bounce for the lower boundary in late November 1995 (right hand arrow).*

future movement of the Index is also shown, so you can see the estimate of the channel into the future was correct. The validity of the lower boundary was confirmed by the bounce upwards of the Index in late November 1995. A series of troughs on November 14 (212.5), November 22 (214,08) and November 30 (215.79) all fell exactly on this extrapolated boundary.

OCCASIONAL FAILURE OF CHANNEL ANALYSIS

The examples discussed so far in this chapter have been ones where channel analysis has been vital in deciding what course of action should be followed. Obviously, since there is a large amount of random behavior in the stock market, predictions made in this way can turn out to be incorrect. Occasionally, a stock can fall so rapidly down through a lower channel boundary that a considerable loss has accrued before remedial action can be taken. However, in the majority of cases where a prediction is incorrect, the initial penetration of a boundary occurs to only a limited extent so a decision can be taken in good time. The only reason for a larger loss to be made in such circumstances is the psychological one of an investor being convinced that the move in the wrong direction is a limited one, and things will change for the better within a few days. The investor then holds on for too long until what would have been a small, acceptable loss, becomes a large, unacceptable one. The only way to avoid this mistake is to sell immediately. It is obvious the price has not stopped at a lower boundary but has continued down through it.

An example that demonstrates this approach is that of **Broken Hill** in January 1997. The channels drawn for this stock are shown in Figure 9.30. The outer channel is based on a 101-day average while the inner is based on a 25-day At the last calculated point for the outer channel the extrapolation of the gently rising curve was a very smooth extension with a curve of slowly increasing

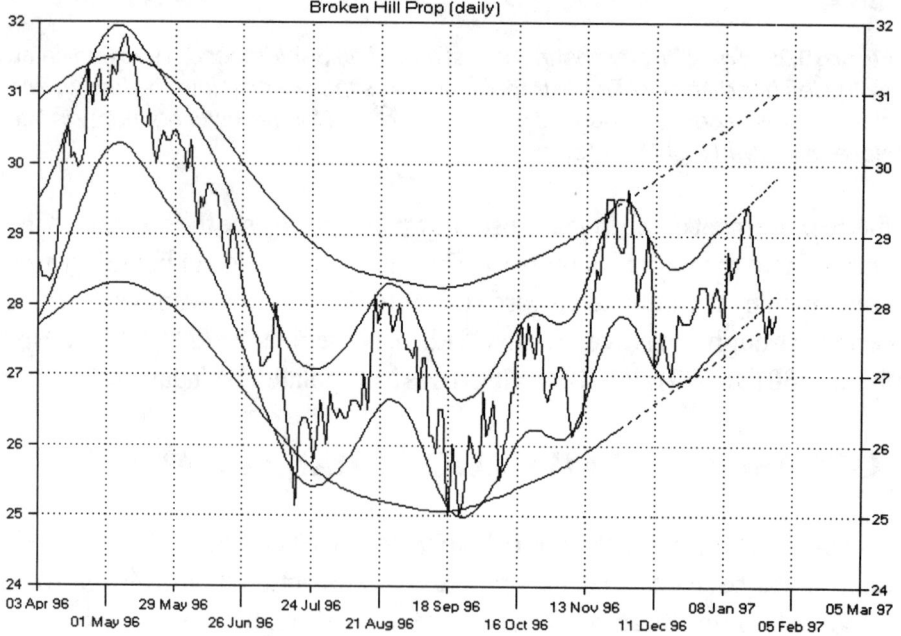

Figure 9.30. *Channels drawn on the daily closings of **Broken Hill** on January 29, 1997. The estimated channels are drawn as dashed lines. The outer is based on a centered 101-day average and the inner on a centered 5-day average.*

slope. The peak on November 28 at $29^1/_2$ occurred before the cut-off, so the slight penetration of the upper boundary had to be accepted. This meant the peak close to it, at $29^5/_8$ on November 29, although after the cutoff, also had to be left penetrating the extrapolated upper boundary, since to do otherwise would have meant a major distortion of the channel.

The stock dropped quite rapidly from that point to the trough at $27 on December 18, but this trough was still above the lower boundary of the outer channel, since again, to force the lower boundary to touch this trough would have meant an extreme upward bend in the outer channel. From that point **Broken Hill** rose in a series of small peaks and troughs to a peak of $29^3/_8$ on January 17, 1995 before falling rapidly to $27^1/_2$ on January 24. This fall took the stock just a fraction of a dollar below the estimated boundary, but this level was well within tolerance. The stock rose, fell and rose again from over three days until January 29 where it hovered above the boundary, as shown in Figure 9.30. At this point, at a level of $27^7/_8$, there was nothing to suggest the estimated channel was not in the correct position. The investor would be contemplating buying the stock with a useful rise to well over $30 in prospect.

An investor, buying at this level, would find that this was the best price reached by **Broken Hill** for some time, since it fell the very next day. The movement over the next few months is shown in Figure 9.31. By April 1, the stock was down to $26^1/_4$ and still falling. More importantly, a calculation of the outer 101-day channel on this date showed that the channel had changed direction around December 24 - 27, 1996 and was already on its way down before any extrapolation was made.

The extrapolation of the channel from the last calculated point is difficult because it can be seen that the peaks and trough following the major peak on December 17 are all bunched within a narrow vertical band, and therefore we are not in the position of having any features that will define the upper and lower boundaries. In the absence of these features the principle of symmetry has to be applied as giving the best estimation on the available evidence of the channel direction.

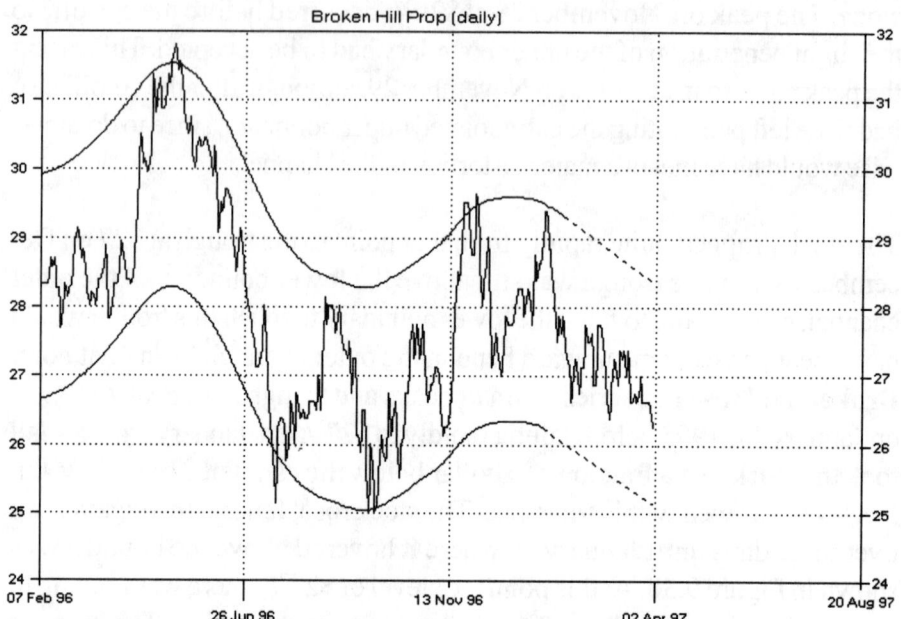

Figure 9.31. *The outer channel drawn for **Broken Hill** on April 2, 1997 shows that path of the channel as estimated on January 29, was totally incorrect. Rather than continuing to rise, the channel had turned at a point between the peaks on November 29, 1996 and the lower peak on January 17, 1997.*

The result is shown by the dashed boundaries in Figure 9.31, and this places the stock just below the mid-channel position and moving down. With the short term trend in the stock now clearly headed downwards and the medium term 101-day channel also falling, the stock is a definite loser for the immediate future. The confirmation of this view of the prospects for **Broken Hill** is a low of just above $15 was reached in June 1998.

This example shows why it is imperative to sell a stock as soon as it violates the estimated position of a lower boundary. In this case the fall through the boundary was of limited extent, and there was a limited recovery so the loss would have been quite small. Failure to take action would have increased the eventual loss to an unacceptable 45%.

There are several ways in which a stock can fall through a lower boundary:

1.   Limited fall below boundary with recovery to a point
        above the boundary

2.   Limited fall below boundary with partial recovery to a
        point below the boundary or sideways hesitation

3.   Limited fall below boundary with further fall after
        one time period

4.   Large fall below boundary

The investor should exit the stock in each of these cases at the first instance of penetration of the lower boundary, although case **1** might cause some indecision. This is because in this circumstance the channel could continue upwards after this one-off penetration of the boundary, but cannot be guaranteed. The investor could stay with the stock while recognizing there is an increased level of risk, these situations where the penetration is only temporary are not common. In most cases a turn down in the channel direction is being signaled.

Cases **2** and **3** are the ones that the investor should give thanks for, since it enables a dignified exit to be made from the stock at a small loss, as long as this exit is made immediately, as was the case with **Broken Hill**.

The effect of case **4** is to cause a very large and unavoidable loss, and it is not uncommon to see a loss of 20% upwards in a day. Since such a movement is totally unpredictable, the investor has only two decisions to make: either to sell or to hold. To hold evidences faith that the stock will experience a short term recovery. During the holding period, the best case is that the loss will not increase, and the worst that a further drop will increase the loss. The best advice is to sell and seek an opportunity to recover the loss in another better-positioned issue..

CHAPTER 10

Channel Turning Points

In the last chapter most of the examples were concerned with determining if a channel had changed direction. The point was made that knowing that a channel, and hence a trend, had changed direction was the most important piece of information that could be derived from a study of channels. In this chapter we will look more closely at the issue in an effort to improve on the excellent results obtained in the last chapter. The main improvement would be a reduction in the time lag between the actual turn in the channel and the point where it becomes obvious that the turn has occurred. The time lag is due to the unavoidable property of centered moving averages that the last calculated (*i.e.* the true) point, and hence the last real position of the calculated channel, derived from it, terminates half a span in the past. We try to estimate what has happened to the average between the last calculated point and the present. From this we can also guess what the average will do in the future.

The first step, if carried out by the simple graphical method, is to project the channel forwards from the last true point by drawing the smoothest and most obvious continuation of the last few points in the calculated channel boundaries. If done by a computer, the procedure is to use a curve-fitting routine, such as a quadratic or cubic fit, to the last few points of the calculated average to decide how it might have crossed the gap between the last true point and the present time. A small mathematical adjustment has to be applied so the value estimated by the routine at the position of the last true point coincides with the true value. If this is not

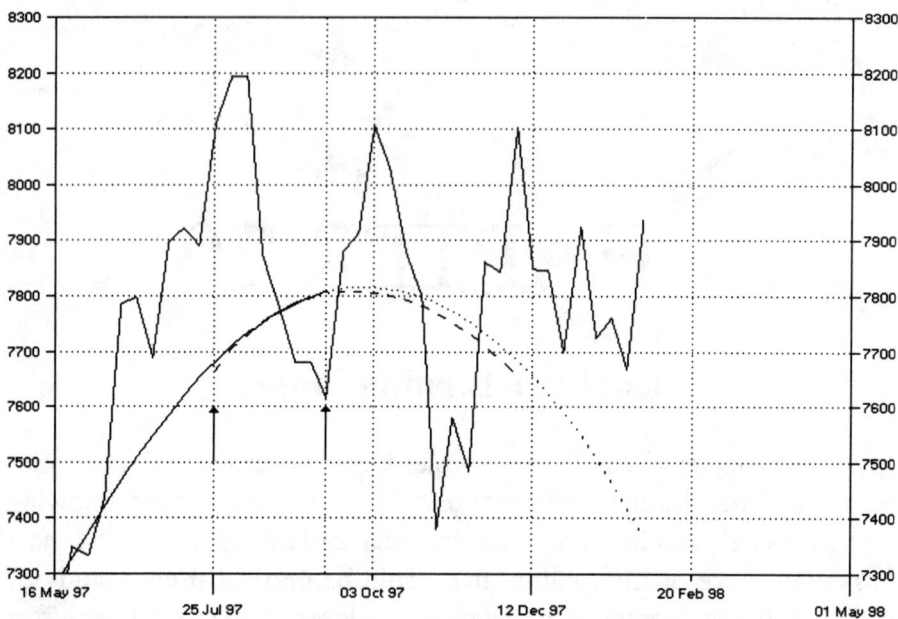

Figure 10.1. *The extrapolation of a 41-week average. The last calculated point is at the position of the right hand arrow. A quadratic fit is calculated using the average points that lie between the two arrows. This is plotted as the dashed line. It is then adjusted so that it coincides with the actual average at the positions of the two arrows before being calculated and plotted up to date as the dotted line.*

done, then the extrapolation starts out being in error from the first. The process is shown in Figure 10.1. The right hand vertical arrow shows the position of the last calculated point of a 41-week average. The left hand arrow shows the point eight weeks before this. These last eight points of the actual centered average are used to calculate a least squares quadratic fit. This is plotted as the dashed line. Although not easy to see, this line does not coincide with the actual calculated average at either the first arrow or the second arrow. It is then adjusted so that it does coincide at both of these points, and its adjusted position is shown by the dotted line.

A computer program such as **Microvest 5.0™** does this calculation and adjustment before using the calculation as a template for the channel boundaries, allowing the specified number of points to lie outside of the boundaries. With a small amount of practice, a graphical estimation of how the centered average crosses the gap from the last calculated point to the present time will be quite close to this curve-fitted version. This can then be used as a template for the channel boundaries.

In a great many cases, this graphical or computational exercise is all that needs to be done to produce a channel accurate in terms of containing all of the price movement across the gap until the present time, and that will also be valid into the near future.

TURNING POINT DELAY

There is almost inevitably a delay between a trough or peak in the data and the corresponding change in the direction of an average. The delay gets larger as the span of the average increases. The reason for the delay is found in the way averages are calculated, with the next data point being added in and the drop point, *i.e.* the data point a complete span back in time, being subtracted from the running total. With, for example, a falling average, the running total will only become larger than its previous value if the next data point is larger in value than the drop point.

Minimum delay

The minimum delay between a peak or trough in the data and a change in the direction of the average is obviously one point, *i.e.* a day for daily data and a week for weekly data. The probability of an average changing by the time the next data point comes in decreases rapidly as the span of the average increases. The further back we go from the peak or trough in the data, the larger the gap between the value at that point in time and the value at the peak or trough. In order to cause the average to change direction as the next data point after the trough comes in we need a larger and larger change between this next datapoint and the peak or trough datapoint.

For averages of small spans, this required change, while large, may still be within the range of changes that have occurred historically (see sec-

tion on probability in chapter 3). As the span increases, the change necessary between the peak or trough and the next data point becomes so large
that it becomes larger than any previous known change, and therefore it
becomes highly improbable that it will occur. Occasionally, a five point
average will change direction after this minimum delay, but the probability of averages with the spans we have been using in previous examples,
such as 41 and 201, changing direction with this minimum delay is so low
it is extremely unlikely to happen.

Maximum delay

The maximum delay between a peak or trough in the data, a change in
direction of the average is one point less than the span of the average. For
example, 200 days for a 201-day average, or 40 weeks for a 41-week
average. This will only happen in the special case that the change between the peak or trough and the point previous to it is so large that this
price level is not reached until another **n** points have elapsed, where **n** is
the span of the average.

Typical delay

We have seen the delay between a peak or trough in the data and a turning average ranges between 1 point and **n** - 1 points, where **n** is the span
of the average. If a large number of average turning points is studied,you
can see the delays form a flattened distribution, with limits of 1 and **n** -1.
The most frequently occurring delay is one of half of the span of the
average. Although this means the most likely delay is one of half a span of
the average, because the distribution is flattened, delays of up to a few
points more or less than the half span are also quite common. The exact
delay that occurs for an average depends solely upon the scatter of the
data around the peak or trough, and is not predictable in advance for any
specific average.

The delays in a 41-week average as the point of calculation moves past
the trough in the data is illustrated by the example of the turning point in

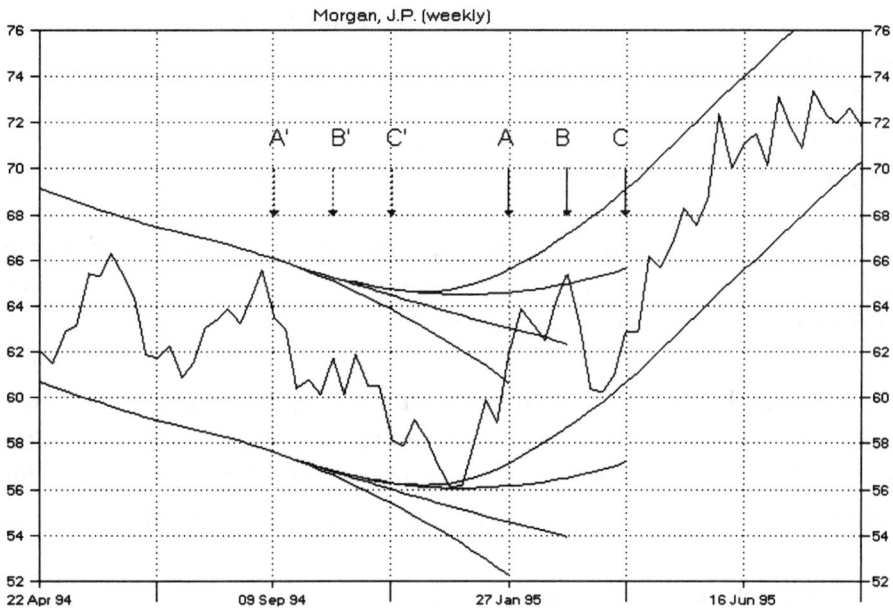

Figure 10.2. *The effect of delays in calculating 41-week channels. The continuous channel running from left to right is the actual channel, calculated some time in the future. The minimum in the channel occurred on December 2, 1994. The channel was calculated successively at points A (January 27, 1995), B (March 3, 1995) and C (April 7, 1995), with the extrapolations from the last true points at A, B and C being shown. The first indication of a turn in the channel was on March 10, 1995. By point C the turn was now obviously well established although the extrapolation is still not very close to the true channel.*

the **J. P. Morgan** stock price in late 1994/ early 1995 as shown in Figure 10.2. The actual 41-week channel, as calculated some time in the future is shown, as are three successive calculations of the channel based of course on the 41-week centered average. The turning point in the actual channel, as calculated in the future, occurred on December 2, 1994.

The first calculation of the channel, at point A on January 27, 1995, gave the extrapolation from point A, with the channel apparently headed downwards at an ever increasing rate. The next calculation, at point B on March 3, gave the extrapolation from point B, with the channel still headed downwards, but at a more or less constant rate or fall. By the time the calculation was carried out on April 7, the extrapolation from point C now gave a channel that had begun to rise, even though comparison with the true channel shows its positioning was not all that good.

Not shown is the point where the first indication that the channel had stopped falling might be about to turn up. That was given on March 3, 1995, some thirteen weeks after the actual turn. The penalty to the investor of this unavoidable delay in the channel changing direction is of course lost profit, since the price may have risen considerably from its low point by the time the change in the channel direction becomes apparent.

Although in this exercise the channels have been extrapolated by the computer from the calculated centered average, the investor who drew the extrapolation by eye across the gap from the last calculated point to the present time would end up with very similar channel boundaries.

At this point, it should be noted that no account has been taken of the violation of these channel boundaries by peaks or troughs in the data and any bending or change in direction of these features might force on the channel.

FACTORS THAT FORCE A CHANGE IN CHANNEL DIRECTION

Although some of these have been illustrated in the many examples in previous chapters, it is useful to restate these and add some additional ones before examining them in greater depth.

Moderate changes in direction

Once the boundaries have been extrapolated by either of the methods just discussed, then there are three factors that will cause a minor adjustment. The first is the penetration of either the upper boundary by a peak or the lower boundary by a trough (but not both) formed in the gap between the last calculated point and the latest data point. The second is the penetration of the boundary by an unexpected or unusually large movement in the most recent data where a peak or trough has not yet formed. The third is an unexpected or unusually large movement in the data around the section that is one complete span back in time (the drop point, see chapter 7).

Boundary penetration by a peak or trough

A minor violation of either the upper boundary by a peak or the lower boundary by a trough is acceptable, since a tolerance will have been allowed over the complete history of the channel. The prime aim though is to allow troughs and peaks to lie on the boundary rather than outside of it. If the penetration appears to be larger than is acceptable, then the channel has to be bent enough to accommodate the peak or trough causing the violation.

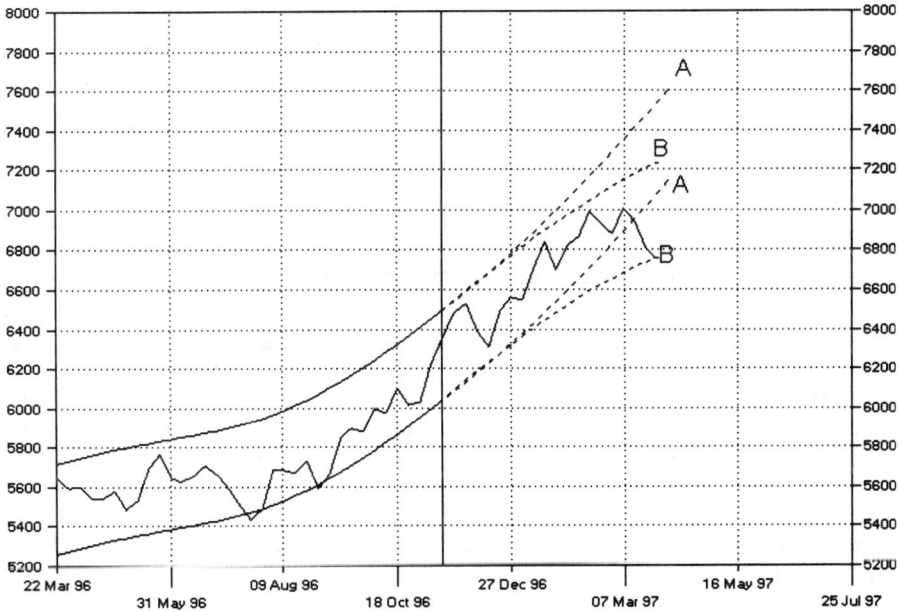

Figure 10.3. *A modest adjustment has to be made from the original extrapolated boundaries (A) to the new boundaries (B) because of the latest fall in the value of the data. The boundary can only stay in position B if the next data point is higher than the latest, thus forming a trough that can lie on the boundary, otherwise the boundary will have to be adjusted downwards again.*

Boundary penetration by most recent data

The situation when the latest data point is penetrating a boundary is rather different. Although the only adjustment that can be made is to move the boundary to allow the data point to lie on it, it is only if the next data point, yet to occur, makes this latest point a peak or a trough that this estimated position for the boundary will be correct. If the next data point continues the move in the same direction, then the boundary will have to be adjusted yet again. Thus, today's adjustment of the boundary must be seen as only temporary until the next data point shows otherwise. In such circumstances with adjustments being made each time new data becomes available, the investor should not take action. To take action is to predict the current short term trend has finally changed direction when there is no evidence to support this belief. This scenario is shown in Figure 10.3.

The original estimation of the boundaries before any adjustment is made is shown as channel A. The recent fall in the value of the data requires the boundary to be moved down to position B. The adjustment at this time is not large enough to cause a reversal in the channel direction, but simply a falling off in the rate of the rising channel.

Unusual movement a complete span in the past

The comment was made early in chapter 7 that the change in the value of an average is brought about not only by the value of the next data point being added into the running total, but also by the value of the point, in the past, which is being subtracted.

Taking a rising average as an example, the rate at which it rises will slow down if the difference between the data point being added in and the point being dropped becomes smaller than it was at the time of the previous point. In the extreme, of course, if the data point being added in is less than the point being dropped, then the calculated value of the average will be less than it was at the previous data point and the average will reverse direction.

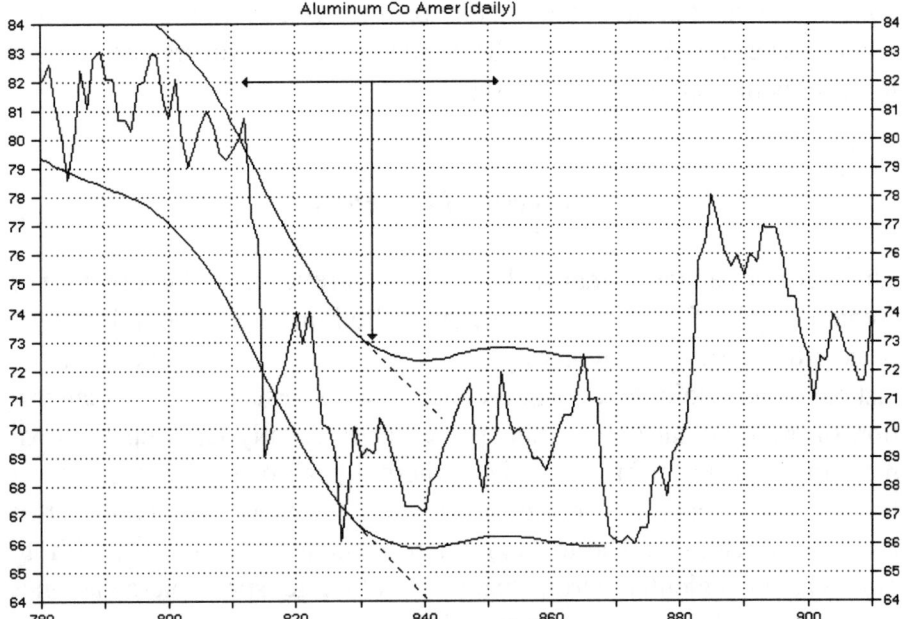

Figure 10.4. *There are 41 points between the ends of the double headed arrow. These produce the averaged point at the position of the vertical arrow. The normal extrapolation of the average would give the dashed line. There is an abnormally large fall between points 812 and 815, while the changes between points 843 and 846 are more normal. This imbalance accounts for the decrease in the rate of descent of the channel, shown as the solid line from the vertical arrow forward.*

If therefore we examine the section of the data around one whole span of the average in the past and find unusually large rises, then we must expect the rate of increase of the average to start to slow down. This is because we will be dropping larger values of the data and replacing them with smaller, more normal values. This concept is illustrated in Figure 10.4. The average of the 41 points starting from point 812 is shown by the vertical arrow. The extrapolation of the channel from the mid-point of this set of data follows the dashed line. The next few points from 812 to 815 show an abnormally large fall, while at the other end of the section, between points 843 and 846, the changes are more normal. When these two ends of the range of points used for the calculation are taken into account, the rate of descent of the channel decreases rapidly. Once these abnormal falls pass out of the calculation, the average moves more or less sideways because the values of the points being added in are very similar to those being dropped.

Reversal of Direction

There are three factors that will cause a total reversal of the direction of a channel. The first is the penetration of both the upper boundary by a peak and the lower boundary by a trough formed in the gap between the last calculated point and the latest data point. The second is the penetration of the boundary by an unexpected or unusually large up or down movement in the most recent data where a peak or trough has not yet formed, but where a previous trough or peak forces a reversal rather than a minor adjustment. The third is where a channel will collide with an outer channel calculated from an average of longer span unless the inner channel is made to change direction.

In all of these cases, unless there are a considerable number of peaks and troughs to establish the boundaries with a high degree of validity, the principle of symmetry can be employed in order to help decide on the new position for the channel.

Boundary penetration by both a peak and a trough

In the case of moderate changes in direction, it was only necessary to bend the channel to accommodate whichever feature was penetrating the boundary. Where we have both a peak and trough, we find that bending the channel one way to accommodate one of the features will make the penetration by the other feature even worse. The only solution will be to bend the channel to reverse direction. Obviously the bend will be somewhere between the last calculated point the latest feature that would otherwise penetrate a boundary. In the absence of other information, the bending point has to be taken as the position of the first feature that would penetrate the boundary.

This exercise was carried out in nearly all of the examples in the last chapter, but one more example is given here for completeness. The 41-week channel is shown for **J.P Morgan** in Figure 10.5. On February 10, 1995 the stock had fallen from a level of $63³/₈ the previous week, forming a peak on February 3. The extrapolated channel, falling in a more or less straight line, allows this peak to sit on the upper boundary while also keeping the trough of $56 on December 23, 1994 within the channel, so that the extrapolation (dotted line) looks good at this point in time.

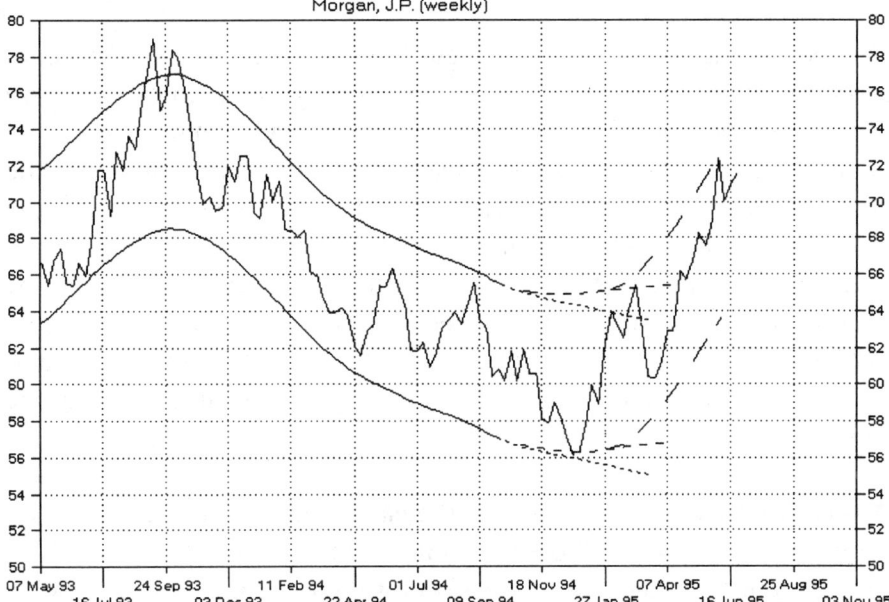

Figure 10.5. *The extrapolated boundaries of a 41-week channel have to be adjusted twice to accommodate the two peaks in the stock price at March 3, 1995 ($65³/₈) and June 2, 1995 ($72³/₈) while keeping the trough at December 23, 1994 ($56) on or within the lower boundary.*

However, within another four weeks another peak had formed at $65³/₈ on March 3. This peak can only be kept within the channel if the fall in the channel is brought to an end and a slight rise is built in. The lower boundary of this adjusted channel passes just through the December trough, but still allows the peak of March 3 to also lie on the upper boundary, so that again, the newly estimated channel appears to be in a reasonable position.

Before long, another adjustment of the channel was called for, since the price rose to form a peak of $72³/₈ on June 2. This calls for a definite upward bend in the channel, otherwise this peak would penetrate well above the current estimated position of the channel. In this particular case this high peak means the level of symmetry around the turning point is quite low. The channel is now rising at a much faster rate.

PROBABILITY METHODS

The recently developed Sigma-p algorithms (see Appendix) offer a considerable improvement on the way that turning points in channels are estimated. One algorithm (Sigma-p A) calculates a better channel across the gap between the last true average point to the current time than the curve-fit method. The other (Sigma-p B) calculates a window where the channel should change direction, although it does not, however give any indication of a price level at which the turn will occur; this has to be deduced from a consideration of where the channel boundaries are likely to be at that point in time. The interesting point about Sigma-p B is that it can calculate the position of the next turning point well into the future, sometimes more than a year ahead.

A predictability score is given for the calculation, so that action is not taken by the investor in those situations where the predictability is low. Predictability is highest when weekly closing prices are used, and varies according to the span being used as the basis of the channel calculation.

The percentage predictability for each of the Dow 30 constituent companies is shown in Table 10.1 for both 41-week and 53-week channels. Often there can be a wide variation between the two channels for the same company. For example in the case of the **Aluminum Company**, where it changes from 80.1% for the 41-week channel to 38.7% for the 53-week channel. The most predictable 41-week channels in July 1998 are those for the **Aluminum Company** and **Woolworth**, while the least predictable are **Du Pont** and **Merck**. For 53-week channels, the most predictable are **AT &T** and **3M**, while the least are the **Aluminum Com-**

pany and **Caterpillar**.

Stocks	41-week predictability	53-week predictability
AT&T	72.8	78.3
Allied Signal	55.3	72.9
Aluminum Co	80.1	38.7
American Express	65.2	64.5
Bethlehem Steel	73.9	67.2
Boeing Company	70.3	75.3
Caterpillar Inc.	75.8	32.8
Chevron Corp	63.5	58.1
Coca Cola	62.9	49.2
Disney	66.4	68.8
Du Pont	42.9	75.1
Eastman Kodak	75.1	64.8
Exxon	71.1	58.6
General Electric	58.5	71.4
General Motors	77.3	53.5
Goodyear Tire	70.5	64.2
IBM	50.5	56.5
Internl Paper Co	63.7	71.8
J P Morgan	78.0	73.1
MacDonalds	62.3	71.2
Merk & Co	41.5	54.7
Minnesota M M	71.3	78.2
Philip Morris	75.2	63.4
Proctor & Gamble	61.9	52.6
Sears Roebuck	68.3	75.8
Texaco Inc	51.1	46.4
Union Carbide	75.0	71.3
United Technols	62.5	71.0
Westinghouse	78.2	65.2
Woolworth Corp	82.9	59.8

Table 10.1

Predictability for a channel turn normally lies within the range of 35 to 85%. The investor should only work with stocks whose predictability lies above 70%.

A few examples serve to show the advantage of these methods over the traditional extrapolation of channel boundaries.

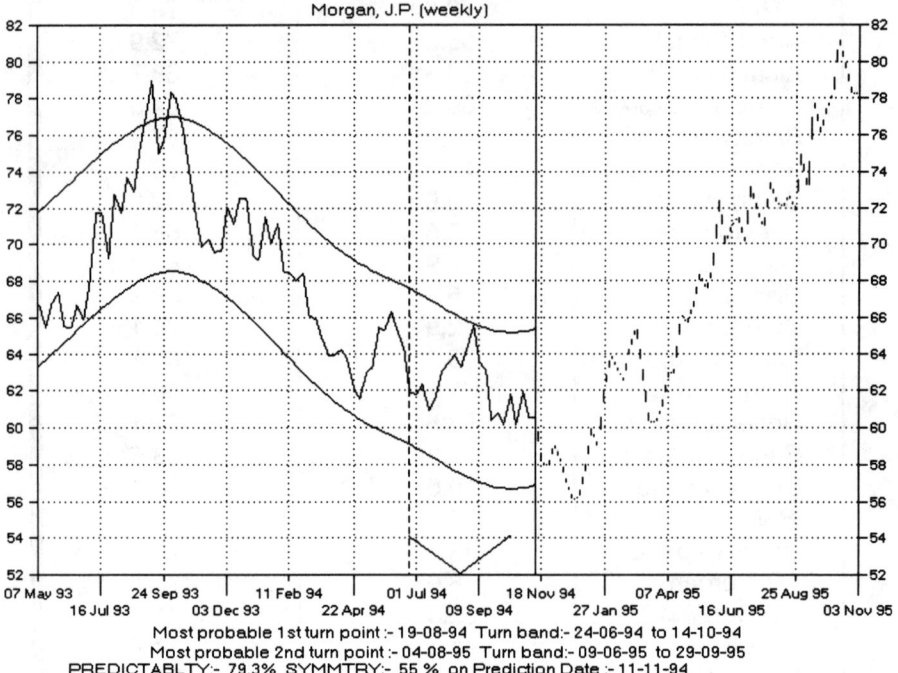

Most probable 1st turn point :- 19-08-94 Turn band:- 24-06-94 to 14-10-94
Most probable 2nd turn point :- 04-08-95 Turn band:- 09-06-95 to 29-09-95
PREDICTABLTY:- 79.3% SYMMTRY:- 55 % on Prediction Date :- 11-11-94

Figure 10.6. *Prediction of the 41-week channel turning point for **J.P Morgan** on November 11, 1994. The dashed vertical line is the last true channel position. The channel boundaries between the latter and the time that the prediction is made (solid vertical line) are estimated by a probability algorithm, while the downward pointing chevron is a different calculation of the most likely turning point window. Future movement of the stock is shown by the broken line. (Note: dates are European style)*

J. P. Morgan

A chart produced for **J.P Morgan** on November 11, 1994 is shown in Figure 10.6. This should be compared with Figure 10.5. You can see that the channel turning upwards only became apparent after the peak was formed on June 2, 1995. Now we can see that Sigma-p A produced a 41-week channel some six months earlier that had obviously changed direction even though the major trough on December 23, had not yet been formed. Sigma-p B confirmed this prospect of a newly rising channel by estimating that the most likely turning point was on August 19, 1994, *i.e.* in the gap between the last true channel position and the current time. This would have allowed the investor in early enough to take full advantage of the ensuing rise that took the stock up to over $80 by the following October.

By March 3, 1995, with the stock having risen to $65 $^3/_8$, Sigma-p B has now calculated that the turning point in the 41-week channel is real, so that it calculates the next probable turn, that now lies in the future. The estimation is for a turn between June and July of that year. It can be seen from Figure 10.7 that by June the progress of the stock had flattened out, so that it appeared that the up trend was coming to an end. However, the

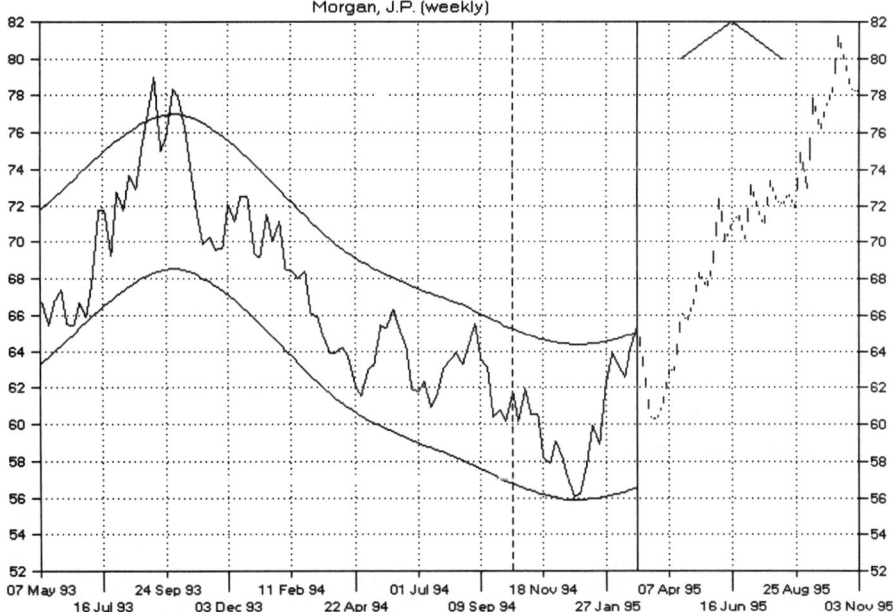

Morgan, J.P. (weekly)

Figure 10.7. *By March 3, 1995 the chevron has disappeared from the gap between the last true channel point (vertical dashed line) and the current time (solid vertical line) and is now estimating a down turn in the channel in June 1995.*

investor would have been waiting for a signal based on the position in June, at which time the prediction of the time of the turning point had moved further into the future, allowing the investor to continue to take advantage of the rise that took the stock even higher over the next few months.

Eastman Kodak (May 1998)

The position on May 17, 1996 for **Eastman Kodak** is shown in Figure 10.8. This example is chosen because at the time the predictability at 84.1% was extremely high. The channel direction, estimated by Sigma-p can be seen to have probably topped out. This is confirmed by the estimation of the most likely turning point having been on February 23, many weeks somewhere in the gap between the last true channel point and the present time.

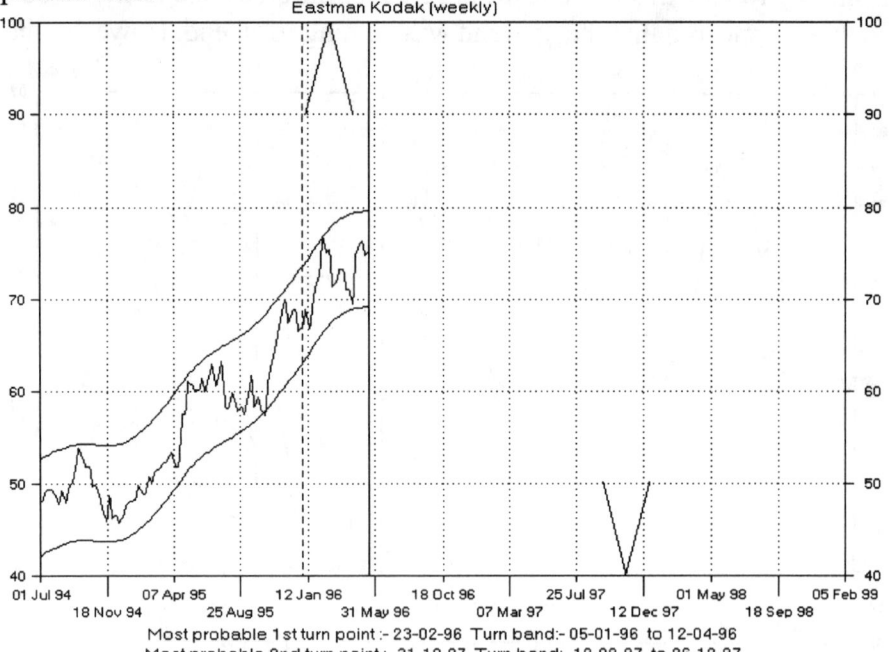

Figure 10.8. *The Sigma-p prediction for **Eastman Kodak** on May 17, 1996 is for the 41-week channel to have already turned down on the previous February, and for a fall to continue until October 1997 where the channel should begin to rise again.*

It is interesting to see that the prediction of the most likely point for the next turn, made on May 17, 1996, was in late October 1997, some 76 weeks into the future!

The astonishing accuracy of this prediction can be seen from Figure 9.9, where the 41-week channel has been calculated at the time of writing of this chapter, July 24, 1998. The calculated channel terminates some 20 weeks prior to this, but the turning point occurs prior to this cut-off and is therefore the true turning point. This turn was on December 5, 1997, only five weeks later than the prediction made more than 19 months previously in May 1996!

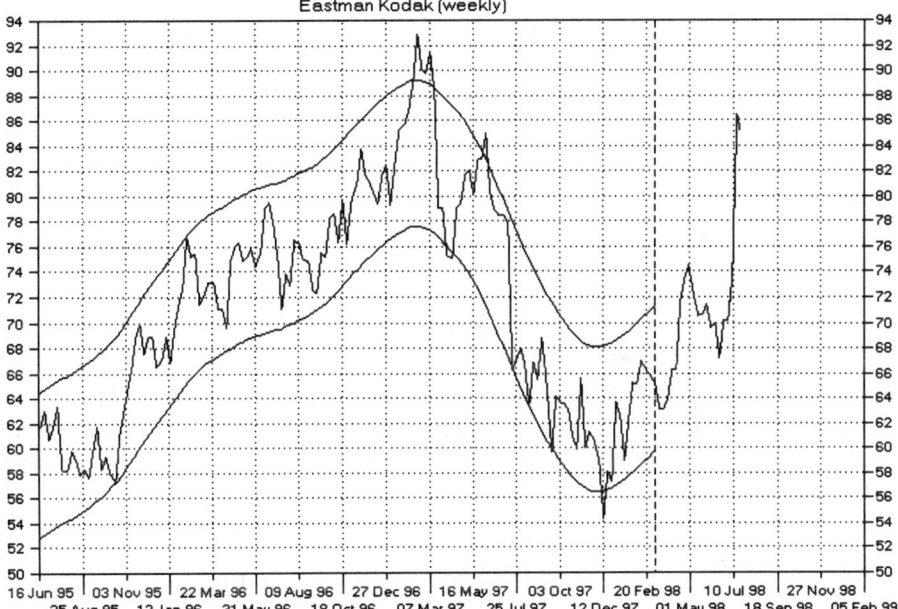

Figure 10.9. *The recent history of **Eastman Kodak** on July 24, 1998. The calculated 41-week channel terminates 20 weeks back at the position of the dashed line. This shows that the turning point occurred on December 5, 1997. The estimation for this turn, made in May 1996, 19 months earlier, was only 5 weeks out!*

One point the reader will have noticed when comparing Figure 10.9 with Figure 10.8 is the fact that the original turn down in the channel was predicted, on May 17, 1996, as having occurred in February 1996. The subsequent channel movement right up until October 1996 remained in line with this prediction, but a shorter wavelength cycle then became prominent, taking the price level higher for around six more months. The kink in the channel from May 1996 forward can be seen quite clearly in Figure 10.9.

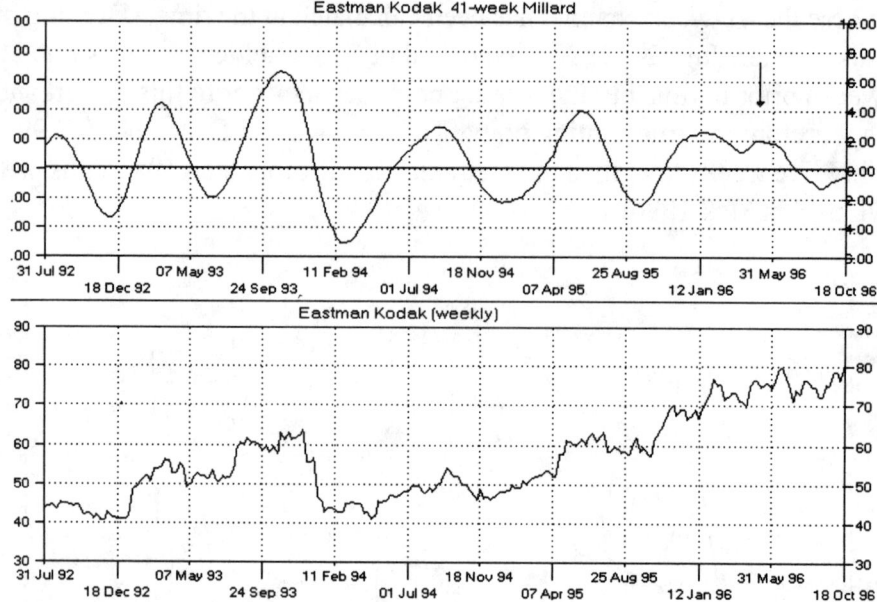

Figure 10.10. *The plot of the 41-week cycle for **Eastman Kodak** (upper panel) shows a distortion due to interference by a shorter wavelength cycle at the point in May 1996 indicated by the arrow. This is the reason the predicted turning point in February 1996 was delayed.*

The interference by another cycle is confirmed by the plot of the 41-week cycle, isolated by the cycle highlighter, shown in Figure 10.10. You can see there was indeed another, short wavelength cycle distorting the normal shape of the cycle at this point. It was this unpredictable cycle that was responsible for the delay in the turn down of the 41-week channel.

Finally, since the later part of this chapter has been concerned with the prediction of channel turning points, it is necessary for this author to stick his neck out and make a prediction on the day before the electronic manuscript is sent to the publisher! Since at the time of writing, **Eastman Kodak** has a high predictability rating, it is sensible to stay with this one, although, due to the interference by the shorter wavelength cycle in May 1996, the predictability has now fallen to 75.1%. The fact that the predictability is not forecast as being 100% will be my get out if my forecast turns out to be slightly in error!

Figure 10.11 shows the prediction for the channel turning point as July 24, 1998. The turning band lies between July 31, 1998 and January 1, 1999, *i.e.* a turn can be expected at any time in this window, with the most likely turning point (downwards) being October 18, 1998.

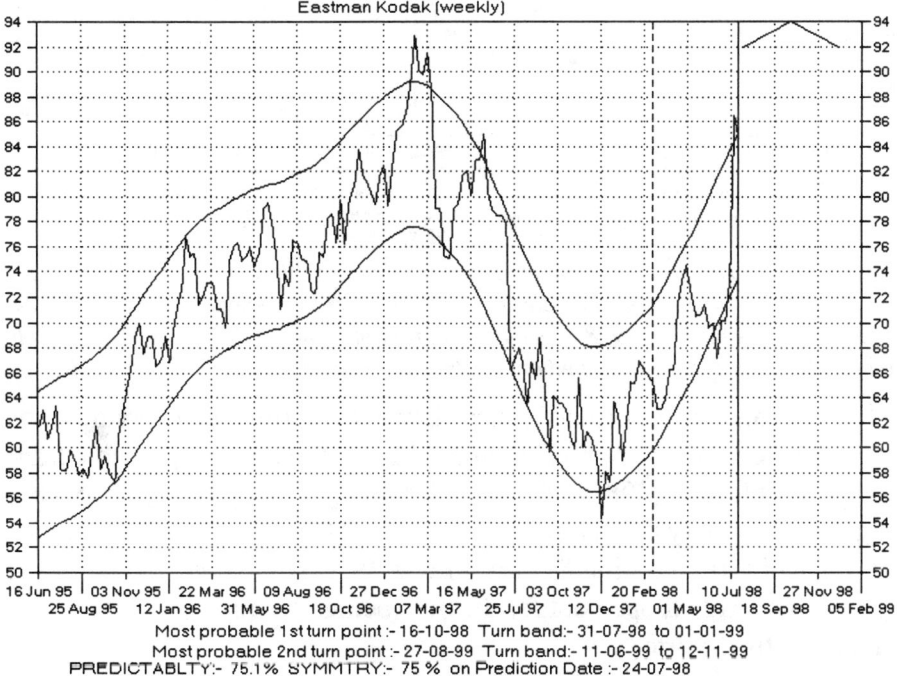

Figure 10.11. *The prediction for the turning point in the 41-week channel for* **Eastman Kodak** *made on July 24, 1998. The turn is predicted to occur between July 24, 1998 and January 1, 1999 with the most probably point being October 16, 1998.*

As far as the Dow is concerned (Figure 10.12), Sigma-p shows that the

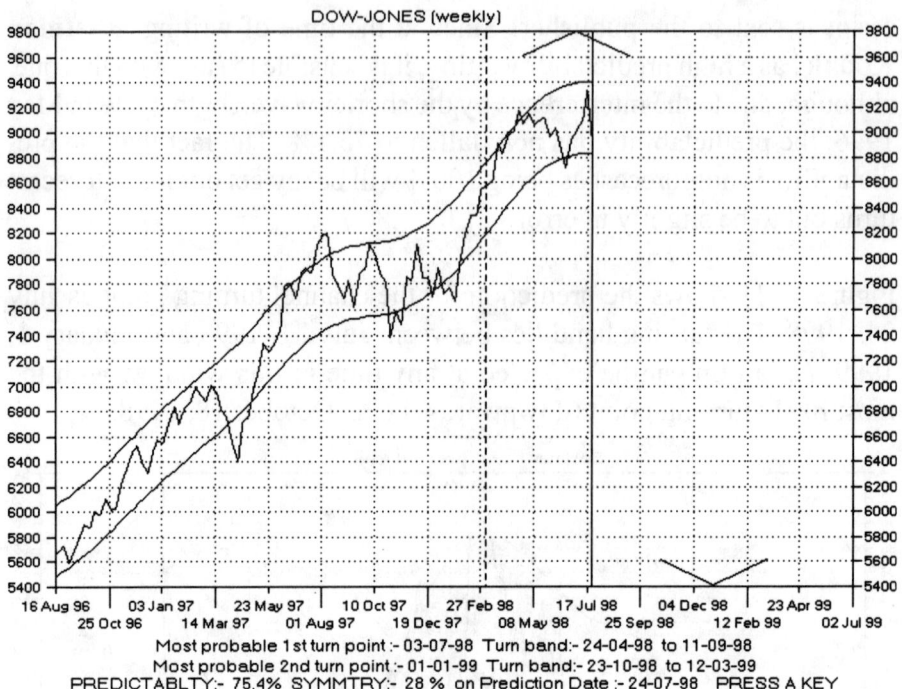

Figure 10.12. *The prediction made for the turning point in the 41-week channel for the Dow Jones Index, made on July 24, 1998. The turn is predicted between April 24, 1998 and September 11, 1998 with the most probable point as July 3, 1998. It is likely that the Dow has already topped out for the time being.*

41-week channel has probably turned, with the turning band predicted as lying between April 24 and September 11, 1998. The most probable turning point is July 3, 1998, with the predictability, at 75.4, being reasonably high. A cautionary note is sounded by the fact that the symmetry estimate of channel turning points is very low at 28%. Although it is likely the Dow has already topped out for the time being, the turning point may be significantly distorted.

It has to be remembered that these turning point estimations by Sigma-p gives no indication as to the amount that the channel will subsequently fall. It sometimes happens in retrospect, a predicted turning point can be seen to appear as a slight inflection in the channel because a shorter wavelength cycle then becomes dominant and the channel continues forwards in the same direction. Such a case can be seen for the Dow in Figure 10.12 around October 1997. Prior to that point Sigma-p predicted a turn in October 1997, but while a turn did begin, the sharp rise in the Dow in early 1998 reversed this process.

APPENDIX

Information on **Microvest 5.0** and **Sigma-p** can be obtained from:

Qudos Publication Ltd.
PO Box 27, Bramhall,
Stockport,
Cheshire SK7 1JH
England

Telephone +44 161 439 3926
Fax +44 161 439 2327
E-mail: qudospubs@aol.com

TRADERS PRESS, INC.®
PO BOX 6206
Greenville, SC 29606
Books and Gifts
for Investors and Traders

Publishers of:

A Complete Guide to Trading Profits (Paris)
A Professional Look at S&P Day Trading (Trivette)
Beginner's Guide to Computer Assisted Trading (Alexander)
Chart Reading for Professional Traders (Jenkins)
Commodity Spreads: Analysis, Selection and Trading Techniques (Smith)
Comparison of Twelve Technical Trading Systems (Lukac, Brorsen, & Irwin)
Day Trading with Short Term Price Patterns (Crabel)
Fibonacci Ratios with Pattern Recognition (Pesavento)
Geometry of Stock Market Profits (Jenkins)
Harmonic Vibrations (Pesavento)
How to Trade in Stocks (Livermore)
Jesse Livermore: Speculator King (Sarnoff)
Magic of Moving Averages (Lowry)
Planetary Harmonics of Speculative Markets (Pesavento)
Point & Figure Charting (Aby)
Point & Figure Charting: Commodity and Stock Trading Techniques (Zieg)
Profitable Grain Trading (Ainsworth)
Reminiscences of a Stock Operator (Lefevre)
Stock Market Trading Systems (Appel & Hitschler)
Stock Patterns for Stock Trading (Rudd)
Study Helps in Point & Figure Techniques (Wheelan)
Technically Speaking (Wilkinson)
Technical Trading Systems for Commodities and Stocks (Patel)
The Professional Commodity Trader (Kroll)
The Taylor Trading Technique (Taylor)
The Traders (Kleinfeld)
*The Trading Rule That Can Make You Rich** (Dobson)
Traders Guide to Technical Analysis (Hardy)
Trading Secrets of the Inner Circle (Goodwin)
Trading S&P Futures and Options (Lloyd)
Understanding Bollinger Bands (Dobson)
Understanding Fibonacci Numbers (Dobson)
Viewpoints of a Commodity Trader (Longstreet)
Wall Street Ventures & Adventures Through Forty Years (Wyckoff)
Winning Market Systems (Appel)

Please contact **Traders Press** to receive our current 100 page catalog describing
these and many other books and gifts of interest to investors and traders.
800-927-8222 Fax 864-298-0221 864-298-0222 tradersprs@aol.com

http://www.traderspress.com

LEGENDARY J.M. HURST CYCLES TRADING & TRAINING COURSE AVAILABLE AGAIN FOR THE FIRST TIME IN A QUARTER OF A CENTURY

The JM Hurst Cycles Trading and Training Course

In the late 1960's, a small group of private investors in California rented time on a mainframe computer—the only kind that existed at that time—and asked an aerospace engineer, J.M. Hurst, to help them in their stock market research. The results of over 20,000 hours of computerized data analysis were distilled and revealed in Hurst's 1970 book, THE PROFIT MAGIC OF STOCK TRANSACTION TIMING, which has become a classic work on cycle analysis.

In the early 1970's, Hurst authored a full-length course on cyclical analysis and on how to apply it to actual trading. It was published by Cyclitech Services, and Hurst taught the principles of this course in a series of seminars for a year or two. The material in this course is considered by many to be the clearest and most thorough material ever made available for those interested in learning about cycles and how to trade profitably with them. There were only 250 copies of the course ever sold. It has been out of print for the past 25 years.

In the mid 1970's, Hurst an intensely private individual, disappeared and has not been heard from again. We have had many customers over the years who were tremendously interested in Hurst and his work and were extremely interested in contacting him. They wanted anything he had written or done beyond his PROFIT MAGIC book, but until now, there has been nothing available. I had only heard about this course in "rumor" form for years. Only recently did I actually locate a copy of this course. It had been a dream of mine for years to preserve this course for posterity and to make it available again to the trading and investing community.

Consisting of ten manuals panning nearly sixteen hundred pages and eleven full length audio tapes, reproducing it has proven to be an expensive, but exciting and fulfilling challenge. We at Traders Press are proud to make this superb course available once again. It is available <u>exclusively</u> direct from Traders Press.

Edward D. Dobson
President
Traders Press

This course is written by J.M Hurst, author of *THE PROFIT MAGIC OF STOCK TRANSACTION TIMING,* a clasic work on cyclical analysis. Mr. Hurst is a mathematical analyst who, after 25 years in the aerospace field, spent 30,000 hours researching the nature of stock and commodity price motion.

HERE IS WHAT WELL-KNOWN INVESTMENT
EXPERTS FAMILIAR WITH THE
WORK OF J. M. HURST HAVE TO SAY ABOUT IT.

"The work of J.M. Hurst is highly regarded by technical analysts interested in the cyclical approach. Those who want a thorough education on this topic should avil themselves of the opportunity to acquire his full length course, which has been unavailable for many years until recently. The principles it teaches are just as valid today as they were 25 years ago."
—Tim Slater, President, Dow Jones Telerate Seminars

In the world of channels, bands, and envelopes, J.M. Hurst stands out as a primary source. (*THE PROFIT MAGIN OF STOCK TRANSACTION TIMING* constitutes the ealier stock-market citation for envelopes I have found.) So it is with great pleasure, and not a little excitement, that I greet 'lost' material from this venerable source. Long out of print and known to but a few, Hurst's course should prove to be an invaluable asset to the research-oriented technical analyst."
—John Bollinger, CFA, CMT

"My copy of "The Profit Magic of Stock Transaction Timing," by J. M. Hurst was only $5.95, when purchased in March of 1979; it remains on of few treasured and frequently referenced volumes. Being an engineer, it is gratifying to find a book that is not full of hocus-pocus and magical methods. Hurst's tome clarifies cycles, channels, and brings a host of believable and useful methods for price analysis. Ed Dobson should be 'publisher of the decade' for uncovering and producing a course written by such a major contributor to market analytics. If you have not read his book, you need this course. If you have read his book, you have probably already ordered the course."
—Gregory L. Morris, CEO MURPHYMORRIS, Inc. Author of *CandlePower and Candlestick Charting Explained*

"Jim Hurst's original cycle work laid the foundation for most of the cycle analysis being done in today's futures and stock markets. The cycle concepts and forecasting techniques are as valid today as they were then. His book and course should be read and studied by all serious students of the markets."
—Walter Bressert, Co-founder of Computrac

"Every since I read about Hurst's method of "phasing," I have looked forward to learning more about his work. His apparently pragmatic approach to technical analysis is very appealing and should adapt well to the more advanced tools now in our hands."
—Perry Kaufman, Author of *Commodity Trading Systems and Methods* and numerous other financial titles.

"I am delighted that Ed Dobson is preserving the Hurst Cycles Course for posterity. It is superb material and should be in the library of every serious technician. I have relied heavily on this material in my own cyclical analysis and in my writings on the subject."
—John J. Murphy, Noted technical analyst, Author of *Technical Analysis of the Futures Market* and *Intermarket Technical Analysis*

"Anyone interested in stock or commodity cycles should be enlightened by the work of James Hurst. His pioneering into the cyclical nature of stocks and commodities is the background of modern cyclic theory. Hurst's entry and exit methods are by themselves worth the price of the course."
—Larry Pesavento, Professional trader and author of numerous financial titles

."After studying technical analysis for several years my perspective was changed forever by reading Hurst's book on cycles and studying his course in the early 1970s. This was the first true explanation of the rhythm in chart formations and has been a valuable tool to this day. It adds tremendously to an understanding of the markets."
—Jim Tillman, Publisher of *Cycle trend Market Letter*

"When Ed Dobson told me he had located the workbooks and audio tapes of J. M. Hurst's course on market cycles, I felt as if a past market master had been resurrected from the dead. Hurst was such a brilliant original thinker that I can't imagine anyone who is serious about technical and cycle analysis would be without this material if given the opportunity to acquire it. Hurst's original book written in the late 1960s was the genesis of my career in cycles and contributed to a significant degree to any success I have enjoyed in this business."
—Peter Eliades, Stockmarket Cycles

...carefully researched work on cycles and envelopes, backed up by solid and verifiable facts... brilliant application of mathematical analysis to the stock market... he developed a simple technique, which we now call channel analysis, which could easily be applied by the pencil and paper investor." ... man whose work must be considered a landmark in the field of investment."
—Brian J. Millard, Author of *Channels and Cycles: A Tributt to J.M. Hurst*

HURST CYCLE TRAINING COURSE CONTAINS...

🔊 200 HOUR COURSE

🔊 10 FULL LESSONS OVER 400 PAGES

🔊 MORE THAN 100 ILLUSTRATIONS

🔊 10 CASSETTE NARRATIONS

🔊 TEXT MATERIAL AND WORKBOOK

🔊 SELF-EXAMINATION WITH KEY

🔊 PERMANENT BINDER WITH CASSETTE STORAGE

 *Course Contents:*

- **LESSON 1**: How Price Action Works
- **LESSON 2**: From Cyclic Concepts to Trading Decisions
- **LESSON 3**: Setting up the Cyclic Model
- **LESSON 4**: Setting up a Transaction
- **LESSON 5**: How to Deal with Tops and Short
- **LESSON 6**: Cyclic Analysis During A Transaction
- **LESSON 7**: Terminating a Transaction
- **LESSON 8**: How to Shape Strategy and Plan Capabilities
- **LESSON 9**: Refining Your Capabilities
- **LESSON 10**: A Reference Summary of Cyclic Analysis

Eleven professionally produced audio tapes accompany approximately 1,600 pages of written material, which includes hundreds of 11 x 17 foldout, full scale illustrative charts. A workshop and final self-examination are included.

Item #1400 **$495** *40% restocking fee*
Shipping weight 18 pounds. Please add the following shipping costs to your order: Domestic UPS: $15, DHL Domestic $23, Foreign: by courier service: $100 Canada: UPS $40